BOLLINGEN SERIES XX

THE COLLECTED WORKS

OF

C. G. JUNG

VOLUME 1

EDITORS

SIR HERBERT READ

MICHAEL FORDHAM, M.D., M.R.C.P.

GERHARD ADLER, PH.D.

WILLIAM MC GUIRE, *executive editor*

PSYCHIATRIC STUDIES

C. G. JUNG

SECOND EDITION

TRANSLATED BY R. F. C. HULL

BOLLINGEN SERIES XX

PRINCETON UNIVERSITY PRESS

PUBLISHED BY PRINCETON UNIVERSITY PRESS
41 WILLIAM STREET, PRINCETON, NEW JERSEY 08540
99 BANBURY ROAD, OXFORD OX2 6JX

PRESS.PRINCETON.EDU

FIRST PUBLISHED IN 1957
NEW PAPERBACK PRINTING, 2024

CLOTH ISBN 9780691097688
PAPERBACK ISBN 9780691259321

LIBRARY OF CONGRESS CATALOG CARD NUMBER: 75-156

EDITORIAL PREFACE

The publication of the first complete collected edition, in English, of the works of C. G. Jung is a joint endeavour by Routledge and Kegan Paul, Ltd., in England and, under the sponsorship of Bollingen Foundation, by Princeton University Press in the United States. The edition contains revised versions of works previously published, such as *The Psychology of the Unconscious*, which is now entitled *Symbols of Transformation*; works originally written in English, such as *Psychology and Religion*; works not previously translated, such as *Aion*; and, in general, new translations of the major body of Professor Jung's writings. The author has supervised the textual revision, which in some cases is extensive.

In presenting the Collected Works of C. G. Jung to the public, the Editors believe that the plan of the edition * may require a short explanation.

The editorial problem of arrangement was difficult for a variety of reasons, but perhaps most of all because of the author's unusual literary productivity: Jung has not only written several new books and essays since the Collected Works were planned, but he has frequently published expanded versions of texts to which a certain space had already been allotted. The Editors soon found that the original framework was being subjected to severe stresses and strains; and indeed, it eventually was almost twisted out of shape. They still believe, however, that the programme adopted at the outset, based on the principles to be outlined below, is the best they can devise.

An arrangement of material by strict chronology, though far the easier, would have produced a rather confusing network of subjects: essays on psychiatry mixed in with studies of religion, of alchemy, of child psychology. Yet an arrangement according to subject-matter alone would tend to obscure a view

* See announcement at end of this volume.

of the progress of Jung's researches. The growth of his work, however, has made a combination of these two schemes possible, for the unfolding of Jung's psychological concepts corresponds, by and large, with the development of his interests.

C. C. Jung was born in northeastern Switzerland in 1875, a Protestant clergyman's son. As a young man of scientific and philosophical bent, he first contemplated archaeology as a career, but eventually chose medicine, and qualified with distinction in 1900. Up to this time, Jung had expected to make physiological chemistry his special field, in which a brilliant future could be expected for him; but, to the surprise of his teachers and contemporaries, he unexpectedly changed his aim. This came about through his reading of Krafft-Ebing's famous *Text-Book of Insanity*, which caught his interest and stimulated in him a strong desire to understand the strange phenomena he there found described. Jung's inner prompting was supported by propitious outer circumstances: Dr. Eugen Bleuler was then director of the Burghölzli Mental Hospital, in Zurich, and it was under his guidance that Jung embarked on his now well-known researches in psychiatry.

The present volume, first of the Collected Works, though not large, is sufficient to contain the studies in descriptive psychiatry. It opens with Jung's first published work, his dissertation for the medical degree: "On the Psychology and Pathology of So-called Occult Phenomena" (1902), a study that adumbrates very much of his later work. But clearly a man of Jung's cast of mind could not be content with simple descriptive research, and soon he embarked upon the application of experimental psychology to psychiatry. The copious results of these researches make up Volume 2 and Volume 3. Jung's work brought about the transformation of psychiatry, as the study of the psychoses, from a static system of classification into a dynamic interpretative science. His monograph "The Psychology of Dementia Praecox" (1907), in Volume 3, marks the peak of this stage of his activity.

It was these experimental researches that led Jung to a fruitful if stormy period of collaboration with Freud, which is represented by the psychoanalytic papers in Volume 4. The chief work in this volume, "The Theory of Psychoanalysis" (1913), gives at length his first critical estimation of psychoanalysis. Volume 5, *Symbols of Transformation* (originally 1912), and Volume 7, *Two Essays on Analytical Psychology* (originally 1912 and 1916), restate his critical position but also make new contributions to the foundation of analytical psychology as a system.

The constant growth of analytical psychology is reflected in Jung's frequent revision of his publications. The first of the *Two Essays on Analytical Psychology*, for example, has passed through several different editions. *Psychology of the Unconscious*, as it was titled in its first (1916) edition in English, appears in the Collected Works, extensively revised by Jung, with the title *Symbols of Transformation*. The Editors decided to leave these works in the approximate chronological positions dictated by the dates of their first editions, though both are published in revised form. Revision and expansion also characterize the group of studies that form Volume 12, *Psychology and Alchemy* (originally 1935–36), as well as many single essays in other volumes of the present edition.

Psychological Types (Volume 6), first published in 1921, has remained practically unchanged; it marks the terminus of Jung's move away from psychoanalysis. No further long single work appeared till 1946. During the intervening period, when Jung's professional work and his teaching occupied a large part of his time, he was abstracting, refining, and elaborating his basic theses in a series of shorter essays, some of which are collected in Volume 8, *The Structure and Dynamics of the Psyche*.

Volume 9, part I, contains essays, mostly of the same period, that have special reference to the collective unconscious and the archetypes. Part II of this volume, however, contains a late (1951) major work, *Aion: Researches into the Phenomenology of the Self*. From the chronological point of view, *Aion* should come much later in this sequence, but it has been placed here because it is concerned with the archetype of the self.

From Volume 10 onwards, the material deals with the application of Jung's fundamental concepts, which, with their historical antecedents, can be said by now to have been adequately set out. The subject-matter of Volume 10 to Volume 17—organized, in the main, around several themes, such as religion, society, psychotherapy, and education—is indicated by the volume titles and contents. It will be noted that, in his later years, Jung has returned to writing longer works: *Aion,* the *Mysterium Coniunctionis,* and perhaps others yet to come from his pen. These arise, no doubt, out of the reflective stage of his life, when retirement from his analytical practice has at last given him time to work out ideas that those who know him have long wanted to see in print.

In 1956, Professor Jung announced that he would make available to the Editors of the Collected Works two accessions of material which will have the effect of enhancing and rounding out the edition: first, a selection of his correspondence on scientific subjects (including certain of his letters to Freud); and second, the texts of a number of the seminars conducted by Jung. Accordingly, Volume 18, and thereafter such additional volumes as may be needed, will be devoted to this material.

The Editors have set aside a final volume for minor essays, reviews, newspaper articles, and the like. These may make a rather short volume. If this should be so, an index of the complete works and a bibliography of Jung's writings in original and in translation will be combined with them; otherwise, the index and bibliography will be published separately.

*

In the treatment of the text, the Editors have sought to present Jung's most recent version of each work, but reference is made where necessary to previous editions. In cases where Professor Jung has authorized or himself made revisions in the English text, this is stated.

In a body of work covering more than half a century, it cannot be expected that the terminology would be standardized; indeed, some technical terms used by Jung in an earlier period were later replaced by others or put to different use. In view of their historical interest, such terms are translated faithfully according to the period to which they belong, except where Professor Jung has himself altered them in the course of his revision. Occasionally, editorial comment is made on terms of particular interest. The volumes are provided with bibliographies and are fully indexed.

*

Of the contents of Volume 1, nothing has previously been translated into English except the monograph "On the Psychology and Pathology of So-called Occult Phenomena." The translation of the latter by M. D. Eder has been consulted, but in the main the present translation is new. It may be noted that, except for the 1916 English version of the "Occult Phenomena," none of these papers has ever been republished by Professor Jung.

An effort has been made to fill out the bibliographical details of the material, which were sometimes abbreviated in the medical publications of the 1900's.

Acknowledgment is made to George Allen and Unwin Ltd. for permission to quote passages from Freud's *The Interpretation of Dreams* and from Nietzsche's *Thus Spake Zarathustra*.

EDITORIAL NOTE TO THE SECOND EDITION

Since the above paragraphs were written, and following Jung's death on June 6, 1961, different arrangements for the publication of the correspondence and seminars have been made with the consent of his heirs. These writings will not, as originally stated, comprise Volume 18 and subsequent volumes of the Collected Works (for their contents as now planned, see below). Instead, a large selection of the correspondence, not restricted to scientific subjects though including some letters to Freud, will be issued under the same publishing auspices but outside the Collected Works, under the editorship of Dr. Gerhard Adler. A selection of the seminars, mainly those delivered in English between 1925 and 1939, will also be published outside the Collected Works in several volumes.

Two works usually described as seminars are, however, being published in the Collected Works, inasmuch as the transcripts were approved by Jung personally as giving a valid account of his statements: the work widely known as the Tavistock Lectures, delivered in London in 1935, privately circulated in multigraphed form, and published as a separate volume entitled *Analytical Psychology: Its Theory and Practice* (Routledge & Kegan Paul, London, and Pantheon Books, New York, 1968); and the seminar given in 1938 to members of the Guild of Pastoral Psychology, London, and published in pamphlet form by the Guild in 1954 under the title *The Symbolic Life*. Both of these will be published in Volume 18, which has been given the general title *The Symbolic Life*.

Volume 18 will also include the minor essays, reviews, forewords, newspaper articles, and so on, for which a "final volume" had been set aside. Furthermore, the amount of new material that has come to light since the Collected Works were planned is very considerable, most of it having been discovered after Jung's death and too late to have been placed in the volumes where thematically it belonged. The Editors have therefore assigned the new and posthumous material also to Volume 18, which will be much larger than was first envisaged. The index of the complete works and a bibliography of Jung's writings in the original and in translation will be published as two separate and final volumes.

Jung ended his long years of creative activity with the posthumously published *Memories, Dreams, Reflections,* recorded and edited by Aniela Jaffé and translated by Richard and Clara Winston (Collins with Routledge & Kegan Paul, London, and Pantheon Books, New York, 1963). At his express wish it was not included in the Collected Works.

*

Finally, the Editors and those closely concerned with implementing the publication programme, including the translator, wish to express their deep sense of loss at the death of their colleague and friend, Sir Herbert Read, who died on June 12, 1968.

*

For the second edition of *Psychiatric Studies,* bibliographical citations and entries have been revised in the light of subsequent publications in the Collected Works and essential corrections have been made.

*

In 1970, the Freud and Jung families reached an agreement that resulted in the publication of *The Freud/Jung Letters* (the complete surviving correspondence of 360 letters), under the editorship of William McGuire, in 1974. And a selection from all of Jung's correspondence throughout his career, edited by Gerhard Adler in collaboration with Aniela Jaffé, was published in 1973 (1906–1950) and 1975 (1951–1961). Finally, a selection of interviews with Jung was published in 1977 under the title *C. G. Jung Speaking: Interviews and Encounters.*

TABLE OF CONTENTS

EDITORIAL PREFACE   v

EDITORIAL NOTE TO THE SECOND EDITION   ix

I

On the Psychology and Pathology of So-called Occult Phenomena   3

Translated from *Zur Psychologie und Pathologie sogenannter occulter Phänomene* (Leipzig, 1902).

1. INTRODUCTION

2. A CASE OF SOMNAMBULISM IN A GIRL WITH POOR INHERITANCE (Spiritualistic Medium)
   Anamnesis, 17. — Somnambulistic States, 19. — Records of Séances, 25. — Development of the Somnambulistic Personalities, 30. — The Romances, 36. — Mystic Science, 39. — Termination of the Disorder, 43

3. DISCUSSION OF THE CASE
   The Waking State, 44. — Semi-Somnambulism, 47. — Automatisms, 48. — The Change in Character, 61. — Nature of the Somnambulistic Attacks, 70. — Origin of the Unconscious Personalities, 77. — Course of the Disorder, 78. — Heightened Unconscious Performance, 80

4. CONCLUSION

On Hysterical Misreading   89

Translated from "Über hysterisches Verlesen," *Archiv für die gesamte Psychologie* (Leipzig), III (1904).

xi

II

Cryptomnesia   95

Translated from "Kryptomnesie," *Die Zukunft* (Berlin), 13th
year (1905), L.

III

On Manic Mood Disorder   109

Translated from "Über manische Verstimmung," *Allgemeine
Zeitschrift für Psychiatrie und psychisch-gerichtliche Medizin*
(Berlin), LXI (1903).

IV

A Case of Hysterical Stupor in a Prisoner in Detention   137

Translated from "Ein Fall von hysterischem Stupor bei einer
Untersuchungsgefangenen," *Journal für Psychologie und
Neurologie* (Leipzig), I (1902).

V

On Simulated Insanity   159

Translated from "Über Simulation von Geistesstörung,"
Journal für Psychologie und Neurologie (Leipzig), II (1903).

A Medical Opinion on a Case of Simulated Insanity   188

Translated from "Ärztliches Gutachten über einen Fall von
simulierter geistiger Störung," *Schweizerische Zeitung für
Strafrecht* (Zurich), XVII (1904).

VI

A Third and Final Opinion on Two Contradictory
Psychiatric Diagnoses   209

Translated from "Obergutachten über zwei sich widersprechende psychiatrische Gutachten," *Monatsschrift für*

Kriminalpsychologie und Strafrechtsreform (Heidelberg), II
(1906).

On the Psychological Diagnosis of Facts

219

Translated from "Zur psychologischen Tatbestandsdiagnostik," *Zentralblatt für Nervenheilkunde und Psychiatrie*
(Leipzig), XXVIII (1905).

BIBLIOGRAPHY   225

INDEX   239

I

ON THE PSYCHOLOGY AND PATHOLOGY OF SO-CALLED OCCULT PHENOMENA

ON HYSTERICAL MISREADING

ON THE PSYCHOLOGY AND PATHOLOGY OF SO-CALLED OCCULT PHENOMENA [1]

[1. INTRODUCTION]

1   In that wide domain of psychopathic inferiority from which science has marked off the clinical pictures of epilepsy, hysteria, and neurasthenia, we find scattered observations on certain rare states of consciousness as to whose meaning the authors are not yet agreed. These observations crop up sporadically in the literature on narcolepsy, lethargy, *automatisme ambulatoire*, periodic amnesia, double consciousness, somnambulism, pathological dreaminess, pathological lying, etc.

2   The above-mentioned states are sometimes attributed to epilepsy, sometimes to hysteria, sometimes to exhaustion of the nervous system—neurasthenia—and sometimes they may even be accorded the dignity of a disease *sui generis*. The patients

[1] [Translated from *Zur Psychologie und Pathologie sogenannter occulter Phänomene* (Leipzig, 1902). It was Professor Jung's inaugural dissertation for his medical degree and was delivered before the Faculty of Medicine, University of Zurich. The 1902 title-page stated that the author was at that time "First Assistant Physician in the Burghölzli Clinic" and that the dissertation was approved on the motion of Professor Eugen Bleuler. The book was dedicated to the author's wife, Emma Rauschenbach Jung (1882-1955). A translation by M. D. Eder was published in *Collected Papers on Analytical Psychology* (London and New York, 1916; 2nd edn., 1917). In the following version, the headings have been somewhat re-ordered and some new headings supplied in brackets in an attempt to clarify the structure of the monograph.—EDITORS]

concerned occasionally go through the whole gamut of diagnoses from epilepsy to hysteria and simulated insanity.

3   It is, in fact, exceedingly difficult, and sometimes impossible, to distinguish these states from the various types of neurosis, but on the other hand certain features point beyond pathological inferiority to something more than a merely analogical relationship with the phenomena of normal psychology, and even with the psychology of the supranormal, that of genius.

4   However varied the individual phenomena may be in themselves, there is certainly no case that cannot be related by means of some intermediate case to others that are typical. This relationship extends deep into the clinical pictures of hysteria and epilepsy. Recently it has even been suggested that there is no definite borderline between epilepsy and hysteria, and that a difference becomes apparent only in extreme cases. Steffens, for example, says: "We are forced to the conclusion that in essence hysteria and epilepsy are not fundamentally different, that the cause of the disease is the same, only it manifests itself in different forms and in different degrees of intensity and duration." [2]

5   The delimitation of hysteria and certain borderline forms of epilepsy from congenital or acquired psychopathic inferiority likewise presents great difficulties. The symptoms overlap at every point, so that violence is done to the facts if they are regarded separately as belonging to this or that particular group. To delimit psychopathic inferiority from the normal is an absolutely impossible task, for the difference is always only "more" or "less." Classification in the field of inferiority itself meets with the same difficulties. At best, one can only single out certain groups which crystallize round a nucleus with specially marked typical features. If we disregard the two large groups of intellectual and emotional inferiority, we are left with those which are coloured pre-eminently by hysterical, epileptic (epileptoid), or neurasthenic symptoms, and which are not characterized by an inferiority either of intellect or of emotion. It is chiefly in this field, insusceptible of any sure classification, that the above-mentioned states are to be found. As is well known, they can appear as partial manifestations of a typical epilepsy or hysteria, or can exist separately as psychopathic inferiorities, in which case the qualification "epileptic" or "hys-

2 "Über drei Fälle von 'Hysteria magna'" (1900), p. 928.

terical" is often due to relatively unimportant subsidiary symptoms. Thus somnambulism is usually classed among the hysterical illnesses because it is sometimes a partial manifestation of severe hysteria, or because it may be accompanied by milder so-called "hysterical" symptoms. Binet says: "Somnambulism is not one particular and unchanging nervous condition; there are many somnambulisms." [3] As a partial manifestation of severe hysteria, somnambulism is not an unknown phenomenon, but as a separate pathological entity, a disease *sui generis,* it must be somewhat rare, to judge by the paucity of German literature on this subject. So-called spontaneous somnambulism based on a slightly hysterical psychopathic inferiority is not very common, and it is worth while to examine such cases more closely, as they sometimes afford us a wealth of interesting observations.

6   CASE OF MISS E., aged 40, single, book-keeper in a large business. No hereditary taint, except that a brother suffered from "nerves" after a family misfortune and illness. Good education, of a cheerful disposition, not able to save money; "always had some big idea in my head." She was very kind-hearted and gentle, did a great deal for her parents, who were living in modest circumstances, and for strangers. Nevertheless she was not happy because she felt she was misunderstood. She had always enjoyed good health till a few years ago, when she said she was treated for dilatation of the stomach and tapeworm. During this illness her hair turned rapidly white. Later she had typhoid. An engagement was terminated by the death of her fiancé from paralysis. She was in a highly nervous state for a year and a half. In the summer of 1897 she went away for a change of air and hydrotherapy. She herself said that for about a year there were moments in her work when her thoughts seemed to stand still, though she did not fall asleep. She made no mistakes in her accounts, however. In the street she often went to the wrong place and then suddenly realized that she was not in the right street. She had no giddiness or fainting-fits. Formerly menstruation occurred regularly every four weeks with no bother; latterly, since she was nervous and overworked, every fourteen days. For a long time she suffered from constant headache. As accountant and book-keeper in a large business she had a very strenuous

3 *Alterations of Personality* (orig. 1892), p. 2, modified.

job, which she did well and conscientiously. In the present year, in addition to the strains of her work, she had all sorts of new worries. Her brother suddenly got divorced, and besides her own work she looked after his housekeeping, nursed him and his child through a serious illness, and so on. To recuperate, she went on September 13 to see a woman friend in southern Germany. Her great joy at seeing her friend again after such a long absence, and their celebration of a party, made the necessary rest impossible. On the 15th, quite contrary to her usual habit, she and her friend drank a bottle of claret. Afterwards they went for a walk in a cemetery, where she began to tear up flowers and scratch at the graves. She remembered absolutely nothing of this afterwards. On the 16th she stayed with her friend without anything of importance happening. On the 17th, her friend brought her to Zurich. An acquaintance came with her to the asylum; on the way she talked quite sensibly but was very tired. Outside the asylum they met three boys whom she described as "three dead people she had dug up." She then wanted to go to the neighbouring cemetery, and only with difficulty would be persuaded to enter the asylum.

7   The patient was small, delicately built, slightly anaemic. Left side of the heart slightly enlarged; no murmurs, but a few double beats; accentuated sounds in the mitral region. The liver dulness extended only to the edge of the upper ribs. Patellar reflexes rather brisk, but otherwise no tendon reflexes. No anaesthesia or analgesia, no paralysis. Rough examination of the field of vision with the hands showed no restriction. Hair of a very pale, yellowish-white colour. On the whole, the patient looked her age. She recounted her history and the events of the last few days quite clearly, but had no recollection of what happened in the cemetery at C. or outside the asylum. During the night of the 17th/18th she spoke to the attendant and said she saw the whole room full of dead people looking like skeletons. She was not at all frightened, but was rather surprised that the attendant did not see them too. Once she ran to the window, but was otherwise quiet. The next morning in bed she still saw skeletons, but not in the afternoon. The following night she woke up at four o'clock and heard the dead children in the adjoining cemetery crying out that they had been buried alive. She wanted to go and dig them up but allowed herself to be

restrained. Next morning at seven o'clock she was still delirious, but could now remember quite well the events in the cemetery at C. and on her way to the asylum. She said that at C. she wanted to dig up the dead children who were calling to her. She had only torn up the flowers in order to clear the graves and be able to open them. While she was in this state, Professor Bleuler explained to her that she would remember everything afterwards, too, when she came to herself again. The patient slept for a few hours in the morning; afterwards she was quite clear-headed and felt fairly well. She did indeed remember the attacks, but maintained a remarkable indifference towards them. The following nights, except on those of September 22 and 25, she again had short attacks of delirium in which she had to deal with the dead, though the attacks differed in detail. Twice she saw dead people in her bed; she did not appear to be frightened of them, but got out of bed so as not to "embarrass" them. Several times she tried to leave the room.

8   After a few nights free from attacks, she had a mild one on September 30, when she called to the dead from the window. During the day her mind was quite clear. On October 3, while fully conscious, as she related afterwards, she saw a whole crowd of skeletons in the drawing-room. Although she doubted the reality of the skeletons she could not convince herself that it was an hallucination. The next night, between twelve and one o'clock—the earlier attacks usually happened about this time—she was plagued by the dead for about ten minutes. She sat up in bed, stared into a corner of the room, and said: "Now they're coming, but they're not all here yet. Come along, the room's big enough, there's room for all. When they're all there I'll come too." Then she lay down, with the words: "Now they're all there," and fell asleep. In the morning she had not the slightest recollection of any of these attacks. Very short attacks occurred again on the nights of October 4, 6, 9, 13, and 15, all between twelve and one o'clock. The last three coincided with the menstrual period. The attendant tried to talk to her several times, showed her the lighted street-lamps and the trees, but she did not react to these overtures. Since then the attacks have stopped altogether. The patient complained about a number of troubles she had had during her stay here. She suffered especially from headaches, and these got worse the morning

7

after the attacks. She said it was unbearable. Five grains of
Sacch. lactis promptly alleviated this. Then she complained of
a pain in both forearms, which she described as though it were
tendovaginitis. She thought the bulging of the flexed biceps
was a swelling and asked to have it massaged. Actually, there
was nothing the matter, and when her complaints were ignored
the trouble disappeared. She complained loud and long about
the thickening of a toe-nail, even after the thickened part had
been removed. Sleep was often disturbed. She would not give
her consent to be hypnotized against the night attacks. Finally,
on account of headache and disturbed sleep, she agreed to hypnotic treatment. She proved a good subject, and at the first
sitting fell into a deep sleep with analgesia and amnesia.

9   In November she was again asked whether she could remember the attack of September 19, which it had been suggested she would recall. She had great difficulty recollecting it,
and in the end she could only recount the main facts; she had
forgotten the details.

10   It remains to be said that the patient was not at all supersti-
tious and in her healthy days had never been particularly interested in the supernatural. All through the treatment, which
ended on November 14, she maintained a remarkable indifference both to the illness and its improvement. The following
spring she returned as an outpatient for treatment of the headaches, which had slowly come back because of strenuous work
during the intervening months. For the rest, her condition left
nothing to be desired. It was established that she had no
remembrance of the attacks of the previous autumn, not even
those of September 19 and earlier. On the other hand, under
hypnosis she could still give a good account of the events in
the cemetery, outside the asylum, and during the night attacks.

11   The peculiar hallucinations and general appearance of our
case are reminiscent of those states which Krafft-Ebing describes
as "protracted states of hysterical delirium." He says:

It is in the milder cases of hysteria that such delirious states occur.
. . . Protracted hysterical delirium depends upon temporary exhaustion. . . . Emotional disturbances seem to favour its outbreak. It
is prone to relapse. . . . Most frequently we find delusions of perse-
cution, with often very violent reactive fear. . . then religious and
erotic delusions. Hallucinations of all the senses are not uncom-

mon. The most frequent and most important are delusions of sight, smell, and touch. The visual hallucinations are mostly visions of animals, funerals, fantastic processions swarming with corpses, devils, ghosts, and what not. . . . The auditory delusions are simply noises in the ear (shrieks, crashes, bangs), or actual hallucinations, often with sexual content.[4]

12   The corpse visions of our patient and their appearance during attacks remind us of states occasionally observed in hystero-epilepsy. Here too there are specific visions which, in contrast to protracted delirium, are associated with individual attacks. I will give two examples:

13   A 30-year-old lady with *grande hystérie* had delirious twilight states in which she was tormented by frightful hallucinations. She saw her children being torn away from her, devoured by wild beasts, etc. She had no remembrance of the individual attacks.[5]

14   A girl of 17, also a severe hysteric. In her attacks she always saw the corpse of her dead mother approaching her, as if to draw her to itself. No memory of the attacks.[6]

15   These are cases of severe hysteria where consciousness works at a deep dream level. The nature of the attacks and the stability of the hallucinations alone show a certain affinity to our case, which in this respect has numerous analogies with the corresponding states of hysteria, as for instance with cases where a psychic shock (rape, etc.) occasioned the outbreak of hysterical attacks, or where the traumatic event is re-experienced in stereotyped hallucinatory form. Our case, however, gets its specific character from the identity of consciousness during the different attacks. It is a "second state," with a memory of its own, but separated from the waking state by total amnesia. This distinguishes it from the above-mentioned twilight states and relates it to those found in somnambulism.

16   Charcot [7] divides somnambulism into two basic forms:

    a. Delirium with marked inco-ordination of ideas and actions.

4 *Text-Book of Insanity* (orig. 1879), p. 498, modified.

5 Richer, *Études cliniques* (1881), p. 483.

6 Ibid., p. 487; cf. also Erler, "Hysterisches und hystero-epileptisches Irresein" (1879), p. 28, and Cullerre, "Un Cas de somnambulisme hystérique" (1888), p. 356*.

7 In Guinon, "Documents pour servir à l'histoire des somnambulismes" (1891).

b. Delirium with co-ordinated actions. This comes nearer to the waking state.

17   Our case belongs to the second group. If by somnambulism we understand a state of systematic partial wakefulness,[8] we must when discussing this ailment also consider those isolated attacks of amnesia which are occasionally observed. Except for noctambulism, they are the simplest states of systematic partial wakefulness. The most remarkable in the literature is undoubtedly Naef's case.[8a] It concerns a gentleman of 32 with a bad family history and numerous signs of degeneracy, partly functional, partly organic. As a result of overwork he had, at the early age of 17, a peculiar twilight state with delusions, which lasted a few days and then cleared up with sudden recovery of memory. Later he was subject to frequent attacks of giddiness with palpitations and vomiting, but these attacks were never attended by loss of consciousness. At the end of a feverish illness he suddenly left Australia for Zurich, where he spent some weeks in carefree and merry living, only coming to himself when he read of his sudden disappearance from Australia in the newspapers. He had complete retrograde amnesia for the period of several months that included his journey to Australia, his stay there, and the journey back. A case of periodic amnesia is published by Azam: [9] Albert X., 12½ years old, with hysterical symptoms, had several attacks of amnesia in the course of a few years, during which he forgot how to read, write, count, and even how to speak his own language, for weeks at a stretch. In between times he was normal.

18   A case of *automatisme ambulatoire* on a decidedly hysterical basis, but differing from Naef's case in that the attacks were recurrent, is published by Proust: [10] An educated man, aged 30, exhibited all the symptoms of *grande hystérie*. He was very suggestible, and from time to time, under the stress of emo-

---

[8] "Sleepwalking must be regarded as systematic partial wakefulness, during which a limited but logically consistent complex of ideas enters into consciousness. No opposing ideas present themselves, and at the same time mental activity continues with increased energy within the limited sphere of wakefulness." Loewenfeld, *Hypnotismus* (1901), p. 289.   [8a] [See Bibliography.—EDITORS.]

[9] *Hypnotisme, double conscience* (1887). A similar case in Winslow, *Obscure Diseases of the Brain and Mind* (1863), quoted in *Allg Z f Psych*, XXII (1865), p. 405.

[10] *Tribune médicale*, 23rd year (1890).

tional excitement, had attacks of amnesia lasting from two days to several weeks. While in these states he wandered about, visited relatives, smashed various things in their houses, contracted debts, and was even arrested and convicted for picking pockets.

19   There is a similar case of vagrancy in Boeteau: [11] A widow of 22, highly hysterical, became terrified at the prospect of an operation for salpingitis, left the hospital where she had been till then, and fell into a somnambulistic condition, from which she awoke after three days with total amnesia. In those three days she had walked about thirty miles looking for her child.

20   William James [12] describes a case of an "ambulatory sort": the Reverend Ansel Bourne, itinerant preacher, 30 years old, psychopath, had on several occasions attacks of unconsciousness lasting an hour. One day (January 17, 1887) he suddenly disappeared from Greene, Rhode Island, after having lifted $551 from a bank. He was missing for two months, during which time he ran a little grocery store in Norristown, Pennsylvania, under the name of A. J. Brown, carefully attending to all the purchases himself, although he had never done this sort of work before. On March 14 he suddenly awoke and went back home. Complete amnesia for the interval.

21   Mesnet [13] published this case: F., 27 years old, sergeant in the African regiment, sustained an injury of the parietal bone at Bazeilles. Suffered for a year from hemiplegia, which disappeared when the wound healed. During the illness he had somnambulistic attacks with marked restriction of consciousness; all the sense functions were paralysed except for the sense of taste and a little bit of the sense of sight. Movements were co-ordinated, but their performance in overcoming obstacles was severely limited. During attacks the patient had a senseless collecting mania. Through various manipulations his consciousness could be given an hallucinatory content; for instance, if a stick was placed in his hand, the patient would immediately

---

11 "Automatisme somnambulique avec dédoublement de la personnalité" (1892).
12 *The Principles of Psychology* (1890) I, p. 391.
13 "De l'automatisme de la mémoire et du souvenir dans la somnambulisme pathologique" (1874), pp. 105–12, cited in Binet, *Alterations*, pp. 42ff. Cf. also Mesnet, "Somnambulisme spontané dans ses rapports avec l'hystérie" (1892).

feel himself transported to a battle scene, would put himself on guard, see the enemy approaching, etc.

22   Guinon and Sophie Woltke made the following experiments with hysterics: [14] A blue glass was held in front of a female patient during an hysterical attack, and she regularly saw a picture of her mother in the blue sky. A red glass showed her a bleeding wound, a yellow one an orange-seller or a lady in a yellow dress.

23   Mesnet's case recalls the cases of sudden restriction of memory.

24   MacNish [15] tells of a case of this sort: An apparently healthy young woman suddenly fell into an abnormally long sleep, apparently with no prodromal symptoms. On waking she had forgotten the words for and all knowledge of the simplest things. She had to learn how to read, write, and count all over again, at which she made rapid progress. After a second prolonged sleep she awoke as her normal self with no recollection of the intervening state. These states alternated for more than four years, during which time consciousness showed continuity within the two states, but was separated by amnesia from the consciousness of the normal state.

25   These selected cases of various kinds of changes in consciousness each throw some light on our case. Naef's case presents two hysteriform lapses of memory, one of which is characterized by delusional ideas, and the other by its long duration, restriction of consciousness, and the desire to wander. The peculiar, unexpected impulses are particularly clear in Proust and Mesnet. In our case the corresponding features would be the impulsive tearing up of flowers and the digging up of graves. The patient's continuity of consciousness during attacks reminds us of the way consciousness behaved in the MacNish case; hence it may be regarded as a temporary phenomenon of alternating consciousness. The dreamlike hallucinatory content of restricted consciousness in our case does not, however, appear to justify us in assigning it without qualification to this "double consciousness" group. The hallucinations in the second state show a certain creativeness which seems to be due to its auto-sug-

[14] "De l'influence des excitations des organes des sens sur les hallucinations de la phase passionnelle de l'attaque hystérique" (1891).
[15] *The Philosophy of Sleep* (1830), cited in Binet, p. 4.

gestibility. In Mesnet's case we observe the appearance of hallucinatory processes through simple stimulations of touch. The patient's subconscious uses these simple perceptions for the automatic construction of complicated scenes which then take possession of his restricted consciousness. We have to take a somewhat similar view of the hallucinations of our patient; at any rate the outward circumstances in which they arose seem to strengthen this conjecture.

26   The walk in the cemetery induced the vision of the skeletons, and the meeting with the three boys evoked the hallucination of children buried alive, whose voices the patient heard at night. She came to the cemetery in a somnambulistic condition, which on this occasion was particularly intense in consequence of her having taken alcohol. She then performed impulsive actions of which her subconscious, at least, received certain impressions. (The part played here by alcohol should not be underestimated. We know from experience that it not only acts adversely on these conditions, but, like every other narcotic, increases suggestibility.) The impressions received in somnambulism go on working in the subconscious to form independent growths, and finally reach perception as hallucinations. Consequently our case is closely allied to the somnambulistic dream-states that have recently been subjected to penetrating study in England and France.

27   The gaps of memory, apparently lacking content at first, acquire such through incidental auto-suggestions, and this content builds itself up automatically to a certain point. Then, probably under the influence of the improvement now beginning, its further development comes to a standstill and finally it disappears altogether as recovery sets in.

28   Binet and Féré have made numerous experiments with the implanting of suggestions in states of partial sleep. They have shown, for instance, that when a pencil is put into the anaesthetic hand of an hysteric, she will immediately produce long letters in automatic writing whose content is completely foreign to her consciousness. Cutaneous stimuli in anaesthetic regions are sometimes perceived as visual images, or at least as vivid and unexpected visual ideas. These independent transmutations of simple stimuli must be regarded as the primary phenomenon in the formation of somnambulistic dream pictures. In excep-

tional cases, analogous phenomena occur even within the sphere
of waking consciousness. Goethe,[16] for instance, says that when
he sat down, lowered his head, and vividly conjured up the
image of a flower, he saw it undergoing changes of its own accord, as if entering into new combinations of form. In the half-
waking state these phenomena occur fairly often as hypnagogic
hallucinations. Goethe's automatisms differ from truly somnambulistic ones, because in his case the initial idea is conscious,
and the development of the automatism keeps within the
bounds laid down by the initial idea, that is to say, within the
purely motor or visual area.

29   If the initial idea sinks below the threshold, or if it was never
conscious at all and its automatic development encroaches on
areas in the immediate vicinity, then it is impossible to differ-
entiate between waking automatisms and those of the somnambulistic state. This happens, for instance, if the perception of
a flower associates itself with the idea of a hand plucking the
flower, or with the idea of the smell of a flower. The only criterion of distinction is then simply "more" or "less": in one case
we speak of "normal waking hallucinations" and in the other
of "somnambulistic dream visions." The interpretation of our
patient's attacks as hysterical becomes more certain if we can
prove that the hallucinations were probably psychogenic in
origin. This is further supported by her complaints (headache
and tendovaginitis), which proved amenable to treatment by
suggestion. The only aspect that the diagnosis of "hysteria" does
not take sufficiently into account is the aetiological factor, for
we would after all expect *a priori* that, in the course of an illness which responds so completely to a rest cure, features would
now and then be observed which could be interpreted as symptoms of exhaustion. The question then arises whether the early
lapses of memory and the later somnambulistic attacks can be
regarded as states of exhaustion or as "neurasthenic crises." We

[16] "I had the gift, when I closed my eyes and bent my head, of being able to con-
jure up in my mind's eye the imaginary picture of a flower. This flower did not
retain its first shape for a single instant, but unfolded out of itself new flowers
with coloured petals and green leaves. They were not natural flowers, but fantastic ones, and were as regular in shape as a sculptor's rosettes. It was impossible to fix the creative images that sprang up, yet they lasted as long as I desired
them to last, neither weakening nor increasing in strength." *Zur Naturwissenschaft.*

know that psychopathic inferiority can give rise to various kinds of epileptoid attacks whose classification under epilepsy or hysteria is at least doubtful. To quote Westphal:

On the basis of numerous observations I maintain that the so-called epileptoid attacks form one of the commonest and most frequent symptoms in the group of diseases we reckon among the mental diseases and neuropathies, and that the mere appearance of one or more epileptic or epileptoid attacks is not decisive either for the character and form of the disease or for its course and prognosis. . . . As already mentioned, I have used the term "epileptoid" in the widest sense for the attack itself.[17]

30   The epileptoid elements in our case are not far to seek; on the other hand, one can object that the colouring of the whole picture is hysterical in the extreme. As against this we must point out that not every case of somnambulism is *ipso facto* hysterical. Occasionally states occur in typical epilepsy which to experts seem directly parallel with somnambulistic states, or which can be distinguished from hysteria only by the occurrence of genuine convulsions.[18]

31   As Diehl [19] has shown, neurasthenic inferiority may also give rise to "crises" which often confuse the diagnosis. A definite content of ideas can even repeat itself in stereotyped form in each crisis. Mörchen, too, has recently published the case of an epileptoid neurasthenic twilight state.[20]

32   I am indebted to Professor Bleuler for the following case: An educated gentleman of middle age, with no epileptic antecedents, had worn himself out with years of mental overwork. Without any other prodromal symptoms (such as depression, etc.) , he attempted suicide on a holiday: in a peculiar twilight state he suddenly threw himself into the water from a crowded spot on the river bank. He was immediately hauled out and had only a vague memory of the incident.

17 "Agoraphobie" (1872) , p. 158.
18 Pick, "Vom Bewusstsein in Zuständen sogenannter Bewusstlosigkeit" (1884), p. 202; and Pelman, "Über das Verhalten des Gedächtnisses bei den verschiedenen Formen des Irreseins" (1864), p. 78.
19 Neurasthenische Krisen" (1902): "When the patients first describe their crises, they generally give a picture that makes us think of epileptic depression. I have often been deceived in this way."
20 *Über Dämmerzustände* (1901), case 32, p. 75.

33   With these observations in mind, we must certainly allow neurasthenia a considerable share in the attacks of our patient. The headaches and the "tendovaginitis" point to a mild degree of hysteria, normally latent but becoming manifest under the stress of exhaustion. The genesis of this peculiar illness explains the above-described relationship to epilepsy, hysteria, and neurasthenia. To sum up: Miss E. suffers from a psychopathic inferiority with a tendency to hysteria. Under the influence of nervous exhaustion she has fits of epileptoid stupor whose interpretation is uncertain at first sight. As a result of an unusually large dose of alcohol, the attacks develop into definite somnambulism with hallucinations, which attach themselves to fortuitous external perceptions in the same way as dreams. When the nervous exhaustion is cured, the hysteriform symptoms disappear.

34   In the realm of psychopathic inferiority with hysterical colouring, we meet with numerous phenomena which show, as in this case, symptoms belonging to several different clinical pictures, but which cannot with certainty be assigned to any one of them. Some of these states are already recognized as disorders in their own right: e.g., pathological lying, pathological dreaminess, etc. But many of them still await thorough scientific investigation; at present they belong more or less to the domain of scientific gossip. Persons with habitual hallucinations, and also those who are inspired, exhibit these states; they draw the attention of the crowd to themselves, now as poets or artists, now as saviours, prophets, or founders of new sects.

35   The genesis of the peculiar mentality of these people is for the most part lost in obscurity, for it is only very rarely that one of these singular personalities can be subjected to exact observation. In view of the—sometimes—great historical significance of such persons, it were much to be wished that we had enough scientific material to give us closer insight into the psychological development of their peculiarities. Apart from the now practically useless productions of the pneumatological school at the beginning of the nineteenth century, there is a remarkable dearth of competent observations in the German scientific literature of the subject; indeed, there seems to be a real aversion to investigation in this field. For the facts so far gathered we are indebted almost exclusively to the labours of

French and English workers. It therefore seems at least desirable that our literature should be enlarged in this respect. These reflections have prompted me to publish some observations which will perhaps help to broaden our knowledge of the relations between hysterical twilight states and the problems of normal psychology.

[2.] A CASE OF SOMNAMBULISM IN A GIRL WITH POOR INHERITANCE (SPIRITUALISTIC MEDIUM)

36   The following case was under my observation during the years 1899 and 1900. As I was not in medical attendance upon Miss S. W., unfortunately no physical examination for hysterical stigmata could be made. I kept a detailed diary of the séances, which I wrote down after each sitting. The report that follows is a condensed account from these notes. Out of regard for Miss S. W. and her family, a few unimportant data have been altered and various details omitted from her "romances," which for the most part are composed of very intimate material.

[Anamnesis]

37   Miss S. W., 15½ years old, Protestant. The paternal grandfather was very intelligent, a clergyman who frequently had waking hallucinations (mostly visions, often whole dramatic scenes with dialogues, etc.). A brother of her grandfather was feeble-minded, an eccentric who also saw visions. One of his sisters was also a peculiar, odd character. The paternal grandmother, after a feverish illness in her twentieth year—typhoid fever?—had a trance lasting for three days, from which she did not begin to awake until the crown of her head was burnt with a red-hot iron. Later on, when emotionally excited, she had fainting-fits; these were nearly always followed by a brief somnambulism during which she uttered prophecies. The father too was an odd, original personality with bizarre ideas. Two of his brothers were the same. All three had waking hallucinations. (Second sight, premonitions, etc.) A third brother was also eccentric and odd, talented but one-sided. The mother has a congenital psychopathic inferiority often bordering on psychosis. One sister

17

is an hysteric and a visionary, another sister suffers from "nervous heart-attacks."

38   S. W. is of delicate build, skull somewhat rachitic though not noticeably hydrocephalic, face rather pale, eyes dark, with a peculiar penetrating look. She has had no serious illnesses. At school she passed for average, showed little interest, was inattentive. In general, her behaviour was rather reserved, but this would suddenly give place to the most exuberant joy and exaltation. Of mediocre intelligence, with no special gifts, neither musical nor fond of books, she prefers handwork or just sitting around day-dreaming. Even at school she was often absent-minded, misread in a peculiar way when reading aloud—for instance, instead of the word "Ziege" (goat) she would say "Geiss," and instead of "Treppe" (stair) she would say "Stege"; this happened so often that her brothers and sisters used to laugh at her.[21] Otherwise there were no abnormalities to be noticed about S. W., and especially no serious hysterical symptoms. Her family were all artisans and business people with very limited interests. Books of a mystical nature were never allowed in the family. Her education was deficient; apart from the fact that there were many brothers and sisters, all given a very casual education, the children suffered a great deal from the inconsequent, vulgar, and often brutal treatment they received from their mother. The father, a very preoccupied business man, could not devote much time to his children and died when S. W. was still adolescent. In these distressing circumstances it is no wonder that she felt shut in and unhappy. She was often afraid to go home and preferred to be anywhere rather than there. Hence she was left a great deal with her playmates and grew up without much polish. Her educational level was accordingly pretty low and her interests were correspondingly limited. Her knowledge of literature was likewise very limited. She knew the usual poems of Schiller and Goethe and a few other poets learnt by heart at school, some snatches from a song-book, and fragments of the Psalms. Newspaper and magazine stories probably represented the upper limit in prose. Up to the time of her somnambulism she had never read anything of a more cultured nature.

21 [The alternative terms are Swiss dialect. Cf. par. 73, and also the following paper, pars. 151ff., below.—EDITORS.]

[Somnambulistic States]

39   At home and from friends she heard about table-turning and began to take an interest in it. She asked to be allowed to take part in such experiments, and her desire was soon gratified. In July 1899, she did some table-turning several times in the family circle with friends, but as a joke. It was then discovered that she was an excellent medium. Communications of a serious nature arrived and were received amid general astonishment. Their pastoral tone was surprising. The spirit gave himself out to be the grandfather of the medium. As I was acquainted with the family, I was able to take part in these experiments. At the beginning of August 1899, I witnessed the first attacks of somnambulism. Their course was usually as follows: S. W. grew very pale, slowly sank to the ground or into a chair, closed her eyes, became cataleptic, drew several deep breaths, and began to speak. At this stage she was generally quite relaxed, the eyelid reflexes remained normal and so did tactile sensibility. She was sensitive to unexpected touches and easily frightened, especially in the initial stage.

40   She did not react when called by name. In her somnambulistic dialogues she copied in a remarkably clever way her dead relatives and acquaintances, with all their foibles, so that she made a lasting impression even on persons not easily influenced. She could also hit off people whom she knew only from hearsay, doing it so well that none of the spectators could deny her at least considerable talent as an actress. Gradually gestures began to accompany the words, and these finally led up to "attitudes passionnelles" and whole dramatic scenes. She flung herself into postures of prayer and rapture, with staring eyes, and spoke with impassioned and glowing rhetoric. On these occasions she made exclusive use of literary German, which she spoke with perfect ease and assurance, in complete contrast to her usual uncertain and embarrassed manner in the waking state. Her movements were free and of a noble grace, mirroring most beautifully her changing emotions. At this stage her behaviour during the attacks was irregular and extraordinarily varied. Now she would lie for ten minutes to two hours on the sofa or the floor, motionless, with closed eyes; now she assumed a half-sitting

posture and spoke with altered voice and diction; now she was in constant movement, going through every possible pantomimic gesture. The content of her speeches was equally variable and irregular. Sometimes she spoke in the first person, but never for long, and then only to prophesy her next attack; sometimes— and this was the most usual—she spoke of herself in the third person. She then acted some other person, either a dead acquaintance or somebody she had invented, whose part she carried out consistently according to the characteristics she herself conceived. The ecstasy was generally followed by a cataleptic stage with *flexibilitas cerea,* which gradually passed over into the waking state. An almost constant feature was the sudden pallor which gave her face a waxen anaemic hue that was positively frightening. This sometimes occurred right at the beginning of the attack, but often in the second half only. Her pulse was then low but regular and of normal frequency; the breathing gentle, shallow, often barely perceptible. As we have already remarked, S. W. frequently predicted her attacks beforehand; just before the attacks she had strange sensations, became excited, rather anxious, and occasionally expressed thoughts of death, saying that she would probably die in one of these attacks, that her soul only hung on to her body by a very thin thread, so that her body could scarcely go on living. On one occasion after the cataleptic stage, tachypnoea was observed, lasting for two minutes with a respiration of 100 per minute. At first the attacks occurred spontaneously, but later S. W. could induce them by sitting in a dark corner and covering her face with her hands. But often the experiment did not succeed, as she had what she called "good" and "bad" days.

41   The question of amnesia after the attacks is unfortunately very unclear. This much is certain, that after each attack she was perfectly oriented about the specific experiences she had undergone in the "rapture." It is, however, uncertain how much she remembered of the conversations for which she served as a medium, and of changes in her surroundings during the attack. It often looked as if she did have a vague recollection, for often she would ask immediately on waking: "Who was there? Wasn't X or Y there? What did he say?" She also showed that she was superficially aware of the content of the conversations. She often remarked that the spirits told her before waking what

they had said. But frequently this was not the case at all. If at her request someone repeated the trance speeches to her, she was very often indignant about them and would be sad and depressed for hours on end, especially if any unpleasant indiscretions had occurred. She would rail against the spirits and assert that next time she would ask her guide to keep such spirits away from her. Her indignation was not faked, for in the waking state she could barely control herself and her affects, so that any change of mood was immediately reflected in her face. At times she seemed barely, if at all, aware of what went on around her during the attack. She seldom noticed when anyone left the room or came into it. Once she forbade me to enter the room when she was expecting special communications which she wished to keep secret from me. I went in, nevertheless, sat down with the three other sitters, and listened to everything. S. W. had her eyes open and spoke to the others without noticing me. She only noticed me when I began to speak, which gave rise to a veritable storm of indignation. She remembered better, but still only vaguely, the remarks of participants which referred to the trance speeches or directly to herself. I could never discover any definite rapport in this connection.

42   Besides these "big" attacks, which seemed to follow a certain law, S. W. also exhibited a large number of other automatisms. Premonitions, forebodings, unaccountable moods, and rapidly changing fancies were all in the day's work. I never observed simple states of sleep. On the other hand, I soon noticed that in the middle of a lively conversation she would become all confused and go on talking senselessly in a peculiar monotonous way, looking in front of her dreamily with half-closed eyes. These lapses usually lasted only a few minutes. Then she would suddenly go on: "Yes, what did you say?" At first she would not give any information about these lapses, saying evasively that she felt a bit giddy, had a headache, etc. Later she simply said: "They were there again," meaning her spirits. She succumbed to these lapses very much against her will; often she struggled against them: "I don't want to, not now, let them come another time, they seem to think I'm there only for them." The lapses came over her in the street, in shops, in fact anywhere. If they happened in the street, she would lean against a house and wait till the attack was over. During these attacks, whose intensity

21

varied considerably, she had visions; very often, and especially during attacks when she turned extremely pale, she "wandered," or, as she put it, lost her body and was wafted to distant places where the spirits led her. Distant journeys during ecstasy tired her exceedingly; she was often completely exhausted for hours afterward, and many times complained that the spirits had again drained the strength from her, such exertions were too much, the spirits must get another medium, etc. Once she went hysterically blind for half an hour after the ecstasy. Her gait was unsteady, groping; she had to be led, did not see the light that stood on the table, though the pupils reacted.

43   Visions also came in large numbers even without proper lapses (if we use this word only for higher-grade disturbances of attention). At first they were confined to the onset of sleep. A little while after she had gone to bed the room would suddenly light up, and shining white figures detached themselves from the foggy brightness. They were all wrapped in white veil-like robes, the women had things resembling turbans on their heads and wore girdles. Later (according to her own statement) "the spirits were already there" when she went to bed. Finally she saw the figures in broad daylight, though only blurred and fleetingly if there was no real lapse (then the figures became solid enough to touch). But she always preferred the darkness. According to her account, the visions were generally of a pleasant nature. Gazing at the beautiful figures gave her a feeling of delicious bliss. Terrifying visions of a daemonic character were much rarer. These were entirely confined to night-time or dark rooms. Occasionally she saw black figures in the street at night or in her room; once in the dark hallway she saw a terrible copper-red face which suddenly glared at her from very near and terrified her. I could not find out anything satisfactory about the first occurrence of the visions. She stated that in her fifth or sixth year she once saw her "guide" at night—her grandfather (whom she had never known in life). I could not obtain any objective clues about this early vision from her relatives. Nothing more of the kind is said to have happened until the first séance. Except for the hypnagogic brightness and "seeing sparks" there were never any rudimentary hallucinations; from the beginning the hallucinations were of a systematic nature involving all the sense organs equally. So far as the intellectual

reaction to these phenomena is concerned, what is remarkable is the amazing matter-of-factness with which she regarded them. Her whole development into a somnambulist, her innumerable weird experiences, seemed to her entirely natural. She saw her whole past only in this light. Every in any way striking event from her earlier years stood in a clear and necessary relationship to her present situation. She was happy in the consciousness of having found her true vocation. Naturally she was unshakably convinced of the reality of her visions. I often tried to give her some critical explanation, but she would have none of it, since in her normal state she could not grasp a rational explanation anyway, and in her semi-somnambulistic state she regarded it as senseless in view of the facts staring her in the face. She once said: "I do not know if what the spirits say and teach me is true, nor do I know if they really are the people they call themselves; but that my spirits exist is beyond question. I see them before me, I can touch them. I speak to them about everything I wish as naturally as I'm talking to you. They must be real." She absolutely would not listen to the idea that the manifestations were a kind of illness. Doubts about her health or about the reality of her dream-world distressed her deeply; she felt so hurt by my remarks that she closed up in my presence and for a long time refused to experiment if I was there; hence I took care not to express my doubts and misgivings aloud. On the other hand she enjoyed the undivided respect and admiration of her immediate relatives and acquaintances, who asked her advice about all sorts of things. In time she obtained such an influence over her followers that three of her sisters began to hallucinate too. The hallucinations usually began as night-dreams of a very vivid and dramatic kind which gradually passed over into the waking state—partly hypnagogic, partly hypnopompic. A married sister in particular had extraordinarily vivid dreams that developed logically from night to night and finally appeared in her waking consciousness first as indistinct delusions and then as real hallucinations, but they never reached the plastic clearness of S. W.'s visions. Thus, she once saw in a dream a black daemonic figure at her bedside in vigorous argument with a beautiful white figure who was trying to restrain the black; nevertheless the black figure seized her by the throat and started to choke her; then she awoke. Bending over her she saw a black shadow with human outlines, and near it a cloudy white figure. The vision disappeared only when she lighted the candle. Similar visions were repeated dozens of times. The visions of the other two sisters were similar but less intense.

44   The type of attack we have described, with its wealth of fantastic visions and ideas, had developed in less than a month, reaching a climax which was never to be surpassed. What came later was only an elaboration of all the thoughts and the cycles of visions that had been more or less foreshadowed right at the beginning. In addition to the "big attacks" and the "little lapses," whose content however was materially the same, there was a third category that deserves mention. These were the semi-somnambulistic states. They occurred at the beginning or end of the big attacks, but also independently of them. They developed slowly in the course of the first month. It is not possible to give a more precise date for their appearance. What was especially noticeable in this state was the rigid expression of the face, the shining eyes, and a certain dignity and stateliness of movement. In this condition S. W. was herself, or rather her somnambulist ego. She was fully oriented to the external world but seemed to have one foot in her dream-world. She saw and heard her spirits, saw how they walked round the room among those present, standing now by one person and now by another. She had a clear memory of her visions, of her journeys, and the instructions she received. She spoke quietly, clearly, and firmly, and was always in a serious, almost solemn, mood. Her whole being glowed with deep religious feeling, free from any pietistic flavour, and her speech was in no way influenced by the Biblical jargon of her guide. Her solemn behaviour had something sorrowful and melancholy about it. She was painfully conscious of the great difference between her nocturnal ideal world and the crude reality of day. This state was in sharp contrast to her waking existence; in it there was no trace of that unstable and inharmonious creature, of that brittle nervous temperament which was so characteristic of her usual behaviour. Speaking with her, you had the impression of speaking with a much older person, who through numerous experiences had arrived at a state of calm composure. It was in this state that she achieved her best results, whereas her romances corresponded more closely to her waking interests. The semi-somnambulism usually appeared

spontaneously, as a rule during the table-turning experiments, and it always began by S. W.'s knowing beforehand what the table was going to say. She would then stop table-turning and after a short pause would pass suddenly into an ecstasy. She proved to be very sensitive. She could guess and answer simple questions devised by a member of the circle who was not himself a medium. It was enough to lay a hand on the table, or on her hands, to give her the necessary clues. Direct thought transference could never be established. Beside the obvious broadening of her whole personality the continued existence of her ordinary character was all the more startling. She talked with unconcealed pleasure about all her little childish experiences, the flirtations and love secrets, the naughtiness and rudeness of her companions and playmates. To anyone who did not know her secret she was just a girl of 15½, no different from thousands of other girls. So much the greater was people's astonishment when they came to know her other side. Her relatives could not grasp the change at first; part of it they never understood at all, so that there were often bitter arguments in the family, some of them siding with S. W. and others against her, either with gushing enthusiasm or with contemptuous censure of her "superstition." Thus S. W., during the time that I knew her, led a curiously contradictory life, a real "double life" with two personalities existing side by side or in succession, each continually striving for mastery. I will now give some of the most interesting details of the séances in chronological order.

[Records of Séances]

45   FIRST AND SECOND SITTINGS (August 1899). S. W. at once took control of the "communications." The "psychograph," for which an overturned tumbler was used, the two fingers of the right hand being placed upon it, moved with lightning speed from letter to letter. (Slips of paper, marked with letters and numbers, had been arranged in a circle round the glass.) It was communicated that the medium's grandfather was present and would speak to us. There now followed numerous communications in quick succession, mostly of an edifying religious character, partly in properly formed words and partly with the letters transposed or in reverse order. These latter words and

sentences were often produced so rapidly that one could not follow the meaning and only discovered it afterwards by reversing the letters. Once the messages were interrupted in brusque fashion by a new communication announcing the presence of the writer's grandfather. Someone remarked jokingly: "Evidently the two spirits don't get on very well together." Darkness came on during the experiment. Suddenly S. W. became very agitated, jumped up nervously, fell on her knees, and cried: "There, there, don't you see that light, that star there?" She grew more and more excited, and called for a lamp in terror. She was pale, wept, said she felt queer, did not know what was the matter with her. When a lamp was brought she quieted down. The experiments were suspended.

46   At the next sitting, which took place two days later, also in the evening, similar communications were obtained from S. W.'s grandfather. When darkness fell she suddenly lay back on the sofa, grew pale, closed her eyes to a slit, and lay there motionless. The eyeballs were turned upwards, the eye-lid reflex was present, also tactile sensibility. Respiration gentle, almost imperceptible. Pulse low and feeble. This condition lasted about half an hour, whereupon she suddenly got up with a sigh. The extreme pallor of the face, which had lasted all through the attack, now gave way to her usual rosy colour. She was somewhat confused and embarrassed, said she had seen "all sorts" of things, but would tell nothing. Only after insistent questioning would she admit that in a peculiar waking condition she had seen her grandfather arm-in-arm with my grandfather. Then they suddenly drove past sitting side by side in an open carriage.

47   THIRD SITTING. In this, which took place a few days later, there was a similar attack of more than half an hour's duration. S. W. afterwards told of many white transfigured forms who each gave her a flower of special symbolic significance. Most of them were dead relatives. Concerning the details of their talk she maintained an obstinate silence.

48   FOURTH SITTING. After S. W. had passed into the somnambulistic state she began to make peculiar movements with her lips, emitting at the same time gulping and gurgling noises. Then she whispered something unintelligible very softly. When this had gone on for some minutes she suddenly began speaking in

an altered, deep tone of voice. She spoke of herself in the third person: "She is not here. she has gone away." There now followed several sentences in a religious vein. From their content and language one could see that she was imitating her grandfather, who had been a clergyman. The gist of the talk did not rise above the mental level of the "communications." The tone of voice had something artificial and forced about it, and only became natural when in due course it grew more like the medium's own. (In later sittings the voice only altered for a few moments when a new spirit manifested itself.) Afterwards she had no remembrance of the trance conversation. She gave hints about a sojourn in the other world and spoke of the unimaginable blessedness she felt. It should be noted that during the attack her talk was absolutely spontaneous and not prompted by any suggestions.

49   Immediately after this sitting S. W. became acquainted with Justinus Kerner's book *Die Seherin von Prevorst*.[22] She thereupon began to magnetize herself towards the end of the attacks, partly by means of regular passes, partly by strange circles and figures of eight which she executed symmetrically with both arms at once. She did this, she said, to dispel the severe headaches that came after the attacks. In other August sittings (not detailed here) the grandfather was joined by numerous kindred spirits who did not produce anything very remarkable. Each time a new spirit appeared, the movements of the glass altered in a startling way: it ran along the row of letters, knocking against some of them, but no sense could be made of it. The spelling was very uncertain and arbitrary, and the first sentences were often incomplete or broken up into meaningless jumbles of letters. In most cases fluent writing suddenly began at this point. Sometimes automatic writing was attempted in complete darkness. The movements began with violent jerkings of the whole arm, so that the pencil went right through the paper. The first attempt consisted of numerous strokes and zigzag lines about 8 cm. high. Further attempts first produced illegible words written very large, then the writing gradually grew smaller and more distinct. It was not much different from the

22 ["The Clairvoyante of Prevorst," pub. 1829; trans. as *The Seeress of Prevorst*, 1859.—EDITORS.]

medium's own. The control spirit was once again the grand-father.

50   FIFTH SITTING. Somnambulistic attacks in September 1899. S. W. sat on the sofa, leant back, shut her eyes, breathing lightly and regularly. She gradually became cataleptic. The catalepsy disappeared after about two minutes, whereupon she lay there apparently sleeping quietly, muscles quite relaxed. Suddenly she began talking in a low voice: "No, you take the red, I'll take the white. You can take the green, and you the blue. Are you ready? Let's go." (Pause of several minutes, during which her face assumed a corpse-like pallor. Her hands felt cold and were quite bloodless.) Suddenly she called out in a loud solemn voice: "Albert, Albert, Albert," then in a whisper: "Now you speak," followed by a longer pause during which the pallor of her face reached its highest conceivable intensity. Again in a loud solemn voice: "Albert, Albert, don't you believe your father? I tell you there are many mistakes in N's teaching. Think about it." Pause. The pallor decreased. "He's very frightened, he couldn't speak any more." (These words in her usual conversational tone.) Pause. "He will certainly think about it." She went on speaking in the same conversational tone but in a strange idiom that sounded like French and Italian mixed, recalling now one and now the other. She spoke fluently, rapidly, and with charm. It was possible to make out a few words, but not to memorize them, because the language was so strange. From time to time certain words recurred, like *wena, wenes, wenai, wene,* etc. The absolute naturalness of the performance was amazing. Now and then she paused as if someone were answering her. Suddenly she said, in German: "Oh dear, is it time already?" (In a sad voice.) "Must I go? Goodbye, goodbye!" At these words there passed over her face an indescribable expression of ecstatic happiness. She raised her arms, opened her eyes, till now closed, and looked upwards radiantly. For a moment she remained in this position, then her arms sank down slackly, her face became tired and exhausted. After a short cataleptic stage she woke up with a sigh. "I've slept again, haven't I?" She was told she had been talking in her sleep, whereupon she became wildly annoyed, and her anger increased still more when she learned that she was talking in a foreign language. "But I told the spirits I didn't want to, I can't do it, it tires me too much." (Began to cry.)

28

"Oh God, must everything, everything come back again like last time, am I to be spared nothing?"

51   The next day at the same time there was another attack. After S. W. had dropped off, Ulrich von Gerbenstein suddenly announced himself. He proved to be an amusing gossip, speaking fluent High German with a North German accent. Asked what S. W. was doing, he explained with much circumlocution that she was far away, and that he was here meanwhile to look after her body, its circulation, respiration, etc. He must take care that no black person got hold of her and harmed her. On insistent questioning he said that S. W. had gone with the others to Japan, to look up a distant relative and stop him from a stupid marriage. He then announced in a whisper the exact moment when the meeting took place. Forbidden to talk for a few minutes, he pointed to S. W.'s sudden pallor, remarking that materialization at such great distances cost a corresponding amount of strength. He then ordered cold compresses to be applied to her head so as to alleviate the severe headache which would come afterwards. With the gradual return of colour to her face, the conversation became more animated. There were all sorts of childish jokes and trivialities, then U. v. G. suddenly said: "I see them coming, but they are still very far off; I see her there like a little star." S. W. pointed to the north. We naturally asked in astonishment why they were not coming from the east, whereupon U. v. G. laughingly replied: "They come the direct way over the North Pole. I must go now, goodbye." Immediately afterwards S. W. awoke with a sigh, in a bad temper, complaining of violent headache. She said she had seen U. v. G. standing by her body; what had he told us? She was furious about the "silly chatter," why couldn't he lay off it for once?

52   SIXTH SITTING. Began in the usual way. Extreme pallor; lay stretched out, scarcely breathing. Suddenly she spoke in a loud solemn voice: "Well then, be frightened; I am. I warn you about N's teaching. Look, in hope there is everything needed for faith. You want to know who I am? God gives where one least expects it. Don't you know me?" Then unintelligible whispering. After a few minutes she woke up.

53   SEVENTH SITTING. S. W. soon fell asleep, stretched out on the sofa. Very pale. Said nothing. sighed deeply from time to time. Opened her eyes, stood up, sat down on the sofa, bent forward,

saying softly: "You have sinned grievously, have fallen far."
Bent still further forward as if speaking to someone kneeling in
front of her. Stood up, turned to the right, stretched out her
hand, and pointed to the spot over which she had been bending:
"Will you forgive her?" she asked loudly. "Do not forgive men,
but their spirits. Not she, but her human body has sinned."
Then she knelt down, remained for about ten minutes in an
attitude of prayer. Suddenly she got up, looked to heaven with
an ecstatic expression, and then threw herself on her knees
again, her face in her hands, whispering incomprehensible
words. Remained motionless in this attitude for several minutes.
Then she got up, gazed heavenward again with radiant counte-
nance, and lay down on the sofa, waking soon afterwards.

Development of the Somnambulistic Personalities

54   At the beginning of many séances, the glass was allowed to
move by itself, and this was always followed by the stereotyped
invitation: "You must ask a question." Since several convinced
spiritualists were attending the séances, there was of course an
immediate demand for all manner of spiritualistic marvels,
especially for the "protecting spirits." At these requests the
names of well-known dead persons were sometimes produced,
and sometimes unknown names such as Berthe de Valours, Elisabeth von Thierfelsenburg, Ulrich von Gerbenstein, etc. The
control spirit was almost without exception the medium's
grandfather, who once declared that "he loved her more than
anyone in this world because he had protected her from childhood up and knew all her thoughts." This personality produced
a flood of Biblical maxims, edifying observations, and song-book
verses, also verses he had presumably composed himself, like the
following:

> Be firm and true in thy believing,
> To faith in God cling ever nigh,
> Thy heavenly comfort never leaving,
> Which having, man can never die.
> Refuge in God is peace for ever
> When earthly cares oppress the mind;
> Who from the heart can pray is never
> Bow'd down by fate howe'er unkind.

55   Numerous other effusions of this sort betrayed by their hackneyed, unctuous content their origin in some tract or other. From the time S. W. began speaking in her ecstasies, lively dialogues developed between members of the circle and the somnambulist personality. The gist of the answers received was essentially the same as the banal and generally edifying verbiage of the psychographic communications. The character of this personality was distinguished by a dry and tedious solemnity, rigorous conventionality, and sanctimonious piety (which does not accord at all with the historical reality). The grandfather was the medium's guide and protector. During the ecstasies he offered all kinds of advice, prophesied later attacks and what would happen when she woke, etc. He ordered cold compresses, gave instructions concerning the way the medium should lie on the couch, arrangements for sittings, and so on. His relationship to the medium was exceedingly tender. In vivid contrast to this heavy-footed dream-personage, there appeared a personality who had cropped up occasionally in the psychographic communications of the first sittings. He soon disclosed himself as the dead brother of a Mr. R., who was then taking part in the séances. This dead brother, Mr. P. R., peppered his living brother with commonplaces about brotherly love, etc. He evaded specific questions in every possible way. At the same time he developed a quite astonishing eloquence toward the ladies of the circle, and in particular paid his attentions to a lady whom he had never known in life. He stated that even when alive he had always raved about her, had often met her in the street without knowing who she was, and was now absolutely delighted to make her acquaintance in this unusual manner. His stale compliments, pert remarks to the men, innocuous childish jokes, etc., took up a large part of the séances. Several members of the circle took exception to the frivolity and banality of this spirit, whereupon he vanished for one or two sittings, but soon reappeared, at first well-behaved, often with Christian phrases on his lips, but before long slipping back into his old form.

56   Besides these two sharply differentiated personalities, others appeared who varied but little from the grandfather type; they were mostly dead relatives of the medium. The general atmosphere of the first two months' séances was accordingly solemn and edifying, disturbed only from time to time by P. R.'s trivial

chatter. A few weeks after the beginning of the séances Mr. R. left our circle, whereupon a remarkable change took place in P. R.'s behaviour. He grew monosyllabic, came less often, and after a few sittings vanished altogether. Later on he reappeared very occasionally, and mostly only when the medium was alone with the lady in question. Then a new personality thrust himself to the forefront; unlike P. R., who always spoke Swiss dialect, this gentleman affected a strong North German accent. In all else he was an exact copy of P. R. His eloquence was astonishing, since S. W. had only a very scanty knowledge of High German, whereas this new personality, who called himself Ulrich von Gerbenstein, spoke an almost faultless German abounding in amiable phrases and charming compliments.[23]

57   Ulrich von Gerbenstein was a gossip, a wag, and an idler, a great admirer of the ladies, frivolous and extremely superficial. During the winter of 1899/1900 he came to dominate the situation more and more, and took over one by one all the abovementioned functions of the grandfather, so that the serious character of the séances visibly deteriorated under his influence. All efforts to counteract it proved unavailing, and finally the séances had to be suspended on this account for longer and longer periods.

58   One feature which all these somnambulist personalities have in common deserves mention. They have at their disposal the whole of the medium's memory, even the unconscious portion of it, they are also *au courant* with the visions she has in the ecstatic state, but they have only the most superficial knowledge of her fantasies during the ecstasy. Of the somnambulistic dreams they only know what can occasionally be picked up from members of the circle. On doubtful points they can give no information, or only such as contradicts the medium's own explanations. The stereotyped answer to all questions of this kind is "Ask Ivenes, Ivenes knows." [24] From the examples we have given of the different ecstasies it is clear that the medium's consciousness is by no means idle during the trance, but develops an extraordinarily rich fantasy activity. In reconstructing her somnambulistic ego we are entirely dependent on her subsequent

23 It should be noted that a frequent guest in S. W.'s house was a gentleman who spoke North German.
24 Ivenes is the mystical name of the medium's somnambulistic ego.

statements, for in the first place the spontaneous utterances of the ego associated with the waking state are few and mostly disjointed, and in the second place many of the ecstasies pass off without pantomime and without speech, so that no conclusions about inner processes can be drawn from external appearances. S. W. is almost totally amnesic in regard to the automatic phenomena during ecstasy, in so far as these fall within the sphere of personalities foreign to her ego. But she usually has a clear memory of all the other phenomena directly connected with her ego, such as talking in a loud voice, glossolalia, etc. In every instance, there is complete amnesia only in the first few moments after the ecstasy. During the first half hour, when a kind of semi-somnambulism with reveries, hallucinations, etc. is still present, the amnesia gradually disappears, and fragmentary memories come up of what has happened, though in a quite irregular and arbitrary fashion.

59   The later séances usually began by our joining hands on the table, whereupon the table immediately started to move. Meanwhile S. W. gradually became somnambulistic, took her hands from the table, lay back on the sofa, and fell into an ecstatic sleep. She sometimes related her experiences to us afterwards, but was very reticent if strangers were present. Even after the first few ecstasies, she hinted that she played a distinguished role among the spirits. Like all the spirits, she had a special name, and hers was Ivenes; her grandfather surrounded her with quite particular care, and in the ecstasy with the flower-vision she learnt special secrets about which she still maintained the deepest silence. During the séances when her spirits spoke she made long journeys, mostly to relatives whom she visited, or she found herself in the Beyond, in "that space between the stars which people think is empty, but which really contains countless spirit worlds." In the semi-somnambulistic state that frequently followed her attacks she once gave a truly poetic description of a landscape in the Beyond, "a wonderful moonlit valley that was destined for generations as yet unborn." She described her somnambulistic ego as a personality almost entirely freed from the body: a small but fully grown black-haired woman, of a markedly Jewish type, clothed in white garments, her head wrapped in a turban. As for herself, she understood and spoke the language of the spirits—for the spirits still speak with one another

33

from human habit, although they don't really need to because they can see one another's thoughts. She did not always actually talk with them, she just looked at them and knew what they were thinking. She travelled in the company of four or five spirits, dead relatives, and visited her living relatives and acquaintances in order to investigate their life and way of thinking; she also visited all the places that lay on her ghostly beat. After becoming acquainted with Kerner's book, she (like the Clairvoyante) felt it her destiny to instruct and improve the black spirits who are banished to certain regions or who dwell partly beneath the earth's surface. This activity caused her a good deal of trouble and pain; both during and after the ecstasies she complained of suffocating feelings, violent headaches, etc. But every fortnight, on Wednesdays, she was allowed to spend the whole night in the gardens of the Beyond in the company of the blessed spirits. There she received instruction concerning the forces that govern the world and the endlessly complicated relationships between human beings, and also concerning the laws of reincarnation, the star-dwellers, etc. Unfortunately she expatiated only on the system of world-forces and reincarnation, and merely let fall an occasional remark concerning the other subjects. For instance, she once returned from a railway journey in an extremely agitated state. We thought at first that something unpleasant must have happened to her; but finally she pulled herself together and explained that "a star-dweller had sat opposite her in the train." From the description she gave of this being I recognized an elderly merchant I happened to know, who had a rather unsympathetic face. Apropos of this event, she told us all the peculiarities of the star-dwellers: they have no godlike souls, as men have, they pursue no science, no philosophy, but in the technical arts they are far more advanced than we are. Thus, flying machines have long been in existence on Mars; the whole of Mars is covered with canals, the canals are artificial lakes and are used for irrigation. The canals are all flat ditches, the water in them is very shallow. The excavating of the canals caused the Martians no particular trouble, as the soil there is lighter than on earth. There are no bridges over the canals, but that does not prevent communication because everybody travels by flying machine. There are no wars on the stars, because no differences of opinion exist. The star-dwellers do not have a human shape but the most laughable ones imaginable, such as no one could possibly conceive. Human spirits who get permission to travel in the Beyond are not allowed to set foot on the stars. Similarly, travelling star-dwellers may not touch down on earth but must remain at a distance of some 75 feet above its surface. Should they infringe this law, they remain in the power of the earth and must take on human bodies, from which they are freed only after their natural death. As human beings they are cold, hard-hearted, and cruel. S. W. can recognize them by their peculiar expression, which lacks the "spiritual," and by their hairless, eyebrowless, sharply cut faces. Napoleon I was a typical star-dweller.

60   On her journeys she did not see the places through which she hastened. She had the feeling of floating, and the spirits told her when she was in the right spot. Then, as a rule, she saw only the face and upper part of the person before whom she wished to appear or whom she wanted to see. She could seldom say in what kind of surroundings she saw this person. Occasionally she saw me, but only my head without any background. She was much occupied with the enchanting of spirits, and for this purpose wrote oracular sayings in a foreign tongue on slips of paper which she concealed in all sorts of queer places. Especially displeasing to her was the presence in my house of an Italian murderer, whom she called Conventi. She tried several times to cast a spell on him, and without my knowledge concealed several slips of paper about the place, which were later found by accident. One of them had the following message written on it (in red pencil):

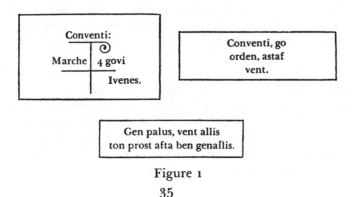

Figure 1

35

61   Unfortunately I never managed to get a translation, for in this matter S. W. was quite unapproachable.

62   Occasionally the somnambulistic Ivenes spoke directly to the public. She did so in dignified language that sounded slightly precocious, but Ivenes was not boringly unctuous or irrepressibly silly like her two guides; she is a serious, mature person, devout and right-minded, full of womanly tenderness and very modest, who always submits to the opinion of others. There is something soulful and elegiac about her, an air of melancholy resignation; she longs to get out of this world, she returns unwillingly to reality, she bemoans her hard lot, her odious family circumstances. With all this she is something of a great lady; she orders her spirits about, despises von Gerbenstein's stupid "chatter," comforts others, succours those in distress, warns and protects them from dangers to body and soul. She is the channel for the entire intellectual output of all the manifestations, though she herself ascribes this to instruction by the spirits. It is Ivenes who directly controls S. W.'s semi-somnambulistic state.

The Romances

63   The peculiar ghostlike look in S. W.'s eyes during her semi-somnambulism prompted some members of the circle to compare her to the Clairvoyante of Prevorst. The suggestion was not without consequences. S. W. gave hints of earlier existences she had already lived through, and after a few weeks she suddenly disclosed a whole system of reincarnations, although she had never mentioned anything of the sort before. Ivenes, she said, was a spiritual being who had certain advantages over the spirits of other human beings. Every human spirit must embody itself in the course of the centuries. But Ivenes had to embody herself at least once every two hundred years; apart from her, only two human beings shared this fate, namely Swedenborg and Miss Florence Cook (Crookes's [24a] famous medium). S. W. called these two personages her brother and sister. She gave no information about their previous existences. At the beginning of the nineteenth century, Ivenes had been Frau Hauffe, the Clairvoyante of Prevorst, and at the end of the eighteenth cen-

24a [Sir William Crookes, the physicist and psychic investigator.—EDITORS.]

tury a clergyman's wife in central Germany (locality unspecified), in which capacity she had been seduced by Goethe and had borne him a son. In the fifteenth century she had been a Saxon countess, with the poetic name of Thierfelsenburg. Ulrich von Gerbenstein was a relative from that time. The lapse of three hundred years before her next incarnation, and the slip-up with Goethe, had to be atoned for by the sorrows of the Clairvoyante. In the thirteenth century, she had been a noblewoman with the name of de Valours, in the south of France, and had been burnt as a witch. From the thirteenth century back to the time of the Christian persecutions under Nero there had been numerous reincarnations, of which S. W. gave no account. During the Christian persecutions she had played a martyr's part. Then came another great darkness, back to the time of David, when Ivenes had been an ordinary Jewess. After her death as such, she had received from Astaf, an angel in one of the higher heavens, the mandate for her wonderful career. In all her pre-existences she had been a medium and an intermediary between this world and the Beyond. Her brothers and sisters were equally old and had the same profession. In each of her pre-existences she had invariably been married, and in this way founded a colossal family tree, with whose endlessly complicated relationships she was occupied in many of her ecstasies. Thus, some time in the eighth century she had been the mother of her earthly father and, what is more, of her grandfather and mine. Hence the remarkable friendship between these two old gentlemen, otherwise strangers. As Mme. de Valours she had been my mother. When she had been burnt as a witch I had taken it very much to heart; I had retired to a monastery in Rouen, wore a grey habit, became prior, wrote a work on botany, and died at over eighty years of age. In the refectory of the monastery there had hung a portrait of Mme. de Valours, in which she was depicted in a half-sitting, half-reclining position. (S. W. in the semi-somnambulistic state often assumed this position on the sofa. It corresponds exactly to that of Mme. Récamier in David's well-known painting.) A gentleman who often took part in the séances and bore a distant resemblance to me was also one of her sons from that time. Around this core of relationships there now grouped themselves, at a greater or lesser distance, all the persons in any way related or known to her. One came from the fifteenth century, another was a cousin from the eighteenth century, and so on.

64   From the three great family stocks there sprang the greater part of the races of Europe. She and her brothers and sisters were descended from Adam, who arose by materialization; the other races then in existence, from among whom Cain took his wife, were descended from monkeys. From these interrelated groups S. W. produced a vast amount of family gossip, a spate of romantic stories, piquant adventures, etc. The special target of her romances was a lady acquaintance of mine, who for some undiscoverable reason was peculiarly antipathetic to her. She declared that this lady was the incarnation of a celebrated Parisian poisoner who had achieved great notoriety in the eighteenth century. This lady, she maintained, still continued her dangerous work, but in a much more ingenious and refined fashion than before. Through the inspiration of the wicked spirits who accompanied her, she had discovered a fluid which when merely exposed to the air attracted any tubercle bacilli flying about and formed a splendid culture medium for them. By means of this fluid, which she was in the habit of mixing with food, she had caused the death of her husband (who had indeed died from tuberculosis), also of one of her lovers and of her own brother, so as to get his inheritance. Her eldest son was an illegitimate child by her lover. During her widowhood she had secretly borne an illegitimate child to another lover, and had finally had illicit relations with her own brother, whom she later poisoned. In this way S. W. wove innumerable stories in which she believed implicitly. The characters in these romances also appeared in her visions, as for instance this lady in the above-mentioned vision with its pantomime of confession and forgiveness of sin. Anything at all interesting that happened in her surroundings was drawn into this system of romances and given a place in the family relationships with a more or less clear account of the pre-existences and influencing spirits. So it fared with all persons who made S. W.'s acquaintance: they were rated as a second or a first incarnation according to whether they had a well-marked or an indistinct character. In most cases they were also designated as relatives and always in the same quite definite way. Only afterwards, often

several weeks later, a new and complicated romance would suddenly make its appearance after an ecstasy, explaining the striking relationship by means of pre-existences or illegitimate liaisons. Persons sympathetic to S. W. were usually very close relatives. These family romances (with the exception of the one described above) were all composed very carefully, so that it was absolutely impossible to check up on them. They were delivered with the most amazing aplomb and often surprised us by the extremely clever use of details which S. W. must have heard or picked up from somewhere. Most of the romances had a pretty gruesome character: murder by poison and dagger, seduction and banishment, forgery of wills, and so forth played a prominent role.

Mystic Science

65   S. W. was subjected to numerous suggestions in regard to scientific questions. Generally, towards the end of the séances, various subjects of a scientific or spiritualistic nature were discussed and debated. S. W. never took part in the conversation, but sat dreamily in a corner in a semi-somnambulistic condition. She listened now to one thing and now to another, catching it in a half dream, but she could never give a coherent account of anything if one asked her about it, and she only half understood the explanations. In the course of the winter, various hints began to emerge in the séances: "The spirits brought her strange revelations about the world forces and the Beyond, but she could not say anything just now." Once she tried to give a description, but only said "on one side was the light, on the other side the power of attraction." Finally, in March 1900, after nothing more had been heard of these things for some time, she suddenly announced with a joyful face that she had now received everything from the spirits. She drew forth a long narrow strip of paper on which numerous names were written. Despite my request she would not let it out of her hands, but told me to draw a diagram [fig. 2].

66   I can remember clearly that in the winter of 1899/1900 we spoke several times in S. W.'s presence of attractive and repulsive forces in connection with Kant's *Natural History and*

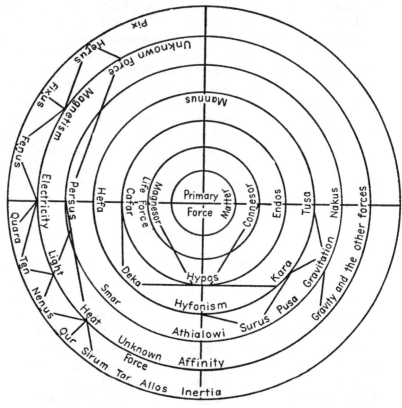

Figure 2

Theory of the Heavens,[25] also of the law of the conservation of energy, of the different forms of energy, and of whether the force of gravity is also a form of motion. From the content of these talks S. W. had evidently derived the foundations of her mystic system. She gave the following explanations: The forces are arranged in seven circles. Outside these there are three more, containing unknown forces midway between force and matter. Matter is found in seven outer circles surrounding the ten inner ones.[26] In the centre stands the Primary Force; this is

[25] [Cf. *Kant's Cosmogony* as in His *"Essay on the Retardation of the Rotation of the Earth"* and His *"Natural History and Theory of the Heavens,"* ed. and trans. W. Hastie (Glasgow, 1900).—EDITORS.]

[26] [Note that the diagram shows only the first seven inner circles.—EDITORS.]

the original cause of creation and is a spiritual force. The first circle which surrounds the Primary Force is Matter, which is not a true force and does not arise from the Primary Force. But it combines with the Primary Force and from this combination arise other spiritual forces: on one side the Good or Light Powers [Magnesor], on the other side the Dark Powers [Connesor]. The Magnesor Power contains the most Primary Force, and the Connesor Power the least, since there the dark power of matter is greatest. The further the Primary Force advances outwards the weaker it becomes, but weaker too becomes the power of matter, since its power is greatest where the collision with the Primary Force is most violent, i.e., in the Connesor Power. In every circle there are analogous forces of equal strength working in opposite directions. The system could also be written out in a single line or column, beginning with Primary Force, Magnesor, Cafar, etc., and then—going from left to right on the diagram—up through Tusa and Endos to Connesor; but in that way it would be difficult to see the different degrees of intensity. Every force in an outer circle is composed of the nearest adjacent forces of the inner circle.

67   THE MAGNESOR GROUP. From Magnesor descend in direct line the so-called Powers of Light, which are only slightly influenced by the dark side. Magnesor and Cafar together form the Life Force, which is not uniform but is differently composed in animals and plants. Man's life-force stands between Magnesor and Cafar. Morally good persons and mediums who facilitate communication between good spirits and the earth have most Magnesor. Somewhere about the middle are the life-forces of animals, and in Cafar those of plants. Nothing is known about Hefa, or rather S. W. can give no information. Persus is the basic force that manifests itself in the forces of motion. Its recognizable forms are Heat, Light, Electricity, Magnetism, and two unknown forces, one of which is to be found only in comets. Of the forces in the sixth circle, S. W. could only name North and South Magnetism and Positive and Negative Electricity. Deka is unknown. Smar is of special significance, to be discussed below; it leads over to:

68   THE HYPOS GROUP. Hypos and Hyfonism are powers which dwell only in certain human beings, in those who are able to exert a magnetic influence on others. Athialowi is the sexual

instinct. Chemical affinity is directly derived from it. In the seventh circle comes Inertia. Surus and Kara are of unknown significance. Pusa corresponds to Smar in the opposite sense.

69   THE CONNESOR GROUP. Connesor is the counterpole to Magnesor. It is the dark and evil power equal in intensity to the good power of Light. What the good power creates it turns into its opposite. Endos is a basic power in minerals. From Tusa (significance unknown) is derived Gravitation, which in its turn is described as the basic power manifesting itself in the forces of resistance (gravity, capillarity, adhesion, and cohesion). Nakus is the secret power in a rare stone which counteracts the effect of snake poison. The two powers Smar and Pusa have a special significance. According to S. W., Smar develops in the bodies of morally good people at the moment of death. This power enables the soul to ascend to the powers of Light. Pusa works the opposite way, for it is the power that leads the morally bad soul into the state of Connesor on the dark side.

70   With the sixth circle the visible world begins; this appears to be so sharply divided from the Beyond only because of the imperfection of our organs of sense. In reality the transition is a very gradual one, and there are people who live on a higher plane of cosmic knowledge because their perceptions and sensations are finer than those of other human beings. Such "seers" are able to see manifestations of force where ordinary people can see nothing. S. W. sees Magnesor as a shining white or bluish vapour which develops when good spirits are near. Connesor is a black fuming fluid which develops on the appearance of "black" spirits. On the night before the great visions began, the shiny Magnesor vapour spread round her in thick layers, and the good spirits solidified out of it into visible white figures. It was just the same with Connesor. These two forces have their different mediums. S. W. is a Magnesor medium, like the Clairvoyante of Prevorst and Swedenborg. The materialization mediums of the spiritualists are mostly Connesor mediums, since materialization takes place much more easily through Connesor on account of its close connection with the properties of matter. In the summer of 1900, S. W. tried several times to produce a picture of the circles of matter, but she never got beyond vague and incomprehensible hints, and afterwards she spoke of it no more.

Termination of the Disorder

71   The really interesting and significant séances came to an end with the production of the power system. Even before this, the vitality of the ecstasies had been falling off considerably. Ulrich von Gerbenstein came increasingly to the forefront and filled the séances for hours on end with his childish chatter. The visions which S. W. had in the meantime likewise seem to have lost much of their richness and plasticity of form, for afterwards she was only able to report ecstatic feelings in the presence of good spirits and disagreeable ones in that of bad spirits. Nothing new was produced. In the trance conversations, one could observe a trace of uncertainty, as if she were feeling her way and seeking to make an impression on her audience; there was also an increasing staleness of content. In her outward behaviour, too, there was a marked shyness and uncertainty, so that the impression of wilful deception became ever stronger. The writer therefore soon withdrew from the séances. S. W. experimented later in other circles, and six months after the conclusion of my observations was caught cheating *in flagrante*. She wanted to revive the wavering belief in her supernatural powers by genuinely spiritualistic experiments like apport, etc., and for this purpose concealed in her dress small objects which she threw into the air during the dark séances. After that her role was played out. Since then, eighteen months have gone by, during which I have lost sight of her. But I learn from an observer who knew her in the early days that now and again she still has rather peculiar states of short duration, when she is very pale and silent and has a fixed glazed look. I have heard nothing of any more visions. She is also said not to take part any longer in spiritualistic séances. S. W. is now an employee in a large business and is by all accounts an industrious and dutiful person who does her work with zeal and skill to the satisfaction of all concerned. According to the report of trustworthy persons, her character has much improved: she has become on the whole quieter, steadier, and more agreeable. No further abnormalities have come to light.

[3. DISCUSSION OF THE CASE]

72   This case, in spite of its incompleteness, presents a mass of psychological problems whose detailed discussion would far exceed the compass of this paper. We must therefore be content with a mere sketch of the more remarkable phenomena. For the sake of clearer exposition it seems best to discuss the different states under separate heads.

The Waking State

73   Here the patient shows various peculiarities. As we have seen, she was often absent-minded at school, misread in a peculiar way, was moody, changeable, and inconsequent in her behaviour, now quiet, shy, reserved, now uncommonly lively, noisy, and talkative. She cannot be called unintelligent, yet her narrow-mindedness is sometimes as striking as her isolated moments of intelligence. Her memory is good on the whole, but is often very much impaired by marked distractibility. Thus, despite numerous discussions and readings of Kerner's *Seherin von Prevorst,* she still does not know after many weeks whether the author is called Koerner or Kerner, or the name of the Clairvoyante, if directly asked. Nevertheless the name "Kerner" appears correctly written when it occasionally turns up in the automatic communications. In general it may be said that there is something extremely immoderate, unsteady, almost protean, in her character. If we discount the psychological fluctuations of character due to puberty, there still remains a pathological residue which expresses itself in her immoderate reactions and unpredictable, bizarre conduct. One can call this character "déséquilibré" or "unstable." It gets its specific cast from certain features that must be regarded as hysterical: above all her distractibility and her dreamy nature must be viewed in this light. As Janet [27] maintains, the basis of hysterical anaesthesias is disturbance of attention. He was able to show in youthful hysterics "a striking indifference and lack of attention towards everything to do with the sphere of the perceptions." A notable instance of this, and one which beautifully illustrates

27 "L'Anesthésie hystérique" (1892).

44

hysterical distractibility, is misreading. The psychology of this process may be thought of somewhat as follows: While reading aloud, a person's attention slackens and turns towards some other object. Meanwhile the reading continues mechanically, the sense impressions are received as before, but owing to the distraction the excitability of the perceptive centre is reduced, so that the strength of the sense impression is no longer sufficient to fix the attention in such a way as to conduct perception along the verbal-motor route—in other words, to repress all the inflowing associations which immediately ally themselves with any new sense impression. The further psychological mechanism permits of two possible explanations:

(1) The sense impression is received *unconsciously*, i.e., below the threshold of consciousness, owing to the rise of the stimulus threshold in the perceptive centre, and consequently it is not taken up by the conscious attention and conducted along the speech route, but only reaches verbal expression through the mediation of the nearest associations, in this case the dialect expressions for the object.

(2) The sense impression is received *consciously*, but at the moment of entering the speech route it reaches a spot whose excitability is reduced by the distraction. At this point the dialect word is substituted by association for the verbal-motor speech-image and is uttered in place of it. In either case, it is certain that the acoustic distraction fails to correct the error. Which of the two explanations is the right one cannot be determined in our case; probably both approach the truth, for the distractibility appears to be general, affecting more than one of the centres involved in the act of reading aloud.

74   In our case this symptom has a special value, because we have here a quite elementary automatic phenomenon. It can be called hysterical because in this particular case the state of exhaustion and intoxication with its parallel symptoms can be ruled out. Only in exceptional circumstances does a healthy person allow himself to be so gripped by an object that he fails to correct the errors due to inattention, especially those of the kind described. The frequency with which this happens in the patient points to a considerable restriction of the field of consciousness, seeing that she can control only a minimum of the elementary perceptions simultaneously flowing in upon her. If

we wish to define the psychological state of the "psychic shadow side" we might describe it as a sleep- or dream-state according to whether passivity or activity is its dominant feature. A pathological dream-state of rudimentary scope and intensity is certainly present here; its genesis is spontaneous, and dream-states that arise spontaneously and produce automatisms are usually regarded as hysterical. It must be pointed out that instances of misreading were a frequent occurrence in our patient and that for this reason the term "hysterical" is appropriate, because, so far as we know, it is only on the basis of an hysterical constitution that partial sleep- or dream-states occur both frequently and spontaneously.

75   The automatic substitution of some adjacent association has been studied experimentally by Binet [28] in his hysterical subjects. When he pricked the anaesthetic hand of the patient, she did not feel the prick but thought of "points"; when he moved her fingers, she thought of "sticks" or "columns." Again, when the hand, concealed from the patient's sight by a screen, wrote "Salpêtrière," she saw before her the word "Salpêtrière" in white writing on a black ground. This recalls the experiments of Guinon and Sophie Woltke previously referred to.

76   We thus find in our patient, at a time when there was nothing to suggest the later phenomena, rudimentary automatisms, fragments of dreaming, which harbour in themselves the possibility that some day more than one association will slip in between the distractibility of her perceptions and consciousness. The misreading also reveals a certain autonomy of the psychic elements; even with a relatively low degree of distractibility, not in any other way striking or suspicious, they develop a noticeable if slight productivity which approximates to that of the physiological dream. The misreading can therefore be regarded as a prodromal symptom of subsequent events, especially as its psychology is the prototype of the mechanism of somnambulistic dreams, which are in fact nothing but a multiplication and infinite variation of the elementary process we have described above. At the time of my observations I was never able to demonstrate any other rudimentary automatisms of this kind; it seems as if the originally low-grade states of distractibility gradually grew beneath the surface of consciousness into those

[28] *Alterations of Personality*, pp. 205f.

remarkable somnambulistic attacks and therefore disappeared from the waking state. So far as the development of the patient's character is concerned, except for a slight increase in maturity no striking change could be noted in the course of observations lasting nearly two years. On the other hand, it is worth mentioning that in the two years since the subsidence (complete cessation?) of the somnambulistic attacks a considerable change of character has taken place. We shall have occasion later on to speak of the significance of this observation.

Semi-Somnambulism

77   In our account of S. W.'s case, the following condition was indicated by the term "semi-somnambulism": For some time before and after the actual somnambulistic attack the patient found herself in a state whose most salient feature can best be described as "preoccupation." She lent only half an ear to the conversation around her, answered absent-mindedly, frequently lost herself in all manner of hallucinations; her face was solemn, her look ecstatic, visionary, ardent. Closer observation revealed a far-reaching alteration of her entire character. She was now grave, dignified; when she spoke, the theme was always an extremely serious one. In this state she could talk so seriously, so forcefully and convincingly, that one almost had to ask oneself: Is this really a girl of 15½? One had the impression that a mature woman was being acted with considerable dramatic talent. The reason for this seriousness, this solemnity of behaviour, was given in the patient's explanation that at these times she stood on the frontier of this world and the next, and associated just as really with the spirits of the dead as with the living. And indeed her conversation was about equally divided between answers to objectively real questions and hallucinatory ones. I call this state semi-somnambulistic because it coincides with Richet's own definition:

Such a person's consciousness appears to persist in its integrity, while all the time highly complex operations are taking place outside consciousness, without the voluntary and conscious ego seeming to be aware of any modification at all. He will have another person within him, acting, thinking, and willing, without his consciousness,

47

that is, his conscious reflecting ego, having the least idea that such is the case.[29]

78   Binet[30] says of the term "semi-somnambulism":

This term indicates the relations in which this state stands to genuine somnambulism; and further, it gives us to understand that the somnambulistic life which shows itself during the waking state is overcome and suppressed by the normal consciousness as it reasserts itself.

Automatisms

79   Semi-somnambulism is characterized by the continuity of consciousness with that of the waking state and by the appearance of various automatisms which point to the activity of a subconscious independent of the conscious self.

80   Our case shows the following automatic phenomena:

    (1) Automatic movements of the table.
    (2) Automatic writing.
    (3) Hallucinations.

81   (1) AUTOMATIC MOVEMENTS OF THE TABLE. Before the patient came under my observation she had been influenced by the suggestion of "table-turning," which she first came across as a parlour game. As soon as she entered the circle, communications arrived from members of her family, and she was at once recognized as a medium. I could only ascertain that as soon as her hands were placed on the table the typical movements began. The content of the communications has no further interest for us. But the automatic character of the act itself merits some discussion, for the objection might very well be made that there was some deliberate pushing or pulling on the part of the patient.

82   As we know from the investigations of Chevreul, Gley, Lehmann, and others,[31] unconscious motor phenomena are not only a frequent occurrence among hysterical persons and those pathologically inclined in other ways, but can also be induced fairly easily in normal persons who exhibit no other spontaneous automatisms. I have made many experiments on these lines and can fully confirm this observation. In the great majority of cases

[29] Richet, "La Suggestion mentale et le calcul des probabilités" (1884), p. 650.
[30] *Alterations*, p. 154.
[31] Detailed references in Binet, pp. 222ff.

all that is required is enough patience to put up with an hour or so of quiet waiting. With most subjects motor automatisms will eventually be obtained in more or less high degree if not hindered by counter-suggestions. In a relatively small number of cases the phenomena arise spontaneously, i.e., directly under the influence of verbal suggestion or of some earlier auto-suggestion. In our case the subject was powerfully affected by suggestion. In general, the disposition of the patient is subject to all those laws which also hold good for normal hypnosis. Nevertheless, certain special circumstances must be taken into account which are conditioned by the peculiar nature of the case. It was not a question here of total hypnosis, but of a partial one, limited entirely to the motor area of the arm, like the cerebral anaesthesia produced by magnetic passes for a painful spot in the body. We touch the spot in question, employing verbal suggestion or making use of some existing auto-suggestion, and we use the tactile stimulus which we know acts suggestively to bring about the desired partial hypnosis. In accordance with this procedure refractory subjects can be brought easily enough to an exhibition of automatism. The experimenter intentionally gives the table a slight push, or better, a series of light rhythmical taps. After a while he notices that the oscillations become stronger, that they continue although he has stopped his own intentional movements. The experiment has succeeded, the subject has unsuspectingly taken up the suggestion. Through this procedure far better results are obtained than by verbal suggestion. With very receptive persons and in all those cases where the movement seems to start spontaneously, the intended tremors,[32] which are not of course perceptible to the subject, take over the role of agent provocateur. In this way persons who by themselves would never achieve automatic movements of the coarser type can sometimes assume unconscious control of the table movements, provided that the tremors are strong enough for the medium to understand their mean-

[32] As is well known, the hands and arms during the waking state are never quite still, but are constantly subject to fine tremors. Preyer, Lehmann, and others have shown that these movements are influenced in high degree by the ideas predominating in the mind. For instance, Preyer shows that the outstretched hand will draw small but more or less successful copies of figures that are vividly imagined. These intended tremors can be demonstrated in a very simple way by experiments with the pendulum.

ing. The medium then takes over the slight oscillations and gives them back considerably strengthened, but rarely at exactly the same moment, mostly a few seconds later, and in this way reveals the agent's conscious or unconscious thought. This simple mechanism may give rise to instances of thought-reading which are quite bewildering at first sight. A very simple experiment that works in many cases even with unpractised persons will serve to illustrate this. The experimenter thinks, say, of the number 4 and then waits, his hands quietly resting on the table, until he feels it making the first move to announce the number thought of. He lifts his hands off the table immediately, and the number will be correctly tilted out. It is advisable in this experiment to stand the table on a soft thick carpet. By paying close attention, the experimenter will occasionally notice a movement of the table that can be represented thus:

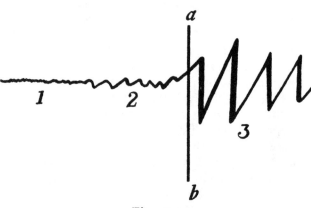

Figure 3

83   *1*: Intended tremors too slight to be perceived by the subject.

2: Very small but perceptible oscillations of the table which show that the subject is responding to them.

3: The big movements ("tilts") of the table, giving the number 4 that was thought of.

ab denotes the moment when the operator's hands are removed.

84   This experiment works excellently with well-disposed but inexperienced persons. After a little practice the phenomenon

usually disappears, since with practice the number can be read and reproduced directly from the intended movements.[33]

85   With a responsive medium these intended tremors work in just the same way as the intentional taps in the experiment cited above: they are received, strengthened, and reproduced, though very gently, almost timidly. Even so, they are perceptible and therefore act suggestively as slight tactile stimuli, and with the increase of partial hypnosis they produce the big automatic movements. This experiment illustrates in the clearest way the gradual increase of auto-suggestion. Along the path of this auto-suggestion all the automatic motor phenomena develop. How the mental content gradually intrudes into the purely motor sphere scarcely needs explaining after the above discussion. No special suggestion is required to evoke the mental phenomena, since, from the standpoint of the experimenter at least, it was a question of verbal representation from the start. After the first random motor expressions are over, unpractised subjects soon begin reproducing verbal products of their own or the intentions of the experimenter. The intrusion of the mental content can be objectively understood as follows:

86   Through the gradual increase of auto-suggestion the motor areas of the arm are isolated from consciousness, that is to say, the perception of slight motor impulses is veiled from the mind.[34] The knowledge received via consciousness of a potential mental content produces a collateral excitation in the speech area as the nearest available means to mental formulation. The intention to formulate necessarily affects the motor component [35] of the verbal representation most of all, thus explaining the unconscious overflow of speech impulses into the motor area,[36] and conversely the gradual penetration of partial hypnosis into the speech area.

33 Preyer, *Die Erklärung des Gedankenlesens* (1886).
34 This is analogous to certain hypnotic experiments in the waking state. Cf. Janet's experiment, when by whispered suggestions he got a patient to lie flat on the ground without being aware of it. *L'Automatisme psychologique* (1913), p. 241.
35 Cf. Charcot's scheme for word-picture composition: (1) auditory image, (2) visual image, (3) motor images, (a) speech image, (b) writing image. In Ballet, *Le Langage intérieur et les diverses formes de l'aphasie* (1886), p. 14.
36 Bain says: "Thinking is restrained speaking or acting." *The Senses and the Intellect* (1894), p. 358.

87   In numerous experiments with beginners, I have noticed, usually at the start of the mental phenomena, a relatively large number of completely meaningless words, often only senseless jumbles of letters. Later all sorts of absurdities are produced, words or whole sentences with the letters transposed all higgledy-piggledy or arranged in reverse order, like mirror-writing. The appearance of a letter or word brings a new suggestion; involuntarily some kind of association tacks on to it and is then realized. Curiously enough, these are not as a rule conscious associations but quite unexpected ones. This would seem to indicate that a considerable part of the speech area is already hypnotically isolated. The recognition of this automatism again forms a fruitful suggestion, since at this point a feeling of strangeness invariably arises, if it was not already present in the pure motor automatism. The question "Who is doing this?" "Who is speaking?" acts as a suggestion for synthesizing the unconscious personality, which as a rule is not long in coming. Some name or other presents itself, usually one charged with emotion, and the automatic splitting of the personality is accomplished. How haphazard and precarious this synthesis is at first can be seen from the following reports from the literature.

88   Myers gives the following interesting observation of a Mr. A., a member of the Society for Psychical Research, who was experimenting on himself with automatic writing:

89

3RD DAY

What is man? — *Tefi hasl esble lies.*
Is that an anagram? — *Yes.*
How many words does it contain? — *Five.*
What is the first word? — *See.*
What is the second word? — *Eeeee.*
SEE? Shall I interpret it myself? — *Try to!*

90   Mr. A. found this solution: "The life is less able." He was astonished at this intellectual pronouncement, which seemed to him to prove the existence of an intelligence independent of his own. He therefore went on to ask:

Who are you? — *Clelia.*
Are you a woman? — *Yes.*
Have you lived on earth? — *No.*
Will you come to life? — *Yes.*

52

When? — *In six years.*
Why are you conversing with me? — *E if Clelia el.*

Mr. A. interpreted this answer as: "I Clelia feel."

91   4TH DAY
Am I the one who asks questions? — *Yes.*
Is Clelia there? — *No.*
Who is here then? — *Nobody.*
Does Clelia exist at all? — *No.*
Then with whom was I speaking yesterday? — *With nobody.*[37]

92   Janet conducted the following conversation with the subconscious of Lucie, who, meanwhile, was engaged in conversation with another observer:

[Janet asks:] Do you hear me? [Lucie answers, in automatic writ-
ing:] *No.*
But one has to hear in order to answer. — *Absolutely.*
Then how do you do it? — *I don't know.*
There must be someone who hears me. — *Yes.*
Who is it? — *Somebody besides Lucie.*
All right. Somebody else. Shall we give the other person a
name? — *No.*
Yes, it will be more convenient. — *All right. Adrienne.*
Well, Adrienne, do you hear me? — *Yes.*[38]

93   One can see from these extracts how the unconscious personality builds itself up: it owes its existence simply to suggestive questions which strike an answering chord in the medium's own disposition. This disposition can be explained by
the disaggregation of psychic complexes, and the feeling of
strangeness evoked by these automatisms assists the process as
soon as conscious attention is directed to the automatic act.
Binet remarks on this experiment of Janet's: "Nevertheless it
should be carefully noted that if the personality of 'Adrienne'
could be created, it was because the suggestion encountered a
psychological possibility; in other words, disaggregated phenomena were existing there apart from the normal consciousness of the subject." [39] The individualization of the subconscious
is always a great step forward and has enormous suggestive

37 Myers, "Automatic writing" (1885).
38 *L'Automatisme,* pp. 317–18.
39 Binet, p. 147.

53

influence on further development of the automatisms.[40] The formation of unconscious personalities in our case must also be regarded in this light.

94   The objection that the table-turning was "simulated" may well be abandoned when one considers the phenomenon of thought-reading from intended tremors, of which the patient gave ample proof. Rapid, conscious thought-reading requires at the very least an extraordinary amount of practice, and this the patient demonstrably lacked. Whole conversations can be carried on by means of these tremors, as happened in our case. In the same way the suggestibility of the subconscious can be demonstrated objectively if, for instance, the operator concentrates on the thought: "The medium's hand shall no longer move the table or the glass," and at once, contrary to all expectation, and to the liveliest astonishment of the subject, the table is immobilized. Naturally all kinds of other suggestions can be realized too, provided that their innervation does not exceed the area of partial hypnosis (which proves at the same time the partial nature of the hypnosis). Hence suggestions aimed at the legs or the other arm will not work.

95   The table-turning was not an automatism confined exclusively to the patient's semi-somnambulism. On the contrary it occurred in its most pronounced form in the waking state, and in most cases then passed over into semi-somnambulism, whose onset was generally announced by hallucinations, as at the first séance.

96   (2) AUTOMATIC WRITING. Another automatic phenomenon, which from the first corresponds to a higher degree of partial hypnosis, is automatic writing. It is, at least in my experience, much rarer and much more difficult to produce than table-turning. Here again it is a question of a primary suggestion, directed to the conscious mind when sensibility is retained, and to the unconscious when it is extinct. The suggestion, however, is not a simple one, since it already contains an intellectual element: "to write" means "to write something." This special property of the suggestion, going beyond the purely motor sphere, often confuses the subject and gives rise to counter-suggestions which prevent the appearance of automatisms. However, I have noticed

40 ' Once baptized, the unconscious personage is more definite and distinct; he shows his psychological characteristics better." Janet, *L'Automatisme*, p. 318.

in a few cases that the suggestion is realized despite its comparative boldness (it is after all directed to the waking consciousness of a so-called normal person!), but that it does so in a peculiar way, by putting only the purely motor part of the central nervous system under hypnosis, and that the deeper hypnosis is then obtained from the motor phenomenon by auto-suggestion, as in the procedure for table-turning described above. The subject,[41] holding a pencil in his hand, is purposely engaged in conversation to distract his attention from writing. The hand thereupon starts to move, making a number of strokes and zigzag lines at first, or else a simple line.

Figure 4

It sometimes happens that the pencil does not touch the paper at all but writes in the air. These movements must be regarded as purely motor phenomena corresponding to the expression of the motor element in the idea of "writing." They are somewhat rare; usually single letters are written right off, and what was said above of table-turning is true here of their combination into words and sentences. Now and then true mirror-writing is observed. In the majority of cases, and perhaps in all experiments with beginners who are not under some special suggestion, the automatic writing is that of the subject. Occasionally its character may be greatly changed,[42] but this is secondary, and is always a symptom of the synthesis of a subconscious personality. As already stated, the automatic writing of our patient never came to very much. The experiments were carried out in the dark, and in most cases she passed over into semi-somnambulism or ecstasy. So the automatic writing had the same result as the preliminary table-turning.

97   (3) HALLUCINATIONS. The manner of transition to somnam-

41 Cf. the experiments of Binet and Féré, in Binet, pp. 99ff.
42 Cf. the tests in Flournoy, *From India to the Planet Mars* (orig. 1900).

bulism in the second séance is of psychological significance. As reported, the automatic phenomena were in full swing when darkness descended. The interesting event in the preceding séance was the brusque interruption of a communication from the grandfather, which became the starting-point for various discussions among members of the circle. These two factors, darkness and a remarkable occurrence, seem to have caused a rapid deepening of hypnosis, which enabled the hallucinations to develop. The psychological mechanism of this process seems to be as follows: The influence of darkness on suggestibility, particularly in regard to the sense organs, is well known.[43] Binet states that it has a special influence on hysterical subjects, producing immediate drowsiness.[44] As may be assumed from the foregoing explanations, the patient was in a state of partial hypnosis, and furthermore a subconscious personality having the closest ties with the speech area had already constituted itself. The automatic expression of this personality was interrupted in the most unexpected way by a new person whose existence no one suspected. Whence came this split? Obviously the patient had entertained the liveliest expectations about this first séance. Any reminiscences she had of me and my family had probably grouped themselves around this feeling of expectation, and they suddenly came to light when the automatic expression was at its climax. The fact that it was my grandfather and no one else—not, for instance, my dead father, who, as the patient knew, was closer to me than my grandfather, whom I had never known—may suggest where the origin of this new person is to be sought. It was probably a dissociation from the already existing personality, and this split-off part seized upon the nearest available material for its expression, namely the associations concerning myself. Whether this offers a parallel to the results of Freud's dream investigations [45] must remain unanswered, for we have no means of judging how far the emotion in question may be considered "repressed." From the brusque intervention of the new personality we may conclude that the patient's imaginings were extremely vivid, with a correspondingly intense expectation which a certain maidenly modesty and embarrassment

43 Cf. Hagen, "Zur Theorie der Hallucination" (1868), p. 10.
44 *Alterations*, pp. 171ff.
45 *The Interpretation of Dreams* (orig. 1900).

56

sought perhaps to overcome. At any rate this event reminds us vividly of the way dreams suddenly present to consciousness, in more or less transparent symbolism, things one has never admitted to oneself clearly and openly. We do not know when the splitting off of the new personality occurred, whether it had been slowly preparing in the unconscious, or whether it only came about during the séance. In any case it meant a considerable increase in the extent of the unconscious area rendered accessible by hypnosis. At the same time this event, in view of the impression it made on the waking consciousness of the patient, must be regarded as powerfully suggestive, for the perception of the unexpected intervention of a new personality was bound to increase still further the feeling of strangeness aroused by the automatism, and would naturally suggest the thought that an independent spirit was making itself known. From this followed the very understandable association that it might be possible to see this spirit.

98   The situation that ensued at the second séance can be explained by the coincidence of this energizing suggestion with the heightened suggestibility occasioned by the darkness. The hypnosis, and with it the chain of split-off ideas, breaks through into the visual sphere; the expression of the unconscious, hitherto purely motor, is objectified (in accordance with the specific energy of the newly created system) in the form of visual images having the character of an hallucination—not as a mere accompaniment of the verbal automatism but as a direct substitute function. The explanation of the unexpected situation that arose in the first séance, at the time quite inexplicable, is no longer given in words, but as an allegorical vision. The proposition "they do not hate one another, but are friends" is expressed in a picture of the two grandfathers arm-in-arm. We frequently come across such things in somnambulism: the thinking of somnambulists proceeds in plastic images which constantly break through into this or that sensory sphere and are objectified as hallucinations. The thought process sinks into the subconscious and only its final terms reach consciousness directly as hallucinations or as vivid and sensuously coloured ideas. In our case the same thing occurred as with the patient whose anaesthetic hand Binet pricked nine times, making her think vividly of the number 9; or Flournoy's Hélène Smith, who, on

being asked in her shop about a certain pattern, suddenly saw before her the figure 18, eight to ten inches high, representing the number of days the pattern had been on loan.[46] The question arises as to why the automatism broke through in the visual sphere and not in the acoustic. There are several reasons for this choice of the visual:

99   (a) The patient was not gifted acoustically; she was for instance very unmusical.

(b) There was no silence (to correspond with the darkness) which might have favoured the occurrence of auditory hallucinations, for we were talking all the time.

(c) The heightened conviction of the near presence of spirits, owing to the feeling of strangeness evoked by the automatism, could easily lead to the idea that it might be possible to see a spirit, thus causing a slight excitation of the visual sphere.

(d) The entoptic phenomena in the darkness favoured the appearance of hallucinations.

100   The reasons given in (c) and (d) are of decisive importance for the appearance of hallucinations. The entoptic phenomena in this case play the same role in producing automatisms by auto-suggestion as do the slight tactile stimuli during hypnosis of the motor centres. As reported, the patient saw sparks before passing into the first hallucinatory twilight state at the first séance. Obviously attention was already at high pitch and directed to visual perceptions, so that the light sensations of the retina, usually very weak, were seen with great intensity. The part played by entoptic perceptions of light in the production of hallucinations deserves closer scrutiny. Schüle says: "The swarm of lights and colours that excite and activate the nocturnal field of vision in the darkness supplies the material for the fantastic figures seen in the air before going to sleep." [47] As we know, we never see absolute darkness, always a few patches of the dark field are dully illuminated; flecks of light bob up here and there and combine into all sorts of shapes, and it only needs a moderately active imagination to form out of them, as one does out of clouds, certain figures known to oneself personally. As one falls asleep, one's fading power of judgment

[46] *India to Mars*, p. 59.
[47] *Handbuch der Geisteskrankheiten* (1878), p. 134.

leaves the imagination free to construct more and more vivid forms. "Instead of the spots of light, the haziness and changing colours of the dark visual field, outlines of definite objects begin to appear." [48] Hypnagogic hallucinations arise in this way. Naturally the chief share falls to the imagination, which is why highly imaginative people are particularly subject to them.[49] The "hypnopompic" hallucinations described by Myers are essentially the same as the hypnagogic ones.

101   It is very probable that hypnagogic images are identical with the dream-images of normal sleep, or that they form their visual foundation. Maury [50] has proved by self-observation that the images which floated round him hypnagogically were also the objects of the dreams that followed. Ladd [51] showed the same thing even more convincingly. With practice he succeeded in waking himself up two to five minutes after falling asleep. Each time he noticed that the bright figures dancing before the retina formed as it were the outlines of the images just dreamed of. He even supposes that practically all visual dreams derive their formal elements from the light sensations of the retina. In our case the situation favoured the development of a fantastic interpretation. Also, we must not underrate the influence of the tense expectation which caused the dull light sensations of the retina to appear with increased intensity.[52] The development

[48] Müller, *Phantastische Gesichtserscheinungen* (1826), quoted by Hagen in "Zur Theorie der Hallucination" (1868), p. 41.

[49] Spinoza had a hypnopompic vision of a "nigrum et scabiosum Brasilianum" (a dirty black Brazilian)—Hagen, "Zur Theorie der Hallucination" (1868), p. 49. In Goethe's *Elective Affinities,* Ottilie sometimes saw in the half darkness the figure of Eduard in a dimly lit room. Cf. also Jerome Cardan, *De subtilitate rerum:* "Imagines videbam ab imo lecti, quasi e parvulis annulis arcisque constantes, arborum, belluarum, hominum, oppidorum, instructarum acierum, bellicorum et musicorum instrumentorum aliorumque huius generis adscendentes, vicissimque descendentes, aliis atque aliis succedentibus" (At the foot of the bed I saw images, consisting as it were of small circles and curves, and representing trees, animals, men, towns, troops drawn up in line, instruments of war and of music and other like things, rising and falling in turn, and coming one after another).

[50] *Le Sommeil et les rêves* (1861), p. 134.

[51] "Psychology of Visual Dreams" (1892).

[52] Hecker says of these states (*Über Visionen,* 1848, p. 16): "There is a simple, elementary vision caused by mental over-activity, without fantastic imagery, without even sensuous ideas: it is the vision of formless light, a manifestation of the visual organ stimulated from within."

of retinal phenomena then followed in accordance with the predominant ideas. Hallucinations have been observed to arise in this way with other visionaries: Joan of Arc saw first a cloud of light,[53] then out of it, a little later, stepped St. Michael, St. Catharine, and St. Margaret. Swedenborg saw nothing for a whole hour but luminous spheres and brilliant flames.[54] All the time he felt a tremendous change going on in his brain, which seemed to him like a "release of light." An hour afterwards he suddenly saw real figures whom he took to be angels and spirits. The sun vision of Benvenuto Cellini in Sant' Angelo probably belongs to the same category.[55] A student who often saw apparitions said: "When these apparitions come, I see at first only single masses of light and hear at the same time a dull roaring in my ears. But after a bit these outlines turn into distinct figures." [56] The hallucinations arise in quite the classical way with Flournoy's Hélène Smith. I cite the relevant passages from his report:

102   *March 18.* Attempt to experiment in the darkness. . . . Mlle. Smith sees a balloon, now luminous, now becoming dark.

103   *March 25.* . . . Mlle. Smith begins to distinguish vague gleams with long white streamers moving from the floor to the ceiling, and then a magnificent star, which in the darkness appears to her alone throughout the whole séance.

104   *April 1.* Mlle. Smith is very much agitated; she has fits of shivering, is very cold. She is very restless, and sees suddenly, hovering above the table, a grinning, very ugly face, with long red hair. Afterwards she sees a magnificent bouquet of roses of different hues. . . . Suddenly she sees a small snake come out from underneath the bouquet; it rises up gently, smells the flowers, looks at them . . .[57]

105   Concerning the origin of her Mars visions, Hélène Smith said: "The red light continues about me, and I find myself surrounded by extraordinary flowers. . . ." [58]

106   At all times the complex hallucinations of visionaries have occupied a special place in scientific criticism. Thus, quite early,

[53] Quicherat, *Procès de condamnation et de réhabilitation de Jeanne d'Arc* (1841–49), V, pp. 116f.
[54] Hagen (1868), p. 57.
[55] *Life of Cellini* (trans. by Symonds), pp. 231f.
[56] Hagen (1868), p. 57.
[57] Flournoy, *India to Mars*, pp. 36ff. (trans. modified).
[58] Ibid., p. 170.

Macario [59] distinguished them as "intuitive" hallucinations from ordinary hallucinations, saying that they occur in persons of lively mind, deep understanding, and high nervous excitability. Hecker expresses himself in a similar manner but even more enthusiastically. He supposes their conditioning factor to be the "congenitally high development of the psychic organ, which through its spontaneous activity calls the life of the imagination into free and nimble play." [60] These hallucinations are "harbingers and also signs of an immense spiritual power." A vision is actually "a higher excitation which adapts itself harmoniously to the most perfect health of mind and body." Complex hallucinations do not belong to the waking state but occur as a rule in a state of partial waking: the visionary is sunk in his vision to the point of complete absorption. Flournoy, too, was always able to establish "a certain degree of obnubilation" during the visions of Hélène Smith.[61] In our case the vision is complicated by a sleeping state whose peculiarities we shall discuss below.

The Change in Character

107   The most striking feature of the "second state" is the change in character. There are several cases in the literature which show this symptom of spontaneous change in the character of a person. The first to be made known in a scientific journal was that of Mary Reynolds, published by Weir Mitchell.[62] This was the case of a young woman living in Pennsylvania in 1811. After a deep sleep of about twenty hours, she had totally forgotten her entire past and everything she had ever learnt; even the words she spoke had lost their meaning. She no longer knew her relatives. Slowly she re-learnt to read and write, but her writing now was from right to left. More striking still was the change in her character. "Instead of being melancholy she was now cheerful to extremity. Instead of being reserved she was buoyant and social. Formerly taciturn and retiring, she was now

59 "Des Hallucinations" (1845), as reviewed in *Allg Z f Psych*, IV (1848), p. 139.
60 *Über Visionen*, pp. 285ff.
61 Flournoy, p. 52.
62 "Mary Reynolds: A Case of Double Consciousness" (1888). Also in *Harper's Magazine*, 1860. Abstracted *in extenso* in William James's *Principles of Psychology* (1891), pp. 391ff.

merry and jocose. Her disposition was totally and absolutely changed." [63]

108   In this state she gave up entirely her former secluded life and liked to set out on adventurous expeditions unarmed, through woods and mountains, on foot and on horseback. On one of these expeditions she encountered a large black bear, which she took for a pig. The bear stood up on his hind legs and gnashed his teeth at her. As she could not induce her horse to go any further, she went up to the bear with an ordinary stick and hit him until he took to flight. Five weeks later, after a deep sleep, she returned to her earlier state with amnesia for the interval. These states alternated for about sixteen years. But the last twenty-five years of her life Mary Reynolds passed exclusively in the second state.

109   Schroeder van der Kolk [64] reports the following case: The patient became ill at the age of sixteen with a periodic amnesia after a previous long illness of three years. Sometimes in the morning after waking she fell into a peculiar choreic state, during which she made rhythmical beating movements with her arms. Throughout the day she would behave in a childish, silly way, as if she had lost all her educated faculties. When normal she was very intelligent, well-read, spoke excellent French. In the second state she began to speak French faultily. On the second day she was always normal again. The two states were completely separated by amnesia.[65]

110   Höfelt [66] reports on a case of spontaneous somnambulism in a girl who in her normal state was submissive and modest, but in somnambulism was impertinent, rude, and violent. Azam's Felida [67] was in her normal state depressed, inhibited, timid, and in the second state lively, confident, enterprising to recklessness. The second state gradually became the dominant one and finally supplanted the first to such an extent that the patient called her normal states, which now lasted only a short time, her

[63] Cf. Emminghaus, *Allgemeine Psychopathologie* (1878), p. 129, Ogier Ward's case.

[64] *Pathologie und Therapie der Geisteskrankheiten* (1863), p. 31, quoted in *Allg Z f Psych*, XXII (1865), 406–7.

[65] Cf. Donath, "Über Suggestibilität" (1892), quoted in *Arch f Psych u Nerv*, XXXII (1899), 335.

[66] "Ein Fall von spontanem Somnambulismus" (1893).

[67] *Hypnotisme* (1887), pp. 63ff.

"crises." The amnesic attacks had begun at the age of 14½. In time the second state became more moderate, and there was a certain approximation in the character of the two states. A very fine example of change in character is the case worked out by Camuset, Ribot, Legrand du Saule, Richer, and Voisin and put together by Bourru and Burot.[68] It is that of Louis V., a case of severe male hysteria, with an amnesic alternating character. In the first state he was rude, cheeky, querulous, greedy, thievish, inconsiderate. In the second state he showed an agreeable, sympathetic character and was industrious, docile, and obedient. The amnesic change in character has been put to literary use by Paul Lindau [69] in his play *Der Andere*. A case that parallels Lindau's criminalistic public prosecutor is reported on by Rieger.[70] The subconscious personalities of Janet's Lucie and Léonie,[71] or of Morton Prince's patient,[72] can also be regarded as parallels of our case, though these were artificial therapeutic products whose importance lies rather in the domain of dissociated consciousness and memory.

111   In all these cases the second state is separated from the first by an amnesic split, and the change in character is accompanied by a break in the continuity of consciousness. In our case there is no amnesic disturbance whatever; the transition from the first to the second state is quite gradual, continuity of consciousness is preserved, so that the patient carries over into the waking state everything she has experienced of the otherwise unknown regions of the unconscious during hallucinations in the second state.

112   Periodic changes in personality without an amnesic split are found in cyclic insanity, but they also occur as a rare phenomenon in hysteria, as Renaudin's case shows.[73] A young man, whose behaviour had always been exemplary, suddenly began to display the worst tendencies. No symptoms of insanity were observed, but on the other hand the whole surface of his body was found to be anaesthetic. This state was periodic, and, in the

68 *Variations de la personnalité* (1888).
69 See Moll, "Die Bewusstseinsspaltung in Paul Lindau's neuem Schauspiel" (1893), pp. 306ff.
70 *Der Hypnotismus* (1884), pp. 109ff.
71 *L'Automatisme psychologique.*
72 "An Experimental Study of Visions" (1898).
73 Quoted in Ribot, *Die Persönlichkeit* (1894).

same way, the patient's character was subject to fluctuations. As soon as the anaesthesia disappeared he became manageable and friendly. The moment it returned he was dominated by the worst impulses, including even the lust for murder.

113   If we remember that our patient's age at the beginning of the disturbances was 15½, i.e., that the age of puberty had just been reached, we must suppose that there was some connection between these disturbances and the physiological changes of character at puberty.

At this period of life there appears in the consciousness of the in-dividual a new group of sensations together with the ideas and feel-ings arising therefrom. This continual pressure of unaccustomed mental states, which constantly make themselves felt because their cause is constantly at work, and which are co-ordinated with one another because they spring from one and the same source, must in the end bring about far-reaching changes in the constitution of the ego.[74]

We all know the fitful moods, the confused, new, powerful feel-ings, the tendency to romantic ideas, to exalted religiosity and mysticism, side by side with relapses into childishness, which give the adolescent his peculiar character. At this period he is making his first clumsy attempts at independence in every direc-tion; for the first time he uses for his own purposes all that family and school have inculcated into him in childhood; he conceives ideals, constructs lofty plans for the future, lives in dreams whose main content is ambition and self-complacency. All this is physiological. The puberty of a psychopath is a serious crisis. Not only do the psychophysical changes run an exceed-ingly stormy course, but features of an inherited degenerate character, which do not appear in the child at all or only sporad-ically, now become fixed. In explaining our case we are bound to consider a specifically pubertal disturbance. The reasons for this will appear from a more detailed study of her second per-sonality. For the sake of brevity we shall call this second person-ality Ivenes, as the patient herself christened her higher ego.

114   Ivenes is the direct continuation of her everyday ego. She comprises its whole conscious content. In the semi-somnam-bulist state her relation to the external world is analogous to that of the waking state—that is to say, she is influenced by re-

[74] Ribot, p. 69.

current hallucinations, but no more than persons who are subject to non-confusional psychotic hallucinations. The continuity
of Ivenes obviously extends to the hysterical attacks as well,
when she enacts dramatic scenes, has visionary experiences, etc.
During the actual attack she is usually isolated from the external world, does not notice what is going on around her, does
not know that she is talking loudly, etc. But she has no amnesia
for the dream-content of the attack. Nor is there always amnesia for her motor expressions and for the changes in her surroundings. That this is dependent on the degree of somnambulistic stupor and on the partial paralysis of individual sense
organs is proved by the occasion when the patient did not notice
me, despite the fact that her eyes were open and that she probably saw the others, but only perceived my presence when I spoke
to her. This is a case of so-called *systematic anaesthesia* (negative
hallucination), which is frequently observed among hysterics.

115   Flournoy,[75] for instance, reports of Hélène Smith that during the séances she suddenly ceased to see those taking part,
although she still heard their voices and felt their touch; or that
she suddenly stopped hearing, although she saw the speakers
moving their lips, etc.

116   Just as Ivenes is a continuation of the waking ego, so she
carries over her whole conscious content into the waking state.
This remarkable behaviour argues strongly against any analogy
with cases of double consciousness. The characteristics reported
of Ivenes contrast favourably with those of the patient; she is
the calmer, more composed personality, and her pleasing modesty and reserve, her more uniform intelligence, her confident
way of talking, may be regarded as an improvement on the patient's whole being; thus far there is some resemblance to
Janet's Léonie. But it is no more than a resemblance. They are
divided by a deep psychological difference, quite apart from the
question of amnesia. Léonie II is the healthier, the more normal; she has regained her natural capacities, she represents the
temporary amelioration of a chronic condition of hysteria.
Ivenes gives more the impression of an artificial product; she
is more contrived, and despite all her excellent points she strikes
one as playing a part superlatively well. Her world-weariness, her
longing for the Beyond, are not mere piety but the attributes

[75] *India to Mars,* p. 63.

of saintliness. Ivenes is no longer quite human, she is a mystic being who only half belongs to the world of reality. Her mournful features, her suffering resignation, her mysterious fate all lead us to the historical prototype of Ivenes: Justinus Kerner's Clairvoyante of Prevorst. I assume that the content of Kerner's book is generally known, so I omit references to the features they have in common. Ivenes, however, is not just a copy of the Clairvoyante; the latter is simply a sketch for an original. The patient pours her own soul into the role of the Clairvoyante, seeking to create out of it an ideal of virtue and perfection; she anticipates her own future and embodies in Ivenes what she wishes to be in twenty years' time—the assured, influential, wise, gracious, pious lady. In the construction of the second personality lies the deep-seated difference between Léonie II and Ivenes. Both are psychogenic, but whereas Léonie I obtains in Léonie II what properly belongs to her, the patient builds up a personality beyond herself. One cannot say that she deludes herself into the higher ideal state, rather she dreams herself into it.[76]

117   The realization of this dream is very reminiscent of the psychology of the pathological swindler. Delbrück[77] and Forel[78] have pointed out the importance of auto-suggestion in the development of pathological cheating and pathological daydreaming. Pick[79] regards intense auto-suggestion as the first symptom of hysterical dreamers which makes the realization of "daydreams" possible. One of Pick's patients dreamt herself into a morally dangerous situation and finally carried out an attempt at rape on herself by lying naked on the floor and tying herself to the table and chairs. The patients may create some dramatic personage with whom they enter into correspondence by letter,

[76] "[Somnambulistic dreams:] . . . romances of the subliminal imagination analogous to those 'continued stories' which so many people tell themselves in their moments of idleness, or at times when their routine occupations offer only slight obstacles to day-dreaming, and of which they themselves are generally the heroes. Fantastic constructions, taken up and pursued over and over again, but seldom seen through to the end, in which the imagination allows itself free play and revenges itself on the dull and drab matter-of-factness of everyday reality." Ibid., pp. 9f.

[77] *Die pathologische Lüge* (1891). [A reference in the 1953 edn. of *Two Essays on Analytical Psychology* (*Coll. Works*, 7), p. 134, n. 4, to this par. is in error. Instead see pars. 138ff., as indicated in the revised (1966) edn., p. 137, n. 3.—EDITORS.]

[78] *Hypnotism* (orig. 1889).

[79] "Über pathologische Träumerei" (1896), pp. 280–301.

as in Bohn's case,[80] where the patient dreamt herself into an engagement with a completely imaginary lawyer in Nice, from whom she received letters which she had written herself in disguised handwriting. This pathological dreaming, with its auto-suggestive falsifications of memory sometimes amounting to actual delusions and hallucinations, is also found in the lives of many saints.[81] It is only a step from dreamy ideas with a strong sensuous colouring to complex hallucinations proper.[82] For instance, in Pick's first case, one can see how the patient, who imagined she was the Empress Elizabeth, gradually lost herself in her reveries to such an extent that her condition must be regarded as a true twilight state. Later it passed over into an hysterical delirium in which her dream fantasies became typical hallucinations. The pathological liar who lets himself be swept away by his fantasies behaves exactly like a child who loses himself in the game he is playing,[83] or like an actor who surrenders completely to his part. There is no fundamental distinction between this and the somnambulistic dissociation of the personality, but only a difference of degree based on the intensity of the primary auto-suggestibility or disaggregation of the psychic elements. The more consciousness becomes dissociated the greater becomes the plasticity of the dream situations, and the less, too, the amount of conscious lying and of consciousness in general. This state of being carried away by one's interest in the object is what Freud calls hysterical identification. For instance, Erler's patient,[84] a severe hysteric, had hypnagogic visions of little riders made of paper, who so took possession of her imagination that she had the feeling of being herself one of them. Much the same sort of thing normally happens to us in dreams, when we cannot help thinking "hysterically." [85] Complete surrender to the interesting idea explains the wonderful

---

80 *Ein Fall von doppeltem Bewusstsein* (1898).

81 Görres, *Die christliche Mystik* (1836–42).

82 Cf. Behr, "Erinnerungsfälschungen und pathologische Traumzustände" (1899), pp. 918ff.; also Ballet, *Le Langage intérieur*, p. 44.

83 Cf. Redlich, "Pseudologia phantastica" (1900), p. 66.

84 "Hysterisches und hystero-epileptisches Irresein" (1879), p. 21.

85 Binet, p. 89: "I may say in this connection that hysterical patients have been my chosen subjects, because they exaggerate the phenomena that must necessarily be found to some degree in many persons who have never shown hysterical symptoms."

naturalness of these pseudological or somnambulistic performances, which is quite beyond the reach of conscious acting. The
less the waking consciousness intervenes with its reflection and
calculation, the more certain and convincing becomes the objectivation of the dream.[86]

118   Our case has still another analogy with *pseudologia phantastica*: the development of fantasies during the attacks. Many
cases are known in the literature of fits of pathological lying,
accompanied by various hysteriform complaints.[87] Our patient
develops her fantasy systems exclusively during the attack. In
her normal state she is quite incapable of thinking out new
ideas or explanations; she must either put herself into the
somnambulistic state or await its spontaneous appearance. This
exhausts the affinities with *pseudologia phantastica* and pathological dreaming.

119   Our patient differs essentially from pathological dreamers
in that it could never be proved that her reveries had previously
been the object of her daily interests; her dreams came up ex-
plosively, suddenly bursting forth with amazing completeness
from the darkness of the unconscious. The same thing happened with Flournoy's Hélène Smith. At several points, however, it is possible in our case to demonstrate the link with
perceptions in the normal state [see next par.], so it seems probable that the roots of those dreams were originally feeling-toned
ideas which only occupied her waking consciousness for a short
time.[88] We must suppose that hysterical forgetfulness [89] plays

86 As, for instance, in the roof-climbing of somnambulists.

87 Delbrück, *Die Lüge;* and Redlich, op. cit. Cf. also the development of delusional ideas in epileptic twilight states mentioned by Mörchen, *Über Dämmerzustände* (1901), pp. 51, 59.

88 Cf. Flournoy's interesting conjecture as to the origin of H. S.'s Hindu cycle:
"I should not be surprised if Marlès' remark on the beauty of the Kanara women
were the sting, the tiny jab, which aroused the subliminal attention and riveted
it, quite naturally, on this single passage and the two or three lines that followed it, to the exclusion of all the much less interesting context" (Swiss edn.,
p. 285).

89 Janet says (*The Mental State of Hystericals*, orig. 1893, p. 78); "It is from
forgetfulness that there arise, not always, but very often, the supposed lies of
hysterical subjects. In the same way we can also explain their caprices, their
changes of mood, their ingratitude, in a word their inconsistencies, for the connection of the past with the present, which gives seriousness and unity to conduct, depends largely upon memory."

a not inconsiderable role in the origin of such dreams: many ideas which, in themselves, would be worth preserving in consciousness, sink below the threshold, associated trains of thought get lost and, thanks to psychic dissociation, go on working in the unconscious. We meet the same process again in the genesis of our own dreams.[90] The apparently sudden and unexpected reveries of the patient can be explained in this way. The total submersion of the conscious personality in the dream role is also the indirect cause of the development of simultaneous automatisms:

A second condition may also occasion the division of consciousness. It is not an alteration of sensibility, but it is rather a peculiar attitude of the mind—the concentration of attention on a single thing. The result of this state of concentration is that the mind is absorbed to the exclusion of other things, and to such a degree insensible that the way is opened for automatic actions; and these actions, becoming more complicated, as in the preceding case, may assume a psychic character and constitute intelligences of a parasitic kind, existing side by side with the normal personality, which is not aware of them.[91]

120   Our patient's "romances" throw a most significant light on the subjective roots of her dreams. They swarm with open and secret love-affairs, with illegitimate births and other sexual innuendoes. The hub of all these ambiguous stories is a lady whom she dislikes, and who gradually turns into her polar opposite, for whereas Ivenes is the pinnacle of virtue this lady is a sink of iniquity. But the patient's reincarnation theory, in which she appears as the ancestral mother of countless thousands, springs, in all of its naïve nakedness, straight from an

90 Cf. Freud, *The Interpretation of Dreams*, p. 593: "The course of our conscious reflections shows us that we follow a particular path in our application of attention. If, as we follow this path, we come upon an idea which will not bear criticism, we break off: we drop the cathexis of attention. Now it seems that the train of thought which has thus been initiated and dropped can continue to spin itself out without attention being turned to it again, unless at some point or other it reaches a specially high degree of intensity which forces attention to it. Thus, if a train of thought is initially rejected (consciously, perhaps) by a judgment that it is wrong or that it is useless for the immediate intellectual purposes in view, the result may be that this train of thought will proceed, unobserved by consciousness, until the onset of sleep."
91 Binet, *Alterations*, pp. 93f., modified.

exuberant fantasy which is so very characteristic of the puberty period. It is the woman's premonition of sexual feeling, the dream of fertility, that has created these monstrous ideas in the patient. We shall not be wrong if we seek the main cause of this curious clinical picture in her budding sexuality. From this point of view the whole essence of Ivenes and her enormous family is nothing but a dream of sexual wish-fulfilment, which differs from the dream of a night only in that it is spread over months and years.

[Nature of the Somnambulistic Attacks]

121   So far there is one point in S. W.'s history that has not been discussed, and that is the nature of her attacks. In the second séance she was suddenly seized with a sort of fainting-fit, from which she awoke with a recollection of various hallucinations. According to her own statement, she had not lost consciousness for a moment. Judging from the outward symptoms and course of these attacks, one is inclined to think of narcolepsy or lethargy, of the kind described, for instance, by Loewenfeld. This is the more plausible since we know that one member of her family—the grandmother—had once had an attack of lethargy. So it is conceivable that our patient inherited the lethargic disposition (Loewenfeld). One often observes hysterical fits of convulsions at spiritualistic séances. Our patient never showed any symptoms of convulsions, but instead she had those peculiar sleeping states. Aetiologically, two elements must be considered for the first attack:

(1) The influence of hypnosis.
(2) Psychic excitation.

122   (1) INFLUENCE OF PARTIAL HYPNOSIS. Janet observed that subconscious automatisms have a hypnotic influence and can bring about complete somnambulism.[92] He made the following experiment: While the patient, who was fully awake, was engaged in conversation by a second observer, Janet stationed him-

---

[92] L'Automatisme psychologique, p. 329: "Another consideration emphasizes the resemblance between these two states, namely, that subconscious acts have a kind of hypnotizing effect, and one that helps by their very performance to induce somnambulism."

self behind her and by means of whispered suggestions made her unconsciously move her hand, write, and answer questions by signs. Suddenly the patient broke off the conversation, turned round, and with supraliminal consciousness continued the previously subconscious talk with Janet. She had fallen into hypnotic somnambulism.[93] In this example we see a process similar to our case. But, for certain reasons to be discussed later, the sleeping state cannot be regarded as hypnotic. We therefore come to the question of:

123   (2) PSYCHIC EXCITATION. It is reported that the first time Bettina Brentano met Goethe, she suddenly fell asleep on his knee.[94] Ecstatic sleep in the midst of extreme torture, the so-called "witch's sleep," is a well-known phenomenon in the annals of witchcraft.[95]

124   With susceptible subjects, comparatively small stimuli are enough to induce somnambulistic states. For example, a sensitive lady had to have a splinter cut out of her finger. Without any kind of bodily change she suddenly saw herself sitting beside a brook in a beautiful meadow, plucking flowers. This condition lasted all through the minor operation and then vanished without having any special after-effects.[96]

125   Loewenfeld observed the unintentional induction of hysterical lethargy by hypnosis.[97] Our case has certain resemblances to hysterical lethargy as described by Loewenfeld: [98] superficial respiration, lowering of the pulse, corpse-like pallor of the face, also peculiar feelings of dying and thoughts of death.[99] Retention of one or more senses is no argument against lethargy: for instance in certain cases of apparent death the sense of hearing remains.[100] In Bonamaison's case,[101] not only was the sense of

93 Ibid., p. 329.

94 Gustave Flaubert made literary use of this falling asleep at the moment of supreme excitement in his novel *Salammbô*. When the hero, after many struggles, at last captures Salammbô, he suddenly falls asleep just as he touches her virginal bosom.

95 Cases of emotional paralysis may also come into this category. Cf. Baetz, "Über Emotionslähmung" (1901), pp. 717ff.

96 Hagen, "Zur Theorie der Hallucination" (1868), p. 17.

97 "Über hysterische Schlafzustände" (1892), p. 59.

98 Cf. Flournoy, *India to Mars*, pp. 67f.

99 Loewenfeld (1891), p. 737.

100 Ibid., p. 734.

101 "Un Cas remarquable d'hypnose spontanée" (1890), p. 234.

touch retained, but the senses of hearing and smell were sharpened. Hallucinations and loud speaking of hallucinatory persons are also met with in lethargy.[102] As a rule there is total amnesia for the lethargic interval. Loewenfeld's case D. had a vague memory afterwards,[103] and in Bonamaison's case there was no amnesia. Lethargic patients do not prove accessible to the usual stimuli for rousing them, but Loewenfeld succeeded, with his patient St., in changing the lethargy into hypnosis by means of mesmeric passes, thus establishing contact with the rest of her consciousness during the attack.[104] Our patient proved at first absolutely inaccessible during lethargy; later she started to speak spontaneously, was indistractible when her somnambulistic ego was speaking, but distractible when the speaker was one of her automatic personalities. In the latter case, it seems probable that the hypnotic effect of the automatisms succeeded in achieving a partial transformation of the lethargy into hypnosis. When we consider Loewenfeld's view that the lethargic disposition must not be "identified outright with the peculiar behaviour of the nervous apparatus in hysteria," then the assumption that this disposition was due to family heredity becomes fairly probable. The clinical picture is much complicated by these attacks.

126   So far we have seen that the patient's ego-consciousness was identical in all states. We have discussed two secondary complexes of consciousness and followed them into the somnambulistic attack, where, owing to loss of motor expression, they appeared to the patient in the second séance as a vision of the two grandfathers. These complexes completely disappeared from view during the attacks that followed, but on the other hand they developed an all the more intense activity during the twilight state, in the form of visions. It seems that numerous secondary sequences of ideas must have split off quite early from the primary unconscious personality, for soon after the first two séances "spirits" appeared by the dozen. The names were inexhaustible in their variety, but the differences between the various personalities were exhausted very quickly, and it became apparent that they could all be classified under two

102 Loewenfeld (1891), p. 737.
103 Ibid., p. 737.
104 Loewenfeld (1892), pp. 59ff.

types, the *serio-religious* and the *gay-hilarious*. It was really only a question of two different subconscious personalities appearing under various names, which had however no essential significance. The older type, the grandfather, who had started the automatisms off in the first place, was also the first to make use of the twilight state. I cannot remember any suggestion that might have given rise to the automatic speaking. According to our previous explanations, the attack can in these circumstances be thought of as a partial self-hypnosis. The ego-consciousness which remains over and, as a result of its isolation from the external world, occupies itself entirely with its hallucinations, is all that is left of the waking consciousness. Thus the automatism has a wide field for its activity. The autonomy of the individual centres, which we found to be present in the patient from the beginning, makes the act of automatic speaking more understandable. Dreamers, too, occasionally talk in their sleep, and people in the waking state sometimes accompany intense thought with unconscious whispering.[105] The peculiar movements of the speech muscles are worth noting. They have also been observed in other somnambulists.[106] These clumsy attempts can be directly paralleled by the unintelligent and clumsy movements of the table or glass; in all probability they correspond to the preliminary expression of the motor components of an idea, or they correspond to an excitation limited to the motor centres and not yet subordinated to a higher system. I do not know whether anything of the sort occurs with people who talk in their dreams, but it has been observed in hypnotized persons.[107]

127   Since the convenient medium of speech was used as the means of communication, it made the study of the subconscious personalities considerably easier. Their intellectual range was relatively narrow. Their knowledge comprised all that the patient knew in her waking state, plus a few incidental details

[105] Cf. Lehmann's researches into involuntary whispering, in *Aberglaube und Zauberei* (1898), pp. 386ff.

[106] Flournoy, for instance, writes (p. 103): "In a first attempt, Leopold [H. S.'s control] only succeeded in giving Hélène his intonation and pronunciation; after a séance in which she suffered acutely in her mouth and in her neck, as though her vocal organs were being manipulated or removed, she began to talk in a natural voice."

[107] Loewenfeld (1892), p. 60.

such as the birthdays of unknown persons who were dead, etc. The source of this information is rather obscure, since the patient did not know how she could have procured knowledge of these facts in the ordinary way. They were cryptomnesias, but are too insignificant to deserve more detailed mention. The two subconscious personalities had a very meagre intelligence; they produced almost nothing but banalities. The interesting thing is their relation to the ego-consciousness of the patient in the somnambulistic state. They were well informed about everything that took place during the ecstasies and occasionally gave an exact report, like a running commentary.[108] But they had only a very superficial knowledge of the patient's fantasies; they did not understand them and were unable to answer a single question on this subject correctly; their stereotyped reply was "Ask Ivenes." This observation reveals a dualism in the nature of the subconscious personalities which is rather difficult to explain; for the grandfather, who manifests himself through automatic speech, also appears to Ivenes, and according to her own statement "knew all her thoughts." How is it that when the grandfather speaks through the mouth of the patient he knows nothing about the very things he teaches Ivenes in the ecstasies?

128   Let us go back to what we said at the first appearance of the hallucinations [par. 98]. There we described the vision of the grandfathers as an irruption of hypnosis into the visual sphere. That irruption did not lead to a "normal" hypnosis but to "hystero-hypnosis"; in other words, the simple hypnosis was complicated by an hysterical attack.

129   It is not a rare occurrence for normal hypnosis to be disturbed, or rather to be replaced, by the unexpected appearance of hysterical somnambulism; the hypnotist in many cases then loses rapport with the patient. In our case the automatism arising in the motor area plays the part of the hypnotist, and the suggestions emanating from it (objectively described as auto-suggestions) hypnotize the neighbouring areas which have grown susceptible. But the moment the hypnosis affects the visual

108 This reminds us of Flournoy's observations: while H. S. speaks somnam-bulistically as Marie Antoinette, her arms do not belong to the somnambulistic personality but to the automatist Leopold, who converses by gestures with the observer. Cf. Flournoy, pp. 130f.

sphere the hysterical attack intervenes, and this, as we have remarked, effects a very profound change over large portions of the psychic area. We must picture the automatism as standing in the same relation to the attack as the hypnotist to a pathological hypnosis: it loses its influence on the subsequent development of the situation. The hallucinatory appearance of the hypnotic personality, or of the suggested idea, may be regarded as its last effect on the personality of the somnambulist. Thereafter the hypnotist becomes a mere figure with whom the somnambulistic personality engages autonomously; he can only just make out what is going on, but can no longer condition the content of the attack. The autonomous ego-complex—in this case Ivenes—now has the upper hand, and she groups her own mental products around the personality of her hypnotist, the grandfather, now diminished to a mere image. In this way we are able to understand the dualism in the nature of the grandfather. *Grandfather I, who speaks directly to those present, is a totally different person and a mere spectator of his double, Grandfather II, who appears as Ivenes' teacher.* Grandfather I maintains energetically that both are one and the same person, that Grandfather I has all the knowledge which Grandfather II possesses and is only prevented from making it public because of language difficulties. (The patient herself was naturally not conscious of this split, but took both to be the same person.) On closer inspection, however, Grandfather I is not altogether wrong, and he can appeal to an observation which apparently confirms the identity of I and II, i.e., the fact that they are never both present together, When I is speaking automatically, II is not present, and Ivenes remarks on his absence. Similarly, during her ecstasies, when she is with II, she cannot say where I is, or she only learns on returning from her journeys that he has been guarding her body in the meantime. Conversely, the grandfather never speaks when he is going on a journey with Ivenes or when he gives her special illumination. This behaviour is certainly remarkable, for if Grandfather I is the hypnotist and completely separate from the personality of Ivenes, there seems no reason why he should not speak objectively at the same time that his double appears in the ecstasy. Although this might have been supposed possible, as a matter of fact it was never observed. How is this dilemma to be resolved? Sure enough there is an identity of I and II, but it does not lie in the realm of the personality under discussion; it lies rather in the basis common to both, namely in the personality of the patient, which is in the deepest sense one and indivisible.

130   Here we come upon the characteristic feature of all hysterical splits of consciousness. They are disturbances that only touch the surface, and none of them goes so deep as to attack the firmly knit basis of the ego-complex. Somewhere, often in an extremely well-concealed place, we find the bridge which spans the apparently impassable abyss. For instance, one of four playing cards is made invisible to a hypnotized person by suggestion; consequently he calls only the other three. A pencil is then put into his hand and he is told to write down all the cards before him; he correctly adds the fourth one.[109] Again, a patient of Janet's [110] always saw, in the aura of his hystero-epileptic attacks, the vision of a conflagration. Whenever he saw an open fire he had an attack; indeed, the sight of a lighted match held before him was sufficient to induce one. The patient's visual field was limited to 30° on the left side; the right eye was closed. The left eye was then focused on the centre of a perimeter while a lighted match was held at 80°. An hystero-epileptic attack took place immediately. Despite extensive amnesia in many cases of double consciousness, the patients do not behave in a way that corresponds to the degree of their ignorance, but as though some obscure instinct still guided their actions in accordance with their former knowledge. Neither this relatively mild amnesic split nor even the severe amnesia of the epileptic twilight state, formerly regarded as an *irreparabile damnum*, is sufficient to sever the innermost threads that bind the ego-complex of the twilight state to that of the normal state. In one case it was possible to articulate the content of the twilight state with the waking ego-complex.[111]

131   If we apply these discoveries to our case, we arrive at the explanatory hypothesis that, under the influence of appropriate suggestions, the layers of the unconscious which are beyond reach of the split try to represent the unity of the automatic

109 Dessoir, *Das Doppel-Ich* (1896), p. 29.

110 Janet, "L'Anesthésie hystérique," p. 69.

111 Graeter, "Ein Fall von epileptischer Amnesie durch Hypermnesie beseitigt" (1899), p. 129.

personality, but that this endeavour comes to grief on the profounder and more elementary disturbance caused by the hysterical attack.[112] This prevents a more complete synthesis by appending associations which are, as it were, the truest and most original property of the "supraconscious" personality. The dream of Ivenes, as it emerges into consciousness, is put into the mouths of the figures who happen to be in the field of vision, and henceforth it remains associated with these persons.

[Origin of the Unconscious Personalities]

132   As we have seen, the various personalities are grouped round two types, the grandfather and Ulrich von Gerbenstein. The grandfather produces nothing but sanctimonious twaddle and edifying moral precepts. Ulrich von Gerbenstein is simply a silly schoolgirl, with nothing masculine about him except his name. We must here add, from the anamnesis, that the patient was confirmed at the age of fifteen by a very pietistic clergyman, and that even at home she had to listen to moral sermons. The grandfather represents this side of her past, Gerbenstein the other half; hence the curious contrast. So here we have, personified, the chief characters of the past: here the compulsorily educated bigot, there the boisterousness of a lively girl of fifteen who often goes too far.[113] The patient herself is a peculiar mixture of both; sometimes timid, shy, excessively reserved, at other times boisterous to the point of indecency. She is often painfully conscious of these contrasts. This gives us the key to the origin of the two subconscious personalities. The patient is obviously seeking a middle way between two extremes; she endeavours to repress them and strives for a more ideal state. These strivings lead to the adolescent dream of the ideal Ivenes, beside whom the unrefined aspects of her character fade into the background. They are not lost; but as repressed thoughts,

---

112 Karplus, "Über Pupillenstarre im hysterischen Anfall" (1898), p. 52, says: "The hysterical attack is not a purely psychic process. . . . The psychic processes merely release a pre-existing mechanism, which in itself has nothing to do with them."

113 This objectivation of associated complexes has been used by Carl Hauptmann in his play *Die Bergschmiede* (1902), where the treasure-seeker is confronted one gloomy night by the hallucination of his entire better self.

analogous to the idea of Ivenes, they begin to lead an independent existence as autonomous personalities.

133 This behaviour calls to mind Freud's dream investigations, which disclose the independent growth of repressed thoughts.[114] We can now understand why the hallucinatory persons are divorced from those who write and speak automatically. They teach Ivenes the secrets of the Beyond, they tell her all those fantastic stories about the extraordinariness of her personality, they create situations in which she can appear dramatically with the attributes of their power, wisdom, and virtue. They are nothing but dramatized split-offs from her dream-ego. The others, the automata, are the ones to be overcome; they must have no part in Ivenes. The only thing they have in common with her spirit companions is the name. It is not to be expected in a case like this, where no clear-cut divisions exist, that two such pregnant groups of characters, with all their idiosyncrasies, should disappear entirely from a somnambulistic ego-complex so closely connected with the waking consciousness. And in fact, we meet them again, partly in those ecstatic penitential scenes and partly in the romances that are crammed with more or less banal, mischievous gossip. On the whole, however, a very much milder form predominates.

Course of the Disorder

134 It only remains now to say a few words about the course of this singular ailment. The whole process reached its climax within four to eight weeks, and the descriptions of Ivenes and the other subconscious personalities refer in general to this period. Thereafter a gradual decline became noticeable; the ecstasies grew more and more vacuous as Gerbenstein's influence increased. The phenomena lost their plasticity and became ever shallower; characters which at first were well differentiated became by degrees inextricably mixed. The psychological yield grew more and more meagre, until finally the whole story assumed the appearance of a first-class fraud. Ivenes herself was severely hit by this decline; she became painfully uncertain, spoke cautiously, as if feeling her way, so that the character of

114 *The Interpretation of Dreams.* Cf. also Breuer and Freud, *Studies on Hysteria* (orig. 1895).

the patient came through in more and more undisguised form. The somnambulistic attacks, too, decreased in frequency and intensity. One could observe with one's own eyes all the gradations from somnambulism to conscious lying.

135   Thus the curtain fell. The patient has since gone abroad. The fact that her character has become pleasanter and more stable may have a significance that is not to be underestimated, if we remember those cases where the second state gradually came to replace the first. We may be dealing here with a similar phenomenon.

136   It is well known that somnambulistic symptoms are particularly common in puberty.[115] The attacks of somnambulism in Dyce's case [116] began immediately before the onset of puberty and lasted just till its end. The somnambulism of Hélène Smith is likewise closely connected with puberty.[117] Schroeder van der Kolk's patient was 16 at the time of her illness; Felida X., 14½. We know also that the future character is formed and fixed at this period. We saw in the cases of Felida X. and Mary Reynolds how the character of the second state gradually replaced that of the first. It is, therefore, conceivable that the phenomena of double consciousness are simply new character formations, or attempts of the future personality to break through, and that in consequence of special difficulties (unfavourable circumstances, psychopathic disposition of the nervous system, etc.) they get bound up with peculiar disturbances of consciousness. In view of the difficulties that oppose the future character, the somnambulisms sometimes have an eminently teleological significance, in that they give the individual, who would otherwise inevitably succumb, the means of victory. Here I am thinking especially of Joan of Arc, whose extraordinary courage reminds one of the feats performed by Mary Reynolds in her second state. This is also, perhaps, the place to point out the like significance of "teleological hallucinations," of which occasional cases come to the knowledge of the public, although they have not yet been subjected to scientific study.

115 Pelman, "Über das Verhalten des Gedächtnisses bei den verschiedenen Formen des Irreseins" (1864), p. 74.
116 Jessen, "Doppeltes Bewusstsein" (1865), p. 407.
117 Flournoy, p. 31.

Heightened Unconscious Performance

137   We have now discussed all the essential phenomena presented by our case which were significant for its inner structure. Certain accompanying phenomena have still to be briefly considered; these are the phenomena of *heightened unconscious performance*. In this field, we meet with a not altogether unjustifiable scepticism on the part of the scientific pundits. Even Dessoir's conception of the second ego aroused considerable opposition and was rejected in many quarters as too enthusiastic. As we know, occultism has claimed a special right to this field and has drawn premature conclusions from dubious observations. We are still very far indeed from being able to say anything conclusive, for up to the present our material is nothing like adequate. If, therefore, we touch on this question of heightened unconscious performance, we do so only to do justice to all sides of our case.

138   By heightened unconscious performance we mean that peculiar automatic process whose results are not available for the conscious psychic activity of the individual. Under this category comes, first of all, thought-reading by means of table movements. I do not know whether there are people who can guess an entire long train of thought by means of inductive inferences from the "intended tremors." At any rate it is certain that, granting this to be possible, such persons must be making use of a routine acquired by endless practice. But in our case routine can be ruled out at once, and there is no choice but to assume for the present a receptivity of the unconscious far exceeding that of the conscious mind. This assumption is supported by numerous observations on somnambulists. Here I will mention only Binet's experiments, where little letters or other small objects, or complicated little figures in relief, were laid on the anaesthesic skin of the back of the hand or the neck, and the unconscious perceptions were registered by means of signs. On the basis of these experiments he comes to the following conclusion: "According to the calculations that I have been able to make, the unconscious sensibility of an hysterical patient is at certain moments *fifty times* more acute than that of

a normal person." [118] Another example of heightened performance that applies to our case and to numerous other somnambulists is the process known as cryptomnesia.[119] By this is meant the coming into consciousness of a memory-image which is not recognized as such in the first instance, but only secondarily, if at all, by means of subsequent recollection or abstract reasoning. It is characteristic of cryptomnesia that the image which comes up does not bear the distinctive marks of the memory-image—that is to say, it is not connected with the supraliminal ego-complex in question.

139   There are three different ways in which the cryptomnesic image may be brought into consciousness:

(1) *The image enters consciousness without the mediation of the senses, intrapsychically.* It is a sudden idea or hunch, whose causal nexus is hidden from the person concerned. To this extent cryptomnesia is an everyday occurrence and is intimately bound up with normal psychic processes. But how often it misleads the scientist, author, or composer into believing that his ideas are original, and then along comes the critic and points out the source! Generally the individual formulation of the idea protects the author from the charge of plagiarism and proves his good faith, though there are cases where the reproduction occurs unconsciously, almost word for word. Should the passage contain a remarkable idea, then the suspicion of more or less conscious plagiarism is justified. After all, an important idea is linked by numerous associations to the ego-complex; it has been thought about at different times and in different situations and therefore has innumerable connecting threads leading in all directions. Consequently it can never disappear so entirely from consciousness that its continuity is lost to the sphere of conscious memory. We have, however, a criterion by which we can always recognize intrapsychic cryptomnesia objectively: the cryptomnesic idea is linked to the ego-complex by the minimum of associations. The reason for this lies in the relation of the individual to the object concerned, in the want of proportion between interest and object.

[118] *Alterations*, p. 139.
[119] Cryptomnesia should not be confused with hypermnesia. By the latter term is meant the abnormal sharpening of the powers of memory, which then reproduce the actual memory-images themselves.

Two possibilities are conceivable: (*a*) The object is worthy of interest, but the interest is slight owing to distractibility or lack of understanding. (*b*) The object is not worthy of interest, consequently the interest is slight. In both cases there is an extremely labile connection with consciousness, the result being that the object is quickly forgotten. This flimsy bridge soon breaks down and the idea sinks into the unconscious, where it is no longer accessible to the conscious mind. Should it now re-enter consciousness by way of cryptomnesia, the feeling of strangeness, of its being an original creation, will cling to it, because the path by which it entered the subconscious can no longer be discovered. Strangeness and original creation are, moreover, closely allied to one another, if we remember the numerous witnesses in *belles-lettres* to the "possessed" nature of genius.[120] Apart from a number of striking instances of this kind, where it is doubtful whether it is cryptomnesia or an original creation, there are others where a passage of no essential value has been reproduced cryptomnesically, and in almost the same words, as in the following example:

140   Nietzsche, *Thus Spake Zara-*   Kerner, *Blätter aus Prevorst* [122]
thustra [121]

Now about the time that Zara-   The four captains and a mer-
thustra sojourned on the Happy   chant, Mr. Bell, went ashore on
Isles, it happened that a ship   the island of Mount Stromboli
anchored at the isle on which   to shoot rabbits. At three o'clock

120 Cf. Nietzsche, *Ecce Homo* (trans. by Ludovici), pp. 101f.: "Has any one at the end of the nineteenth century any distinct notion of what poets of a stronger age understood by the word 'inspiration'? If not, I will describe it. If one had the smallest vestige of superstition left in one, it would hardly be possible completely to set aside the idea that one is the mere incarnation, mouthpiece, or medium of an almighty power. The idea of revelation, in the sense that something which profoundly convulses and upsets one becomes suddenly visible and audible with indescribable certainty and accuracy, describes the simple fact. One hears—one does not seek; one takes—one does not ask who gives; a thought suddenly flashes up like lightning, it comes with necessity, without faltering—I have never had any choice in the matter."

121 Ch. XL, "Great Events" (trans. by Common, p. 180, slightly modified). (Orig. 1883.)

122 Vol. IV, p. 57, headed: "An Extract of Awe-Inspiring Import from the Log of the Ship *Sphinx* in the Year 1686, in the Mediterranean." (Orig. 1831–39.) [Cf. par. 181, below.—EDITORS.]

the smoking mountain stands, and the crew went ashore to shoot rabbits. About the noontide hour, however, when the captain and his men were together again, they suddenly saw a man coming towards them through the air, and a voice said distinctly: "It is time! It is highest time!" But when the figure drew close to them, flying past quickly like a shadow in the direction of the volcano, they recognized with the greatest dismay that it was Zarathustra. . . . "Behold," said the old helmsman, "Zarathustra goes down to hell!"

they mustered the crew to go aboard, when, to their inexpressible astonishment, they saw two men flying rapidly towards them through the air. One was dressed in black, the other in grey. They came past them very closely, in the greatest haste, and to their utmost dismay descended amid the burning flames into the crater of the terrible volcano, Mount Stromboli. They recognized the pair as acquaintances from London.

141   Nietzsche's sister, Elisabeth Förster-Nietzsche, told me, in reply to my enquiry, that Nietzsche had taken a lively interest in Kerner when staying with his grandfather, Pastor Oehler, in Pobler, between the ages of 12 and 15, but certainly not later. It could scarcely have been Nietzsche's intention to commit a plagiarism from a ship's log; had this been the case he would surely have omitted that extremely prosaic and totally irrelevant passage about shooting rabbits. Obviously, when painting the picture of Zarathustra's descent into hell, that forgotten impression from his youth must have slipped half or wholly unconsciously into his mind.

142   This example shows all the peculiarities of cryptomnesia: a quite unimportant detail which only deserves to be forgotten as quickly as possible is suddenly reproduced with almost literal fidelity, while the main point of the story is, one cannot say modified, but re-created in an individual manner. Around the individual core—the idea of the journey to hell—there are deposited, as picturesque details, those old, forgotten impressions of a similar situation. The story itself is so absurd that the young Nietzsche, a voracious reader, probably skimmed through it without evincing any very profound interest in the matter. Here, then, is the required minimum of associative connections,

for we can hardly conceive of a greater jump than from that stupid old tale to Nietzsche's consciousness in the year 1883. If we realize Nietzsche's state of mind [123] at the time when he wrote *Zarathustra,* and the poetic ecstasy that at more than one point verges on the pathological, this abnormal reminiscence will appear more understandable.

143   The other of the two possibilities mentioned above, namely, registering some object, not in itself uninteresting, in a state of distractibility or partial interest due to lack of understanding, and its cryptomnesic reproduction, is found mainly in somnambulists, and also—as curiosities of literature—in people at the point of death.[124] Out of the rich choice of these phenomena we are chiefly concerned here with speaking in foreign tongues, the symptom of glossolalia. This phenomenon is mentioned in practically all cases of ecstasy; it is found in the New Testament, in the *Acta Sanctorum,*[125] in the witch trials, and in recent times in the story of the Clairvoyante of Prevorst, in Judge Edmond's daughter Laura, in Flournoy's Hélène Smith, who was thoroughly investigated on this question too, and also in Bresler's case,[126] which was probably identical with that of Blumhardt's Gottliebin Dittus.[127] As Flournoy has shown, glossolalia, in so far as it is a really independent language, is a cryptomnesic phenomenon par excellence. I would refer the reader to Flournoy's exceedingly interesting study of this subject.[128]

144   In our case glossolalia was observed only once, and then the only intelligible words were the interspersed variations of the word *vena.* The origin of this word is clear: a few days previously the patient had dipped into an anatomical atlas and immersed herself in a study of the veins of the face, which were

---

[123] In *Ecce Homo:* "There is an ecstasy so great that the tremendous strain of it is at times eased by a storm of tears, when your steps now involuntarily rush ahead, now lag behind; a feeling of being completely beside yourself, with the most distinct consciousness of innumerable delicate thrills tingling through you to your very toes; a depth of happiness, in which pain and gloom do not act as its antitheses, but as its condition, as a challenge, as necessary shades of colour in such an excess of light." [Cf. Ludovici trans., p. 102.]

[124] Eckermann, *Conversations with Goethe,* p. 587.

[125] Cf. Görres, *Die christliche Mystik.*

[126] "Kulturhistorischer Beitrag zur Hysterie" (1896), pp. 333ff.

[127] Zündel, *Pfarrer J. C. Blumhardt* (1880).

[128] *From India to the Planet Mars.*

given in Latin, and she used the word *vena* in her dreams, just as a normal person might do. The remaining words and sentences in foreign language reveal at a glance their derivation from the patient's slight knowledge of French. Unfortunately I did not get exact translations of the various sentences, because the patient refused to give them to me; but we can take it that it was the same sort of thing as Hélène Smith's Martian language. Flournoy shows that this Martian language was nothing but a childish translation from the French; only the words were altered, the syntax remained the same. A more probable explanation is that our patient simply strung a lot of meaningless foreign-sounding words together, and, instead of forming any true words,[129] borrowed certain characteristic sounds from French and Italian and combined them into a sort of language, just as Hélène Smith filled in the gaps between the real Sanskrit words with pseudo-linguistic products of her own. The curious names of the mystical system can mostly be traced back to known roots. Even the circles remind one of the planetary orbits found in every school atlas; the inner parallel with the relation of the planets to the sun is also pretty clear, so we shall not go far wrong if we see the names as reminiscences of popular astronomy. In this way the names "Persus," "Fenus," "Nenus," "Sirum," "Surus," "Fixus," and "Pix" can be explained as childish distortions of "Perseus," "Venus," "Sirius," and "fixed star," analogous to the *vena* variations. "Magnesor" is reminiscent of "magnetism," whose mystical significance the patient knew from the Clairvoyante of Prevorst story. "Connesor" being contrary to "Magnesor," the first syllable "Con-" suggests French "contre." "Hypos" and "Hyfonism" remind one of "hypnosis" and "hypnotism," about which the weirdest ideas still circulate amongst laymen. The frequent endings in "-us" and "-os" are the signs by which most people distinguish between Latin and Greek. The other names derive from similar accidents to which we lack the clues. Naturally the modest glossolalia of our case cannot claim to be a classic example of cryptomnesia, for it con-

---

129 ". . . the rapid and confused gibberish whose meaning can never be ascertained, probably because it really has none, but is only a pseudo-language." Flournoy, p. 199. ". . . analogous to the gibberish which children use sometimes in their games of 'pretending' to speak Chinese, Indian, or 'savage'. . ." (p. 159, modified).

sists only in the unconscious use of different impressions, some optical, some acoustic, and all very obvious.

145   (2) *The cryptomnesic image enters consciousness through mediation of the senses, as an hallucination.* Hélène Smith is the classic example of this. See the case cited above, concerning the number 18 [par. 98].

146   (3) *The image enters consciousness by motor automatism.* Hélène Smith had lost a very valuable brooch which she was anxiously looking for everywhere. Ten days later her guide Leopold told her by table movements where it was. From the information received, she found it one night in an open field, covered by sand.[130] Strictly speaking, in cryptomnesia there is no heightened performance in the true sense of the term, since the conscious memory experiences no intensification of function but only an enrichment of content. Through the automatism certain areas which were previously closed to consciousness are made accessible to it in an indirect way, but the unconscious itself is not performing any function that exceeds the capacities of the conscious mind either qualitatively or quantitatively. Cryptomnesia is therefore only an apparent instance of heightened performance, in contrast to hypermnesia, where there is an actual increase of function.[131]

147   We spoke earlier of the unconscious having a receptivity superior to that of the conscious mind, chiefly in regard to simple thought-transference experiments with numbers. As already mentioned, not only our somnambulist but a fairly large number of normal people are able to guess, from tremor movements, quite long trains of thought, provided they are not too complicated. These experiments are, so to speak, the prototype of those rarer and incomparably more astonishing cases of intuitive knowledge displayed at times by somnambulists.[132] Zschokke has shown from his own self-analysis [133] that such phenomena occur in connection not only with somnambulism but with non-somnambulists as well.

130 Ibid., p. 405.
131 For a case of this kind see Krafft-Ebing, *Text-Book of Insanity* (orig. 1879).
132 Loewenfeld (*Hypnotismus,* p. 289) writes: "The restriction of associative processes to, and the steady concentration of attention on, a definite field of representation can also lead to the development of new ideas which no effort of will in the waking state would have been able to bring to light."
133 Zschokke, *Eine Selbstschau* (1843), pp. 227ff.

148   This knowledge seems to be formed in several different ways. The first thing to be considered, as we have said, is the delicacy of unconscious perceptions; secondly, we must emphasize the importance of what proves to be the enormous suggestibility of somnambulists. The somnambulist not only incorporates every suggestive idea into himself, he actually lives himself into the suggestion, into the person of the doctor or observer, with the utter abandon characteristic of suggestible hysterics. Frau Hauffe's relation to Kerner is an excellent example of this. So it not surprising that there is in these cases a high degree of concord of associations, a fact which Richet, for instance, might have taken more account of in his experiments on thought-transference. Finally, there are cases of somnambulistic heightened performance which cannot be explained solely by the hyperaesthetic unconscious activity of the senses, or by the concord of associations, but which postulate a highly developed intellectual activity of the unconscious. To decipher the intended tremor movements requires an extraordinary delicacy of feeling, both sensitive and sensory, in order to combine the individual perceptions into a self-contained unit of thought—if indeed it is permissible at all to make an analogy between the cognitive processes in the unconscious and those of the conscious. The possibility must always be borne in mind that, in the unconscious, feelings and concepts are not so clearly separated, and may even be one. The intellectual exaltation which many somnambulists display during ecstasy, though rather uncommon, is a well-observed fact,[134] and I am inclined to regard the mystical system devised by our patient as just such an example of heightened unconscious performance that transcends her normal intelligence. We have already seen where part of that system probably comes from. Another source may be Frau Hauffe's "life-circles," depicted in Kerner's book. At any rate its outward form seems to be determined by these factors. As we have already noted, the idea of dualism derives from those fragments of conversation overheard by the patient in the dreamy state following her ecstasies.

[134] Gilles de la Tourette (quoted in Loewenfeld, p. 132) says: "We have seen somnambulistic girls, poor, uneducated, and quite stupid in the waking state, whose whole appearance altered as soon as they were put to sleep. Before they were boring, now they are lively and excited, sometimes even witty."

[4. CONCLUSION]

149   This exhausts my knowledge of the sources used by the patient. Where the root idea came from she was unable to say. Naturally I waded through the occult literature so far as it pertained to this subject, and discovered a wealth of parallels with our gnostic system, dating from different centuries, but scattered about in all kinds of works, most of them quite inaccessible to the patient. Moreover, at her tender age, and in her surroundings, the possibility of any such study must be ruled out of account. A brief survey of the system in the light of the patient's own explanations will show how much intelligence was expended on its construction. How high the intellectual achievement is to be rated must remain a matter of taste. At all events, considering the youth and mentality of the patient, it must be regarded as something quite out of the ordinary.

150   In conclusion, I would like to express my warmest thanks to my revered teacher, Professor Bleuler, for his friendly encouragement and the loan of books, and to my friend Dr. Ludwig von Muralt for his kindness in handing over to me the first case mentioned in this book (case of Miss E.).[135]

[135] (Added 1978.) The version published in the *Gesammelte Werke*, Band I, gives for par. 150 the following concluding paragraphs (tr. Lisa Ress), from a later printing of the monograph:

I am far from believing that with this work any sort of final and scientifically satisfying result has been achieved. Primarily, my intention has been to counter general opinion, which dismisses so-called occult phenomena with a contemptuous smile, by demonstrating the manifold connections between these phenomena and the subjects covered by medicine and psychology, as well as to refer to the many important questions which this unexplored territory holds for us. Impetus for this work was given me by the conviction that in this area a rich harvest for experiential psychology is ripening, as well as by the awareness that our German science has not concerned itself sufficiently with these problems. This latter reason also induced me to lead off with the investigation of a case of somnambulism belonging to the purely pathological, so as to locate the place of somnambulists in relation to pathology in general.

I hope that in this sense my work will aid science in preparing a way toward the progressive elucidation and assimilation of the as yet extremely controversial psychology of the unconscious.

ON HYSTERICAL MISREADING [1]

151   In his review of my paper "On the Psychology and Pathology of So-called Occult Phenomena," [2] Mr. Hahn misrepresented my views on "hysterical misreading." Since I regard this phenomenon as being of fundamental importance, perhaps I may be allowed to state my views once again.

152   My patient misread with remarkable frequency at school, and always in a quite definite way: each time she substituted the Swiss dialect word for the word in question, so instead of saying "Treppe" (stair) she said "Stege," and instead of "Ziege" (goat) she said "Geiss," and so on. [3] These expressions are absolutely synonymous. Hence, if the word "Stege" is produced, it proves that the meaning of the word "Treppe" was understood. There are two possible ways of explaining this phenomenon:

153   (1) The word "Treppe" is understood correctly and consciously. In this case there is absolutely no reason for a healthy person to reproduce the word incorrectly, i.e., as a dialect word. But with my patient the dialect word somehow crept in.

154   (2) The word "Treppe" is not understood correctly. In this case any normal person will reproduce nonsense that either

1 [First published as "Über hysterisches Verlesen," *Archiv für die gesamte Psychologie* (Leipzig), III (1904) : 4, 347–50.—EDITORS.]
2 [See the previous paper in this volume. The review by R. Hahn was published in the *Archiv*, III, Literaturbericht, p. 26.—EDITORS.]
3 [Cf. pars. 38 and 73, above.]

sounds like or looks like the word, but he will never reproduce an expression that sounds and looks different but is synonymous. I have made numerous reading-tests with patients suffering from paralysis, mania, alcoholism, senile dementia, etc., who are distractible and unable to concentrate, and on the basis of hundreds of these experiences I can confidently assert that this kind of misreading does not occur in individuals who are not hysterical. Every misreading that occurs in a state of distractibility is based on a phonetic or a textual likeness; with normal persons it is usually caused by momentary constellations. I have found this rule amply confirmed by association tests conducted under conditions of distraction.

155   If, therefore, my patient reproduces dialect words instead of the literary ones without noticing this frequently repeated mistake, she has in the first place a defective acoustic control of what she is saying; and, in the second place, the synonym shows that the meaning of the optic impression was understood correctly. But it is reproduced incorrectly. Where does the cause of the mistake lie? In my paper I left this question open, contenting myself with the general remark that it was an "automatic" phenomenon which I was not able to localize at the time.

156   The most probable explanation is as follows: We know from everyday experience that the ordinary kind of misreading disturbs the sense by substituting for the right word a word akin to it in sound or form. Slips of the tongue in uttering a correctly understood word follow the same rule, and when, as often happens, a Swiss finds himself uttering a dialect word, he very rarely does so when reading out loud, and the words that are confused with one another are mostly those with a strong phonetic affinity. This cannot be said of the example I have deliberately chosen: "Ziege—Geiss." In order to explain their confusion, we have to assume an additional factor. This additional factor is the patient's hysterical disposition.

157   Our dreamy, somewhat drowsy patient reads mechanically; her comprehension of the meaning is therefore practically nil. While her conscious mind is occupied with something quite different, the psychic processes set in motion by her reading remain feeble and indistinct. In normal and sick persons who are distractible but not hysterical, these feebly accentuated psychic processes give rise to misconstructions based on a phonetic or

formal likeness, so that reproduction is falsified at the cost of sense. It is the other way round with my patient: the formal connection breaks down completely but the sense connection is preserved. This can only be explained on the hypothesis of a split consciousness; that is to say, besides the ego-complex, which follows its own thoughts, there is another conscious complex which reads and understands correctly, and allows itself various modifications of expression, as indeed is frequently the case with complexes that function automatically. Hysterical misreading differs from all other types in that, despite the misreading, the sense is preserved during reproduction.

158   If Mr. Hahn fails to understand this well-known automatization of psychic functions in the psychopathology of hysteria, I can only recommend him to a study of the literature and to a little practical observation on his own account. Literature and reality abound in analogous phenomena.

159   The reason why I attach particular importance to hysterical misreading is that it demonstrates in a nutshell the splitting off of psychic functions from the ego-complex, which is such a characteristic of hysteria, and consequently the strong tendency of the psychic elements towards autonomy.

160   In my paper, I cited by way of analogy the observations made by Binet,[4] who, having anaesthetized the subject's hand by hypnosis (split it off from the ego-complex), pricked it with a needle under the cover of a screen, whereupon the subject suddenly thought of a row of dots (corresponding to the number of pricks). Or Binet would move the subject's fingers, and she at once thought of "sticks" or "columns"; or the anaesthetic hand was induced to write the name "Salpêtrière," and the subject suddenly saw "Salpêtrière" before her, in white writing on a black ground.

161   Mr. Hahn is of the opinion that these observations have to do with "something essentially different" from misreading. What is this something? Mr. Hahn does not say.

162   Binet's experiments make it clear that the conscious complex which is split off from the ego-complex, and upon which the anaesthesia of the arm depends, perceives things correctly but reproduces them in modified form.

163   The ego-complex of my patient is displaced from the act of

4 [Cf. par. 75, above.]

reading by other ideas, but the act continues automatically and forms a little conscious complex on its own, which likewise understands correctly but reproduces in modified form.

164   The type of process is therefore the same, for which reason my reference to Binet's experiments is fully justified. It is a type that repeats itself over the whole field of hysteria; for instance, the systematic "irrelevant answers" of hysterical subjects, which have only recently been publicized, would also come into this category.

165   For the rest, I would like to point out that the main emphasis of my paper falls on the fullest possible registration and analysis of the manifold psychological phenomena which are all intimately connected with the development of character at this time of life. The analysis of the clinical picture is not, as Mr. Hahn thinks, based on French writers, but on Freud's investigations of hysteria. Mr. Hahn would like to see the analysis "carried further and pursued more rigorously." I would be very much obliged to Mr. Hahn if, together with his criticism, he would specify new ways of investigating this very difficult field.

II

CRYPTOMNESIA

CRYPTOMNESIA [1]

166   Modern scientific psychology distinguishes between direct
and indirect memory. You have a direct memory when, for
instance, you see a certain house and it then "comes into your
mind" that a friend of yours lived there some years ago. You see
the well-known house, and by the law of association the coexist-
ent memory-image of your friend enters your consciousness. An
indirect memory is different: I walk, deep in thought, past the
house where my friend X used to live. I pay no attention either
to the house or to the street, but am thinking of some urgent
business matter I have to attend to. Suddenly an unexpected
image thrusts itself obtrusively between my thoughts: I see a
scene in which X once discussed similar matters with me many
years ago. I am surprised that this particular memory should
come up, for the conversation was of no importance. Suddenly
I realize that I am in the street where my friend once lived. In
this case the association of the memory-image with the house is
indirect: I did not perceive the house consciously, for my
thoughts distracted me from my surroundings too much. But
the perception of the house nevertheless slipped into the dark
background of consciousness [2] and activated the association

1 [First published as "Kryptomnesie," *Die Zukunft* (Berlin), 13th year (1905), L,
325-34.—EDITORS.]
2 I call "unconscious," in the widest sense, everything that is not represented in
consciousness, whether momentarily or permanently.

with X. As this association was too feebly accentuated to cross the threshold of consciousness, a common association had to intervene as an auxiliary. This mediating association is the memory-image of the conversation that touched on matters similar to those now being revolved in my consciousness. In this way, the memory-image of X enters the sphere of consciousness.

167   The direct and the indirect memory-image have one quality in common: the quality of being known. I recognize the association as an image I remember, and therefore know that it is not a new formation. The images we combine anew lack this quality of being known. I say "combine," because originality lies only in the combination of psychic elements and not in the material, as everything in nature eloquently testifies. If a new combination has the quality of being known it is something abnormal: a deception of memory. The million acts of recollection daily taking place in our brain consist for the most part of direct memories, but a considerable number of them will fall on the side of indirect memory. These last are especially interesting. As our example of indirect memory shows, an unconscious perception that enters the brain passively can spontaneously activate a related association and in this way reach consciousness. The unconscious perception therefore does what our consciousness ordinarily does when we look at the house and ask ourselves "Who lived there?" in order to evoke a clear memory. We thus call back the image of X into our minds. The unconscious perception behaves in exactly the same way; it seeks out the memory-image related to it, and in our example (by a psychological law which I do not propose to go into here) it combines with something that is being gently activated from the other side, namely the image of X talking of similar business matters. We see from this that association can take place without the least assistance from consciousness.

168   From the way it entered my consciousness as an indirect memory, the image of X would commonly be described as a "chance idea," and the German word *Einfall* clearly expresses the apparently fortuitous and groundless nature of the phenomenon. This kind of indirect memory is very common among people who think intuitively rather than in logical sequence—so common that we often forget how strictly determined all psychic processes are. To take a simple example: I am working away at

some casual task, whistling a tune, some popular song whose words I don't even remember at the moment. Somebody asks me what tune it is. I cast round in my memory: it is the student song "Not a cent, not a cent, and my clothes are only lent!" I have no idea how I came to pick on this particular song, which has nothing whatever to do with the associations now engaging my conscious mind. I go back along the train of thought I followed while working. All at once I remember that a few minutes ago I had been thinking, with a certain amount of feeling-tone, of a grand settlement of accounts in the New Year. Hence the song! I need hardly add that one can carry out some very pretty psychological diagnoses on one's fellows in this way. For instance, when a friend of mine was imprudent enough to whistle three little melodies within a space of ten minutes, I could tell him to his face how sorry I was to hear that his love affair had ended unhappily. The melodies were "Im Aargau sind zwei Liebei" ("In Aargau are two lovers,"—a Swiss folksong), "Verlassen, verlassen bin i" ("Forlorn, forlorn am I"), and "Steh ich in finstrer Mitternacht" ("I stand in midnight's gloom"). It even happened that on one occasion I whistled a tune whose text I did not know. On making inquiries I discovered a text that was undoubtedly associated with a strongly feeling-toned [2a] train of thought I had pursued five minutes before.

169   These examples, which one can observe every day in oneself and others, clearly show that a (feeling-toned) train of thought can disappear from the conscious mind without therefore ceasing to exist. On the contrary, it still has sufficient energy to send

2a [The phrases "feeling-toned complex" and "feeling tone" translate the German "gefühlsbetonter Komplex" and "Gefühlston." Although it might be justifiable to follow H. G. and Cary F. Baynes and translate the first phrase as "emotionally-toned" complex (cf. Jung, "On Psychical Energy," in *Contributions to Analytical Psychology*, p. 9), the Editors have decided, in keeping with the general policy of this edition, to retain the original terminology on account both of its historical interest and of Jung's consistent use of the term in his later works. In a re-statement of his theory of complexes published in 1934 (see "A Review of the Complex Theory," Coll. Works, 8, par. 201), Jung defines the feeling-toned complex as "the image of a certain psychic situation which is strongly accentuated emotionally." From this it is clear that the word "feeling" is not used in the later technical sense to designate one of the four psychic functions, but in a more generalized way. It is in the latter sense that the terms "feeling tone" and "feeling-toned complex" will be used throughout the collected edition.—EDITORS.]

up, in the midst of the conscious world of associations that have completely changed in the meantime, an idea that bears no relation to its momentary surroundings.

170　　Still more drastic examples are provided by hysteria, which is nothing other than a caricature of normal psychological mechanisms. Recently I had to treat a hysterical young lady who became ill chiefly because she had been brutally beaten by her father. Once, when we were out for a walk, this lady dropped her cloak in the dust. I picked it up, and tried to get the dust off by beating it with my stick. The next moment the lady hurled herself upon me with violent defensive gestures and tore the cloak out of my hands. She said she couldn't stand the sight, it was quite unendurable to her. I at once guessed the connection and urged her to tell me the motives for her behaviour. She was nonplussed, and could only say that it was extremely unpleasant for her to see her cloak cleaned like that. These symptomatic actions, as Sigmund Freud calls them, are very common among hysterics. The explanation is simple. A feeling-toned memory complex, though not present in consciousness at the moment, motivates certain actions from its invisible seat in the unconscious just as if it were present in the conscious mind.

171　　We can confidently say that our consciousness fairly swarms with strange intruders of this kind, which would be hard put to it to establish their identity. Every day thousands of associations enter the luminous circle of consciousness, and we would question them in vain for a more specific account of their origins. We must always bear in mind that conscious psychic phenomena are only a very small part of our total psyche. By far the greater part of the psychic elements in us is unconscious.

172　　Our consciousness therefore finds itself in a rather precarious position with regard to automatic movements of the unconscious that are independent of our will. The unconscious can perceive, and can associate autonomously; and the trouble is that only those associations which have once passed through our conscious minds have the quality of being known, and many of them can fall into oblivion so completely that they lose any such quality. Our unconscious must therefore harbour an immense number of psychic complexes which would astonish us by their strangeness. The inhibitions imposed by our waking consciousness do something to protect us from invasions of this kind. But in dreams, when the inhibitions of the conscious mind are lifted, the unconscious can play the maddest games. Anyone who has read Freud's dream analyses or, better still, has done some himself, will know how the unconscious can bedevil the most innocent and decent-minded people with sexual symbols whose lewdness is positively horrifying. It is to this unconscious that all those who do creative work must turn. All new ideas and combinations of ideas are premeditated by the unconscious. And when our own consciousness approaches the unconscious with a wish, it was the unconscious that gave it this wish. The unconscious brings the wish and its fulfilment.

173   On this treacherous ground wander all who seek new combinations of ideas. Woe to them if they do not continually exercise the most rigorous self-criticism!

174   Since, in the airy world of thought, one usually finds what one seeks, and gets what one wishes, the man who seeks new ideas will also be the most easily enchanted with the deceptive gifts of the psyche. Not only is the history of religion or the psychology of the masses rich in examples, but so is the intellectual life of anyone who has ever hoped to achieve anything. What poet or composer has not been so beguiled by certain of his ideas as to believe in their novelty? We believe what we wish to believe. Even the greatest and most original genius is not free from human wishes and their all-too-human consequences.

175   Quite apart from this general proposition, what kind of people seek these new combinations? They are the men of thought, who have finely-differentiated brains coupled with the sensitivity of a woman and the emotionality of a child. They are the slenderest, most delicate branches on the great tree of humanity: they bear the flower and the fruit. Many become brittle too soon, many break off. Differentiation creates in its progress the fit as well as the unfit; wits are mingled with nitwits —there are fools with genius and geniuses with follies, as Lombroso has remarked. One of the commonest and most usual marks of degeneracy is hysteria, the lack of self-control and self-criticism. Without succumbing to the pseudo-psychiatric witch-hunting of an author like Nordau,[3] who sees fools every-

3 [Max Simon Nordau, 1849–1923, German physician, author of *Conventional Lies of Civilization* and of *Degeneration*, an attempt to relate genius and degeneracy.—EDITORS.]

99

where, we can assert with confidence that unless the hysterical mentality is present to a greater or lesser degree genius is not possible. As Schopenhauer rightly says, the characteristic of the genius is great sensibility, something of the mimosa-like quality of the hysteric. Geniuses also have other qualities in common with hysterical persons.

176   It may be that the majority of hysterical persons are ill because they possess a mass of memories, highly charged with affect and therefore deeply rooted in the unconscious, which cannot be controlled and which tyrannize the conscious mind and will of the patient. With women it is sometimes disappointed hopes of love, sometimes an unhappy marriage; with men, a bad position in life or unrewarded merits. They try to repress the affect from their daily lives, and so it torments them with horrid dream-symbols at night, plagues them with fits of precordial anxiety by day, saps their energy, drives them into all kinds of crazy sects, and causes headaches that defy all the medicine-men and all the magic remedies of electricity, sun-baths, and food cures. The genius, too, has to bear the brunt of an outsize psychic complex; if he can cope with it, he does so with joy, if he can't, he must painfully perform the "symptomatic actions" which his gift lays upon him: he writes, paints, or composes what he suffers.

177   This applies more or less to all productive individuals. Tapping the depths of the psyche, the instinctively functioning complex sends up from its unknown and inexhaustible treasury countless thoughts to its slave "consciousness," some old and some new, and consciousness must deal with them as best it can. It must ask each thought: Do I know you, or are you new? But when the daemon drives, consciousness has no time to finish its sorting work, the flood pours into the pen—and the next day is perhaps already printed.

178   I said earlier that only the combinations are new, not the material, which hardly alters at all, or only very slowly and almost imperceptibly. Have we not seen all Böcklin's hues already in the old masters? And were not the fingers, arms, legs, noses and throats of Michelangelo's statues all somehow prefigured in antiquity? The smallest parts of a master work are certainly always old, even the next largest, the combined units, are mostly taken over from somewhere else; and in the last resort a

master will not scorn to incorporate whole chunks of the past in a new work. Our psyche is not so fabulously rich that it can build from scratch each time. Neither does nature. One can see from our prisons, hospitals, and lunatic asylums at what enormous cost nature takes a little step forward; she builds laboriously on what has gone before.

179   This process in the world at large is repeated in the smaller world of language: few novel combinations, nearly all of it old fragments taken over from somewhere. We speak the words and sentences learnt from parents, teachers, books; anyone who talks fastidiously, whether because he has a gift for language or because he takes pleasure in it, talks "like a book"—the book he has just been reading; he repeats rather larger fragments than do other people. The ordinary decent person either does not talk that way or openly admits where he got it from. But if somebody reproduces a sentence eight lines long verbatim from somebody else, we cannot, it is true, peremptorily shut the mouths of those who cry "Plagiarism!"—for as a matter of fact plagiarisms do occur—but neither need we immediately drop the person to whom this misfortune happens. For, when nature instituted the faculty of remembrance, she did not tie herself exclusively to the possibility of direct and indirect memories; she also gave, to clever and foolish alike, the power of cryptomnesia.

180   The word "cryptomnesia" is a technical term taken from French scientific literature. The Swiss psychologist Flournoy has made particularly valuable contributions, based on case material, to our knowledge of this phenomenon.[4] Cryptomnesia means something like "hidden memory." What this means in practice is best shown by a concrete example.[5] When, some years ago, I read about Zarathustra's journey to hell, I was particularly struck by the passage where Nietzsche describes how Zarathustra descends into hell through the mouth of a volcano. It seemed to me that I had read this description somewhere before. I thought at first that it must be a falsification of memory on my part (abnormal quality of being known), but finally the

[4] *From India to the Planet Mars* (orig. 1900).
[5] I have used this example before and discussed it in my psychiatric study "On the Psychology and Pathology of So-called Occult Phenomena." [See pars. 140f., above.]

most startling aspect of this quality settled on the passage where the crew of the ship went ashore "to shoot rabbits." This passage preoccupied my thoughts for several days, till at last I remembered having read a similar story some years earlier in Justinus Kerner. I leafed through his *Blätter aus Prevorst*, that antiquated collection of simple-minded Swabian ghost stories, and found the following tale, which I put side by side with the corresponding passage from Nietzsche:

181

Nietzsche, *Thus Spake Zarathustra* [6]	Kerner, *Blätter aus Prevorst* [7]
Now about the time that Zarathustra sojourned on the Happy Isles, it happened that a ship anchored at the isle on which the smoking mountain stands, and the crew went ashore to shoot rabbits. About the noontide hour, however, when the captain and his men were together again, they suddenly saw a man coming towards them through the air, and a voice said distinctly: "It is time! It is highest time!" But when the figure drew close to them, flying past quickly like a shadow in the direction of the volcano, they recognized with the greatest dismay that it was Zarathustra. . . . "Behold," said the old helmsman, "Zarathustra goes down to hell!"	The four captains and a merchant, Mr. Bell, went ashore on the island of Mount Stromboli to shoot rabbits. At three o'clock they mustered the crew to go aboard, when, to their inexpressible astonishment, they saw two men flying rapidly towards them through the air. One was dressed in black, the other in grey. They came past them very closely, in the utmost haste, and to their greatest dismay descended amid the burning flames into the crater of the terrible volcano, Mount Stromboli. They recognized the pair as acquaintances from London.
[Nietzsche introduces this story with the words: "They say . . . that through the volcano itself the narrow path leads down to the gate of the underworld."]	[Kerner goes on to say that when the travellers returned to London, they learnt that two acquaintances had died in the meantime, the very ones whom they saw on Stromboli. From this story it was concluded that Stromboli was the entrance to hell.]

[6] Ch. XL, "Great Events" (trans. by Common, p. 180, slightly modified). (Orig. 1883.)

[7] Vol. IV, p. 57, headed: "An Extract of Awe-Inspiring Import from the Log of the Ship *Sphinx* in the Year 1686, in the Mediterranean." (Orig. 1831–39.)

182   One can see at once that the similarity between the two
stories cannot be mere chance. The main argument in its dis-
favour is the number of verbal correspondences and the reproduction of unimportant details like "to shoot rabbits." A plagiarism, therefore! Everyone will find this supposition absurd.
Why? Because the passage is too unimportant in relation to
Nietzsche's artistic intention. And not only unimportant, but
largely superfluous and unnecessary. The rabbits, for instance,
characterize nothing in particular, whether we imagine the
"Happy Isles" as the Lipari Islands or the Canary Islands. Nor is
the description made any more felicitous by the rabbits—on the
contrary. The thing is not easy to explain psychologically. The
first question is, when did Nietzsche read the *Blätter aus Prevorst*? As I learnt from a letter which Frau Förster-Nietzsche
wrote me, Nietzsche took a lively interest in Justinus Kerner
when staying with his grandfather, Pastor Oehler, in Pobler,
between the ages of 12 and 15, but probably not later. As
Nietzsche had to be very economical in his reading because of
his weak eyes, it is difficult to understand what could have
lured him back to this childish wonder-book in his later years,
and the explanation of the plagiarism then becomes even more
difficult. I think we may take it that Nietzsche read this story
in his early youth and never again afterwards. How then did he
come to reproduce this passage?

183   I believe, though I cannot prove it, that it was not this old
wives' tale that gave Nietzsche the idea of Zarathustra's journey
to hell. Rather, while he was working out the general idea,
Kerner's story would have slipped into his mind because it was
associated with the general idea "journey to hell" by the law of
similarity. The remarkable thing is the verbal fidelity of the
reproduction. The striking agreement between the two texts
strongly suggests that the reproduction did not come from the
sphere of conscious memory, otherwise Nietzsche would have to
be credited with a memory that was absolutely amazing. The
normal powers of memory offer no explanation; it is almost
inconceivable that Nietzsche could have reawakened that old
sequence of words by a voluntary act of evocation. The reappearance of old, long-forgotten impressions is, however, expli-
cable in terms of the physiology of the brain. The brain never
forgets any impression, no matter how slight; every impression

leaves behind it some trace in the memory, no matter how fine. Consciousness, on the other hand, operates with an unending loss of previous impressions, much as the Bank of England always destroys after a certain lapse of time the notes that are daily returned to it. Under special conditions the re-emergence of old memory traces with photographic fidelity is by no means impossible. Literature records not a few cases of dying people, or people in other abnormal mental states, who recited whole chains of earlier impressions which perhaps never belonged to the sphere of conscious memory at all. Eckermann [8] mentions an old man "of low station" who, on his deathbed, suddenly began talking Greek. It turned out that a number of Greek verses had been drummed into him as a child, so that he should serve as a shining example to a lazy pupil of noble birth. I know another case where an old maidservant recited from the Bible passages in Greek and Hebrew on her deathbed. Investigations showed that as a young girl she had worked for a priest who had the habit of walking up and down after meals, reading the Bible aloud in the original tongues. The Viennese psychiatrist, Krafft-Ebing, who died recently, reports the case of a sixteen-year-old hysterical girl who, in an ecstatic state, could repeat without difficulty a poem, two pages long, which she had read shortly before.

184   As these examples show, the physiology of the brain makes such reproductions possible. But, for them to take place, an abnormal mental state is always needed, which can justifiably be conjectured in Nietzsche's case at the time when he wrote *Zarathustra*. One has only to think of the incredible speed with which this work was produced.

There is an ecstasy so great that the tremendous strain of it is at times eased by a storm of tears, when your steps now involuntarily rush ahead, now lag behind; a feeling of being completely beside yourself, with the most distinct consciousness of innumerable delicate thrills tingling through you to your very toes; a depth of happiness, in which pain and gloom do not act as its antitheses, but as its condition, as a challenge, as necessary shades of colour in such an excess of light.[9]

[8] Eckermann, *Conversations with Goethe,* trans. by Moon, p. 587.
[9] *Ecce Homo,* trans. by Ludovici, p. 102, modified.

So he himself describes his mood. These shattering extremes of feeling, far transcending his personal consciousness, were the forces that called up in him the remotest and most hidden associations. Here, as I said before, consciousness only plays the role of slave to the daemon of the unconscious, which tyrannizes over it and inundates it with alien ideas. No one has described the state of consciousness when under the influence of an automatic complex better than Nietzsche himself:

Has any one at the end of the nineteenth century any distinct notion of what poets of a stronger age understood by the word "inspiration"? If not, I will describe it. If one had the smallest vestige of superstition left in one, it would hardly be possible to set aside the idea that one is the mere incarnation, mouthpiece, or medium of an almighty power. The idea of revelation, in the sense that something which profoundly convulses and shatters one becomes suddenly visible and audible with indescribable certainty and accuracy, describes the simple fact. One hears—one does not seek; one takes—one does not ask who gives; a thought suddenly flashes up like lightning, it comes with necessity, without faltering—I never had any choice in the matter.[10]

There could scarcely be a better description of the impotence of consciousness in face of the tremendous automatism driving up from the unconscious. Only this elemental force can wrench from oblivion the oldest and most delicate traces in a man's memory, while yet he retains his full senses. When the brain dies, and consciousness disintegrates, while the cerebral cortex still goes on drowsily working for a bit, automatically and without co-ordination, fragmentary memories may be reproduced together with a mass of morbid rubbish. The same thing happens in insanity. I recently observed a case of compulsive talking in a feeble-minded girl. She rattled away for hours on end about all the warders she had ever met in her life, including their families, their children, the arrangement of the rooms, describing everything down to the craziest detail—a marvellous performance that could not possibly have been a voluntary evocation. The work of genius is very different; it fetches up these distant fragments in order to build them into a new and meaningful structure.

[10] Ibid., pp. 101f.

185   These psychic processes, where an automatic creative force causes lost memories to reappear in sizeable fragments and with photographic fidelity, are what science calls cryptomnesia.

186   The case of Jacobsohn, which I know only from the remarks of Harden and Schnitzler,[11] would seem to have much in common with cryptomnesia; at any rate I could not say why it should not be so. From this one might, perhaps, draw conclusions about the strength of Jacobsohn's talent and his passion for art, but hardly, as Schnitzler ventures to do, about his state of mind, let alone infer a focal lesion of the speech centres. Symptoms of a lesion in Broca's convolution and the neighbouring areas of the brain bear little resemblance to cryptomnesia. I am on the contrary inclined to give Jacobsohn a good prognosis, for the time being, as regards his artistic production. Should any human ill befall him, it would be the purest accident if the cortex of his speech convolutions were also affected.

11 [Maximilian Harden wrote of the case of Siegfried Jacobsohn, a dramatic critic, in his weekly journal *Die Zukunft,* in 1904. Jacobsohn, accused of plagiarizing, claimed that he had not done so knowingly, and Harden suggested that a mental aberration (resembling cryptomnesia) may have been responsible. Arthur Schnitzler, the Viennese physician and playwright, added some medical comments in the next issue. Jung's article on cryptomnesia followed shortly after.—EDITORS.]

III

ON MANIC MOOD DISORDER

ON MANIC MOOD DISORDER [1]

187   Under the term "manic mood disorder" I would like to publish a number of cases whose peculiarity consists in chronic hypomanic behaviour. A constitutional mood disorder characterized by melancholy and irritability has been known for some time, but only recently has attention been drawn to cases which, while still coming into the category of psychopathic inferiority, are remarkable for their excessively "sanguine temperament." So far as I know from the relevant literature, Siefert [2] was the first to publish a case of this kind. It offered clear indications of a manic state, which, as the anamnesis showed, was chronic and could be followed back into youth. The patient was 36 years old on his admission, and had suffered a severe head trauma at the age of nine. He was intelligent and a skilled worker. Later, however, he led a vagabond's life, was a deserter, thief, jailbreaker, and hardened alcoholic. He was arrogant in his behaviour, tremendously active, full of noble intentions and plans for world betterment, showing flight of ideas and surprisingly little need for sleep.

188   In earlier writers we find only the barest hints, which might possibly refer to similar cases, as for instance in Pinel,[3] whose

1 [First published as "Über manische Verstimmung," *Allgemeine Zeitschrift für Psychiatrie und psychisch-gerichtliche Medizin* (Berlin), LXI (1903): 1, 15-39. —Editors.]
2 "Über chronische Manie" (1902), pp. 261ff.
3 *A Treatise on Insanity* (orig. 1801), pp. 150ff.

manie sans délire with unimpaired brain activity and maniac behaviour is nevertheless too wide a frame for the narrowly circumscribed clinical picture we have in mind. The *mania chronica* mentioned in Mendel [4] is a "secondary psychopathic state" with imbecility; a picture that hardly fits here. Even in Koch, Schüle, Krafft-Ebing, and others we find no mention of these states. In 1896, van Deventer [5] published a second case under the term "sanguine inferiority," which comes midway between the "sanguine-tempered normal person on the one hand and the maniac on the other." The patient had an hereditary taint, was excitable and wayward from youth up, of good intelligence, skilled in various crafts, always cheerful and carefree, but with a wild and turbulent character, morally defective in every sense, showing flight of ideas, dangerous recklessness, and immense activity, occasionally also deep depressions.

189   In his *Grundriss der Psychiatrie*,[6] Wernicke gives an excellent description of these cases under the term "chronic mania." He can say "nothing certain" about their causation, but thinks it safe to say that a pure mania never terminates in such a chronic state. The case he cites was preceded by a psychosis of several years' standing, about which no information was available. He describes this state as follows:

Chronic mania has all the essential marks of acute mania, only these are modified in accordance with the conditions of a chronic, stable state. Hence, the flight of ideas keeps within the bounds of moderation, and can still be influenced to some extent by reflection and self-control. The elated mood is less marked, but occasionally it breaks through. On the other hand, the irascible mood is maintained owing to unavoidable conflicts with society. The heightened feeling of self-confidence, though not amounting to real megalomania, is very marked and gives these persons a certainty of address which, combined with their undeniable mental productivity, helps them to get on in the world. At the same time, they create for themselves all sorts of difficulties and conflicts by disregarding all the norms and checks which are imposed on them by custom and law. They have no consideration for others, yet demand every consideration for themselves. No signs of any formal disturbance of thinking need be present in this state.

4 *Die Manie* (1881).
5 "Ein Fall von sanguinischer Minderwerthigkeit" (1894).
6 Pub. 1894.

190   Although this general description fits in very well with the picture of a chronic hypomanic state, it still seems to me rather too broad, since it could also cover a large number of instabilities listed by Magnan—many querulous and morally feeble-minded persons (moral insanity). As experience shows, in many psychopathic illnesses there are persons who think unclearly and are prone to flights of ideas, who are ruthlessly egocentric, irascible, and mentally productive, but who can hardly be said to be suffering from chronic mania. In order to arrive at an accurate diagnosis, we require the symptoms of mania in more definite form. Occasional elation, exaggerated self-confidence, mental productivity, conflicts with law and order are not in themselves sufficient to warrant a diagnosis of "chronic mania." For this we need the cardinal symptoms: emotional lability with predominantly elated mood, flight of ideas, distractibility, over-activity, restlessness, and—dependent on these symptoms—exaggerated self-importance, megalomaniac ideas, alcoholism, and other moral defects.

191   So far as the term "manic mood disorder" is concerned, I would prefer van Deventer's "sanguine inferiority," because in my view it gives a more accurate description of what the term connotes. We have long been familiar with the idea of a constitutional melancholic mood, connoting a picture whose position midway between "healthy" and "diseased" exactly corresponds to that of the constitutional manic mood. As to the term "chronic mania" in the sense used by Siefert and Wernicke, this expression seems to me altogether too strong, for it is not a question of a real mania at all but of a hypomanic state which yet cannot be regarded as psychotic. The relatively mild manic symptoms are not partial manifestations of a periodic mania and are therefore seldom found in isolation; rather, they are frequently mixed with other psychopathic features, and this is only what one would expect, since the borderlines between the various clinical pictures of psychopathic inferiority are extraordinarily indistinct and fluctuating. Over-accentuation of the ego, periodicity of various symptoms, such as irritability, depression, exacerbation of stable abnormalities, hysterical traits, etc., are found in nearly all cases of degeneracy, without there necessarily being any deeper connection with the basic symptoms. This is all the more reason for delimiting the picture as closely

111

as possible, and the first requisite is always the presence of the fundamental manic symptoms.

1

192   The following case presents a very mild form of manic mood disorder bordering on simple psychopathic instability.

193   CASE A, born 1875, business man. Heredity: father contracted paralysis of the insane twelve years after the birth of the patient. Other members of the family healthy. Patient was a bright, clever child, physically rather weak. Scarlet fever at 8 years old. States that at school he was absent-minded and inattentive, always up to tricks. Severe attack of diphtheria in his twelfth year, with subsequent paralysis of accommodation and of the palate. Was afterwards lazy and superficial in his schoolwork, but showed great capabilities if he took the trouble. Easily moved to tears, became much more "difficult to understand" after the diphtheria. Entered high school at 13, found the work very easy, was always at the top of his class, extremely gifted but lacked perseverance. Early tendency to abuse of alcohol, no intolerance. Always in a cheerful mood, without worries. Matriculated with distinction. Afterwards he entered the business firm of a relative. Found it didn't suit him, did little work, let himself be distracted by pleasures of all kinds. A year later, he volunteered for one year's military service in the cavalry. Heavy abuse of alcohol at first only in merry company, then always before military duty, in order to calm his tremor; always had a full bottle by him, "knocked it back like anything." Was the master of ceremonies and life and soul of the party. In the last months of military service, apparently only four hours sleep per night without fatigue next day. Then another year at home. Did practically no work. In recent months he gradually got fits of moodiness which lasted a day and repeated themselves at irregular intervals every two months. At these times he was in an abysmal bad humour, sometimes irritable, sometimes depressed, had gloomy thoughts, took a pessimistic view of the world, was often so irritable that when his mother or sister asked him anything he had to keep a grip on himself so as not to "bang both fists on the table." He couldn't settle down to any work, a "terrible inner restlessness" plagued him continually, an "everlasting restless urge to get away," to change his situa-

tion, kept him from any profitable activity. He chased one pleasure after another and consumed enormous quantities of alcohol. His relatives finally decided to yield to his craving for change and let him go abroad, where he obtained a position in a branch of the firm. But things didn't work there either. He flouted the authority of his uncle, who was his chief, annoyed him in every conceivable way, covered him with insults, and led an utterly dissolute life, indulging in every kind of excess. He didn't do a stroke of work, and after a few months had to be sent home again as a severe alcoholic, in 1899. He was then put into a home for alcoholics, but paid little attention to the regime of abstinence and used his days out for alcoholic and sexual excesses. He stayed there for about six months and then returned home, somewhat better. He did not remain abstinent, but behaved fairly decently until his proposed engagement fell through, which had a shattering effect on him. In despair he took to excessive drinking again, so heavily that he had to be put in the same home for a second time. There he tried as before to dissimulate his use of alcohol, not always successfully. Twice he ran away, the second time to Milan, where he got through several hundred marks in a few days. When his money ran out he telegraphed for more and returned home with a profound moral hangover. When it was suggested to him, in this state, that he should be placed in a closed institution, he readily agreed, and was admitted to Burghölzli on July 22, 1901.

194   On admission the patient was slightly inebriated, euphoric, very talkative, showing flight of ideas. Told that his mother would visit him the next day, he got excited, wept, declared he was not in a fit state to receive her. In regard to his dipsomania he showed insight, but in regard to its cure he displayed a very shallow optimism. Physical examination revealed nothing but a distinct difference in the size of the pupils. For the rest of July things went well. The patient was always very animated, talkative, cheerful, amiable, showing plenty of social talent, and a sophistication that never went very deep and was at best witty. When out for walks he could talk for hours without stopping, and jumped from one thing to another in his flights of ideas. He expressed opinions on every conceivable subject with the greatest superficiality. He proved to be astonishingly well read

113

in German and English novels of the lighter sort, was always on the go but lacked perseverance. In a short space of time he bought over a hundred books, half of which he left unread. His room was crammed with newspapers, comics, picture postcards, photographs. He took drawing lessons and boasted about his artistic gifts. After three or four lessons he gave up drawing, and the same thing happened with his riding lessons. He realized that his superficiality was abnormal and cheerfully admitted it, even priding himself on this specialty of his: "You see, I'm the most cultured and well-read superficial person," he said to me once. By the middle of September his patience was at an end. He became very moody and irritable, suddenly forced his way out, telegraphed home to say he couldn't possibly remain where he was any longer. He wrote a long letter to the doctors in a huffy, aggressive tone, and several more in the same vein to his relatives. Having returned, after a few days he became quieter and more reasonable. Henceforth he was allowed more freedom, and could go out when he wished. He now began to go out every evening, visiting mostly light concerts and variety shows, and spent almost the entire morning in bed. His mood was continuously elated, he did no work but did not feel the least unhappy about it. This vacuous life continued up to his discharge. He was convinced of the necessity for abstinence, but overestimated his energy and powers of resistance. For his former life he lacked all feeling of shame; could talk with broad complacency about how he had worried his uncle almost sick, and felt no trace of gratitude to him for having taken a great deal of trouble to put him on the right road again. Similarly, he revelled in stories of his drinking bouts and other excesses, although there was nothing in the least praiseworthy about them.

195   The manic symptoms in this case can be traced back to the high school period, and the purely psychopathic ones to the diphtheria in his twelfth year. The life the patient led from the time he matriculated was quite abnormal and offers a choice of two diagnoses: psychopathic instability or manic mood disorder. Moral insanity, which one might also think of, appears to be ruled out by the wealth of emotional reactions. It is certainly not a case of simple alcoholism, since the psychic abnormality persisted even during abstinence. If we exclude the features

that could be grouped under ordinary psychopathic inferiority, we are left with definite hypomanic symptoms: mild flight of ideas, predominantly elated but quite inadequate mood, overactivity without consistency or perseverance. The moral defect is sufficiently explained by the superficiality of mood and the transitoriness of affects.

2

196   The next case concerns a woman whose life took a similar course, but whose anamnesis, being more detailed, allows us a deeper insight into the nature of the emotional change.

197   CASE B, born in 1858, married. Father a neurasthenic eccentric and drunkard, died of cirrhosis of the liver. Mother had heart trouble, died of some mental disease, apparently paralysis of the insane. Nothing known of any severe illnesses in youth. Patient was a bright, uncommonly lively child and a good pupil. From an early age she had suffered under disagreeable conditions at home. Her father was a solicitor, her family of good social standing, but between the parents there was continual strife because the father had an illegitimate liaison. In her eighteenth year, a male secretary employed in her father's business made two violent attempts to rape her, but she did not dare to divulge them to her parents, as the secretary threatened to make devastating revelations concerning her father's affairs. She suffered for years from the memory of these assaults and from the continual sexual molestations of the secretary. Gradually she developed hysterical attacks of convulsions, unaccountable moods, mostly depressions with fits of despair, and to deaden them she began drinking wine. According to her relatives, she was good-natured and soft-hearted, but extremely weak-willed. At 22 she married. Before her marriage she got the consent of her parents to travel part of the way to meet her fiancé, who lived in Italy, but did not return with him at once. Instead, she ran around with him for a couple of days before coming home again. She was married with great *éclat*. The marriage, however, was not a happy one. She felt she was misunderstood by her husband and could never get accustomed to social etiquette. At parties given in their house she secretly slipped away and danced in the yard with the servants. After the birth of a child she became very excitable, partly from weakness, partly because

of the visibly increasing estrangement from her husband. From the early days of her marriage she had cultivated a taste for fine wines and liqueurs. Now she drank more and more. On account of her increasing irritability and excitement, her husband sent her on a journey to recuperate. When she returned home she found he had started an intimate relationship with the house-keeper. This was enough to aggravate her already excited condition so gravely that she had to be sent to an institution. She came back after six months and found that the housekeeper, as her husband's mistress, had completely supplanted her. The consequence was renewed alcoholic excesses. She was then admitted to a Swiss mental home.

198   The following points are taken from her clinical record. On her admission, May 13, 1888, she went off into loud self-accusations and complained of an inexplicable inner restlessness (which she said had existed ever since the sexual assault). She was soon in a better mood, began comparing the mental home with the private institution she had been in before, praised the latter, complained that she was being boarded as a second-class patient, criticized the regulations. She was extremely labile, at one moment with tears in her eyes, shouting with laughter the next, up to all sorts of tricks. She was extraordinarily talkative and told quite openly, in front of her fellow patients, without the least shame, how she used to make herself drunk. After the alcoholic symptoms had worn off she continued in a very labile mood, garrulous, eager for applause, fond of ambiguous stories, quick at taking words the wrong way, criticizing the doctors and the treatment, "laughing very loudly like a servant girl at quite ordinary jokes," familiar with the staff, socially very entertaining. This emotional lability lasted throughout her stay in the asylum. The diagnosis was alcoholism with moral defect. In November 1890 her husband was granted a divorce, and this was a heavy blow to the patient. She was discharged in December with the best intentions for the future. Her income amounted to 2000 francs a year for five years. She now lived with a woman friend who had a great influence over her. During this time she appears to have been almost completely abstinent. When, in 1895, her income was exhausted, she took a post with her friend in a Swiss asylum. But she did not feel satisfied, got on badly with her superiors, was very upset when a number

of escapes took place in her ward, and quit the post after a few months. She then lived alone and began drinking again. Before collapsing altogether, she was able to make up her mind to visit a clinic of her own accord,. and was admitted to Burghölzli on October 19, 1895.

199   On her admission she was much the same as on the admission reported above, only less inebriated. The initial depression quickly disappeared, and she soon unbosomed herself in exuberant letters to her friend. She was a "creature of moods," "never able to hide her feelings," allowing herself to be entirely ruled by the mood of the moment. She was extremely active and adapted herself quickly, "cheerful, temperamental, always ready with a bad joke," sometimes bad-tempered, often carrying on in a rather sentimental way. Her behaviour at concerts in the asylum was ostentatious; instead of singing, she would warble with full-throated laughter. In 1896, on one of her days out, she suddenly got engaged to another patient, also an alcoholic. In July 1896 she was discharged. The medical report emphasized that her alcoholism was caused by her moods, which completely dominated her. Further, that her emotional condition was now more evenly balanced, but that there was still a "congenital lability of mood and great emotional excitability." After that she lived "in sin" with her fiancé, who soon had a relapse and started her off drinking again. He was put in a home, and she, left to herself, tried to make a living in the grocery trade, but without much success. Once more she took to heavy drinking, got drunk daily, frequented taverns of ill repute, and on one occasion tore off her clothes in a frenzy of excitement, so that she stood there in her petticoat. She often turned up at the tavern dressed only in petticoat and raincoat. In November 1897 she was brought back to the asylum. On admission she had an hysterical attack with symptoms of delirium tremens. Then followed deep depressions, which lasted in milder form until January 1898, though this did not prevent her from showing great liveliness on festive occasions. Later she became touchy, flaunted her superior social position before others, was at times erotic, tried to flirt with a male patient, singing him sentimental songs from a distance. She was full of optimistic plans for the future, started to learn typewriting and helped in the anatomical laboratory. In March 1898 she suddenly went out and got

117

mildly drunk, and received a reprimand which threw her into a blind rage. Next day she was found in an extreme stage of intoxication, and it turned out that she had made herself drunk in the laboratory with 96% alcohol. She was wildly excited, quite unapproachable at first, uttering threats; then manic, with flight of ideas, pressure of activity, eroticism, and devil-may-care humour. After a few days she was the same as before, unable to adapt to regulations, flirting with a manic patient at a concert. Periods of boisterous merriment. Discharged on October 11, 1900, to take up post as a housekeeper. Worked extraordinarily well and was much appreciated for her continual gaiety and sociability. From a letter written at this time we extract the following passages, which are typical of her extreme self-confidence, exaggerated language abounding in forceful expressions, and her elated mood:

200   The everlasting mistrust, the everlasting disbelief of these pessimists in a final moral cure, saps your strength and breaks your courage. You see yourself abandoned by others and finally you abandon yourself. Then you try to deaden your torments of soul and seize on any and every means that deadens—so long as there's spirit in it. Thank God I no longer need this deadening now. Are you pleased with me? Do you believe in my leonine strength?—!! . . .

201   My talent for educating children is a fact which neither the scepticism of Dr. X nor the shrewdness of Dr. Y can abolish. . . .

202   I am so tired in the evenings that my head throbs, as though it had been used for a drum in the Basel carnival. Under these circumstances you must bear kindly with me if letters from my hand turn into birds of paradise and the inclination to ballet dance in ink is at its last gasp.

203   In July 1901 she went down with influenza, and her employer inadvisedly gave her wine as a tonic (!), whereupon she got a bottle of wine sent up every day. On July 7, she was readmitted to Burghölzli for delirium tremens, having lately drunk methylated spirits and eau de cologne. Now and then she seemed to have deep depressions with a sentimental tinge, but they were never so bad that she could not be provoked into wildly gay laughter. At a concert in August her behaviour was quite manic; she adorned herself with three huge roses, flirted openly, showed motor restlessness, behaved extremely tactlessly with the others. No insight afterwards. Her "excitability reached

the highest degree of mania" (July 1901). At a music rehearsal in the room of an assistant doctor she was "extremely vivacious and talkative, erotic and provocative." She was sexually very excited at this period, but sometimes depressed. She dashed off her copywork in a careless way, wrote pages of sentimental scribble showing flights of ideas. She could be roused to all kinds of activity, but her energy invariably flagged. Very sensitive, reacting to censure with deep depression, all emotional reactions extremely labile and immoderate. She had no insight into her lability, greatly overestimated herself and her powers of resistance, had an inflated sense of her personal value, and often made very disdainful remarks about other people. She felt that she still had "a task in front of her," that she "was destined for something higher and better," that not her inferiority but her unfortunate circumstances were to blame for her degeneration. From August 1902 to April 1903 she followed a weight-reducing course, and towards the spring a more stable depression supervened, during which she took more pains with her copywork than before.

204   The first psychopathic symptoms in this hereditarily tainted patient showed themselves from her eighteenth year in the form of marked hysteria resulting from sexual traumata. Indications of some emotional abnormality apart from the hysteria are present from the age of 22. After her thirtieth year we have an accurate clinical history in which superficiality and emotional lability are already established. Besides alcoholism, a moral defect was diagnosed (1888). In 1896, the alcoholism was recognized as dependent on her emotional lability. In the course of years the manifest hysteria entirely disappeared except for a few symptoms (sentimental tone of the depressions), but the emotional abnormality remained stable. The periodic depressions were always of short duration and never so deep that they could not be banished by a joke. The only depression of longer duration, which had a decidedly improving effect on the patient, occurred under the influence of the reducing course and can therefore be regarded as a specific effect of this treatment. Depressions under such a treatment also occur with normal persons. The patient's depressions often had a reactive character, especially to censure, and were then merely excessive reactions to a depressing stimulus. Spontaneous exacerbations of stable

119

symptoms were never observed with certainty; in most cases they were excessive reactions to the effects of joy or alcohol. The patient was decidedly manic when drunk. In her normal state we find a mild flight of ideas, which expressed itself particularly clearly in her writings; a predominantly elated mood with optimistic outlook, often indicative of her exaggerated self-esteem; great lability of pleasure/pain affects; marked distractibility. Her manic over-activity showed itself as a rule merely in her extreme vivacity and talkativeness, but it only needed some kind of festivity to produce an immediate increase of motor activity. The dependence of alcoholism, and of moral inferiority in general, on emotional abnormality is much clearer here than in the first case.

3

205   The third case concerns a patient who was chiefly remarkable for her social instability.

206   CASE C, born in 1876, nurse, unmarried. Heredity: father a drunkard, died of carcinoma of the liver. Step-sister (by the same father) epileptic. Patient had no severe physical illnesses in youth. Clever at school, also got good marks for behaviour, with few exceptions. Once when she got bad marks for arithmetic, she tore up the report under the teacher's eyes. Once wrote an anonymous letter to the school administration, denouncing certain teachers for assigning too much work. Once she ran away from school for two days. She was a very lively child, passionately fond of reading novels (often half the night). At 16 she left school and went to her sister's to learn how to be a seamstress. But she did little work, read most of the time, never obeyed her sister, quarrelled with her after six months, and then took up another apprentice post, where she stayed only nine months instead of the required two years. She was quick to learn though not very diligent, was usually very merry, but sometimes irritable. Though "good-natured," she "never took anything much to heart." She was "burning with travel fever" and made up her mind to go to Geneva. There she found a job as an apprentice seamstress for a year, remained for the full period, but took occasional time off, paying her employer for the day. Afterwards she returned home. During this period her diet consisted almost entirely of sweets, of which she sometimes consumed

five francs' worth a day. Although it finally sickened her, for a long time afterwards she felt impelled to buy chocolates whenever she passed a confectioner's. She would then give them to children in the street. She borrowed money for her passions in the most frivolous way from everybody, often just took it from her sister or bullied it out of her. After about six months she induced a relative to take her to America. Stayed a month in Chicago without working. Then she worked at a clothes shop, ran away four days later without giving notice. She then changed her job ten times in succession, staying a few hours or at most a couple of days in each of them. Finally found a job that suited her, as a companion. Became ill six months later with stomach ulcer; returned to Switzerland. She left a job as receptionist at a hotel after five days because of a quarrel with her employer, and went back home. A few weeks later she took a job as a housemaid, but got "sick of it" after eight months. She "could only stay in a job until she knew the country and the people, then something else had to come along." Then she worked as a student nurse in a hospital in Bern. "Sick of it" after five months, went to another hospital, four months later became ill again with stomach ulcer, spent several months ill at home. At this point she started an illegitimate relationship with the dissolute son of a neighbour. On recovering from her illness, she worked as a shopgirl in Zurich. Spent considerable sums of money on herself and her friend, whom she supported financially. She borrowed money everywhere and left her father and sister to pay her debts. As a result, she was sent to a faith-healing institution for a cure, where she stayed for six months, working fairly well; then another four months as a maid. She started another intimate relationship, but soon got sick of her lover. Then seven months as a wardress in an institute for epileptics, followed by five months as a children's nurse in a private house, which she left because of quarrels with one of the maids. She then betook herself to her late lover in W., made a violent scene but was finally reconciled. After that she got another job as a maid in Schaffhausen for a fortnight, then for two days in Bern, for some weeks in Zurich, for another four weeks in Bern, then again for a short time in Zurich, then for two months as a nurse in a lunatic asylum, then again for a few days in W., where she ran through her earnings at the hotel and started quarrelling again with her lover. After renewed reconciliation, she returned to Zurich, but soon fell out two more times with her lover, took another job for two months, then went to Chur "for the fun of it," then back to W., in order to make another scene with her lover, then returned to Zurich for a few days, only to go immediately afterwards to W. and make a second and this time final scene with her lover. After that she took a job as a children's nurse in the Valais, where she stayed two and a half months. She became ill again with stomach ulcer and returned to Zurich via W. As she got out of the train at W. the first person she ran into was her lover, which annoyed her so much that she took the train straight back to Zurich. On arrival in Zurich, however, she regretted her sudden decision and immediately seated herself in the train back to W. Alighting on the platform at W., she regretted this decision too and rushed back to Zurich. (The distance between Zurich and W. is an hour and a half by rail.) On returning from W. after one of her quarrels, she went to a hotel with an unknown man whom she picked up at the station in Zurich and spent the night with him. With another she started an erotic conversation and apparently followed him even into the toilet, causing a public scandal.

207   Wherever she worked she was liked, as she was constantly busy and a pleasant companion. She was never quiet, always on the go and excitable. Lately the excitement increased visibly, she also talked much more than before. She had never saved any money; what she earned she spent at once and incurred debts everywhere.

208   On the recommendation of Professor M., the patient was admitted to Burghölzli on April 2, 1903. The report emphasizes the following points: "The patient suffers from a mild degree of maniacal excitement. The outward cause may be considered to be an affair with a young man which came to nothing. For several weeks the patient was expansive, unstable, irritable; she is excessively open-handed, sleeps little at night, cannot bear to be contradicted. Her mood is elated. She is talkative, occasionally showing flight of ideas. She cannot be kept at home because of her expansiveness, she starts something new every minute, and wants to go to W. in order to wreak her vengeance on her former fiancé."

209   She had a lively, intelligent expression of face, talked a great deal. Continuous motor restlessness when talking; in ordinary conversation no very noticeable flights of ideas; these only showed more clearly during longer recitals. She was very elated, very erotic, flirting and laughing a great deal; very labile, weeping easily at the memory of unhappy experiences; liked to sulk ostentatiously, and once made a violent scene when the doctor refused to visit her alone in her room, threatened suicide, so that she had to be removed for a while to the observation room. Soon afterwards she was as euphoric as ever. She was very frank and enjoyed telling of her adventures, but was incapable of putting them down on paper in an orderly fashion. An autobiography still remains to be attempted after several false starts. She expressed a strong desire to go out, but still harboured thoughts of vengeance on her ex-fiancé, threatened to shoot him. Had all sorts of adventurous plans for the future, and once urgently requested to be allowed out in order to answer a newspaper advertisement for an animal trainer, asserting proudly that she did not lack courage. In addition, she had intensive plans for marriage. She took the disorderly life she had lived very lightly, and was convinced that things would go better in future. She showed slight insight into the excitement of the last few weeks before her admission. No major depressions or excited states were observed, and no deterioration of the normal state except the present one. Slight increase of excitement during her periods.

210   In my account of this case I have purposely given a complete chronicle of the changes in social position in order to illustrate the extraordinary instability and restlessness of the patient. Over a period of eleven years, she changed her job no less than thirty-two times, in the great majority of cases simply because she was "sick of it." So far as one can rely on the anamnestic information, the abnormal emotional state can be followed back into childhood. Apart from the menstrual cycle no periodicity was discoverable. Depressions never seemed to arise spontaneously, but were merely the outcome of circumstances. There was no alcoholism, only an enormous abuse of sweets. The findings—mild flight of ideas, talkativeness, predominantly elated mood, lability, distractibility, pressure of activity, eroticism—

123

all bear out the diagnosis of manic mood disorder and explain the patient's erratic and morally defective career.

4

211 The fourth case was under investigation on a charge of theft and was certified by me as of unsound mind, the intensity of manic symptoms being of so high a degree that even "partial responsibility" seemed to me out of the question.

212 CASE D, born 1847, painter. Heredity: father an eccentric person, intelligent, very lively, frivolous, always in a merry mood, went in for politics and litigation, neglected his business and his family, drank and gambled, lost his property and fortune, until he finally came to the poorhouse. First brother intelligent and gifted, head full of ideas, interested in social and political problems, died in poverty leaving a pile of debts. Second sister very extravagant, died in dire poverty. Third brother a moderate drinker, but able to support himself and wife. Fourth brother led a profligate life in every respect, a notorious liar, very much come down in the world, living on poor relief. One son of a normal brother was a notorious scrounger and sot. Patient had no serious illnesses in youth. A lively child, alert and intelligent; excellent school reports. Was apprenticed after leaving school; worked very industriously for the first year, clever, made progress. In the course of the second year he changed, started drinking, neglected his work, extravagant. Remained four years in the same job, then took to roaming. His dissoluteness increased, his work grew more and more uneven and careless, and by way of contrast he developed a "terrific opinion of himself," boasted of his cleverness and gifts, always passing himself off as something quite extraordinary. His roamings began at 19. He never stayed anywhere for longer than a few months, was always drinking, dissatisfied, no master was good enough for him, always had his "special ideas," wanted to "be appreciated," thought "everything should be to his liking," was always "worked up," frequently quit his job without giving notice, sometimes without even collecting his wages. In 1871 he returned home utterly destitute, looking like a tramp. Despite that, he bragged endlessly and told boastful stories about himself and his successes. He remained for some time at home, worked eagerly, "always in a hurry." Suddenly his elated mood

changed, he became irritable, cantankerous, grumbled about the work, his work-mates, former masters, etc., sometimes getting into a rage and "acting like the devil." Now as before he indulged in drink, and the more he drank the more excited he became, giving vent to an unstanchable stream of talk. After a fortnight he suddenly packed his things, set forth on his wanderings again, and finally, in 1873, came to Paris. He found no work there because of the slump, and was sent home again by the authorities after five weeks. In 1875 he went to Nuremberg. According to the report of his employer there, he was a very skilful and efficient worker, but had to be dismissed on account of drunkenness. Because of acute manic excitement he had to be kept in confinement for a few weeks, and as no real remission ensued, he was packed off to Switzerland. He was admitted to Burghölzli on March 21, 1876.

213 The patient was elated, excited, laughing away to himself, showed flight of ideas, made bad jokes, heard voices that told him funny stories, showed immense self-esteem. No essential change subsequently occurred except for a quieting down and cessation of the voices. The illness was taken for mania, and the patient was discharged as cured in August 1876, although at the time of his discharge he certainly did not give the impression of being a normal person. He then began his old wandering life again. He roamed round Switzerland like a vagabond; in November 1876, as a result of great privations and severe cold, he found himself in a delirious state in which it seemed to him that "he was the pope and had ordered a huge dinner." In this state he tried to draw 5000 francs at the post-office and was arrested; on taking food he suddenly became clear again. In 1882 he married. The marriage remained childless. His wife had four or five abortions. He stuck to her for almost a year; then the wanderings were resumed and he stayed with his wife only off and on. In 1885 he found himself in great straits, and in desperation conceived the plan of poisoning himself and his wife. But he was afraid to carry it out, so he fell back on stealing. Up to the beginning of 1886 he committed a series of thefts, was arrested, and in view of his doubtful mental condition was referred to the doctors in St. Pirminsberg for a medical opinion. The following points were emphasized in the report:

214 The patient was in a continuous state of elation, with height-

ened self-confidence, amounting at times to real megalomania. He delighted in making mysterious allusions to his importance: "Great things are impending, here in the madhouse sits the founder of God's kingdom on earth." He composed an eighty-page opus intended for the press, largely incoherent in content, through which there ran like a red thread his unbounded glorification of himself. In it he addressed himself rhetorically to the pope, deeming himself his equal in infallibility, also to Christ, spoke of himself as a new Messiah, compared himself to Hercules and Winkelried, etc. Occasionally he went into real ecstasies, in which he wrote things like: "The greatest artist of all times past and to come shines the shoes of the unfortunate, polishes the floor in St. Pirminsberg. As is the son, so is the father and vice versa.—Hurrah for Helvetia!!! O stone of the wise, how thou shinest! O D—— (his own name), what brilliance! Your God, O my companions, has the heart of a child, the voice of a lion, the innocence of a dove, and the appearance of one of you!" During his stay in the asylum the composition of these pieces formed his main occupation. He wrote several pages a day, and when his paper ran out he would sing patriotic songs for hours on end in a raucous voice. He was always very talkative, spoke in dialect, but when he really got going he fell into a literary style. His thought processes were orderly, but with a tendency to digression and detailed description. His language abounded in choice expressions, with a preference for foreign words, though these were generally used correctly. In keeping with his exaggerated self-esteem he always held himself aristocratically aloof from the other patients; the warders he snubbed, whereas he was always very friendly with the doctors. His situation did not worry him, he lived cheerfully from day to day, full of the greatest hopes for the future. He never showed any insight into his illness. Once he was in a particularly bad mood for several days, very irritable, suspicious, reserved, but occasionally cursing and swearing about the asylum. The diagnosis was "periodic mania, which might pass over into insanity." The thefts were put down to unsoundness of mind.

215   On October 2, 1886, the patient was transferred to Burghölzli. Until December his state was the same as in St. Pirminsberg. At the beginning of December he quieted down a bit;

the earlier symptoms continued but were less intense. He was given some painting to do in the asylum. Among other things he painted the asylum chapel; it was subsequently discovered that between the veins of the marble he had drawn little figures of devils and also a not unskilful caricature of the asylum's priest. He was discharged on February 25, 1887. Even during this quieter phase he still produced the same old ideas, held forth with great pathos on his vocation as a reformer and world improver. After his discharge he resumed his wanderings in Switzerland, working a bit but never staying more than a few months in the same place. In 1891 he stole a great deal of food and was sentenced to six months in the workhouse. In 1893 he got a year for the same reason. In 1894 he was charged with stealing 700 francs. From the fourth day of his detention on, he heard voices whispering outside his door, and thought he could recognize the voice of one of his nieces, saying: "You will be repaid." Six days later he was released. At home the hallucinations persisted for another day and then suddenly vanished. In 1895 he was sentenced to two years in the workhouse for theft. In January 1895 he was sent to the penitentiary. According to the statements of officials there, the patient "had a screw loose" from the beginning and soon aroused suspicions of mental disorder. He accused the officials, quite without reason, of swindling. In solitary confinement he covered the walls with senseless daubs, asserting that he was a great artist. At night he was restless, talking loudly to himself about his "daily occupation." Now and then he was very irritable. On August 19, 1895, another medical report was made on him. The following points were emphasized: "The condition of the patient is much the same as that described in 1886 in the report from St. Pirminsberg. He showed manic excitement, flight of ideas, extraordinary elation, and self-esteem, boasting of his capabilities, his physical prowess, saying that he had known for 25 years how, 'by means of a certain substance, as with a breath, everything could be decked in the most gorgeous, dazzling colours'; he could 'change a dog into the most beautiful golden scarab in the twinkling of an eye.' " He came out with a lot of similar stories. On November 9 he was moved to Burghölzli. His condition was the same as in the penitentiary. He gave more or less logical reasons for his exaggerations. For instance, he got his gilding effects by brushing over with the right colour; gave up his plan for world improvement after he had seen how incorrigible the world was. His behaviour varied as before; mostly he was elated and excited, but intermittently he was irritable, with stormy moods. Though he quieted down somewhat, his condition remained the same until his discharge on January 16, 1897.

216   In the weeks preceding his recent arrest he wandered round the neighbourhood of his home village and spent the nights in a barn, the walls of which he scribbled over with verses and sayings. His clothes were in rags, his shoes were tied to his feet with string. Between September 13 and October 3, 1901, he committed three burglaries with theft at night, taking food, drink, tobacco, and clothes. He stated that on the occasion of one of these thefts he was very agitated because, while in the cellar, he heard a voice saying: "Go down quickly and leave something for me too." He was arrested on October 8, 1901. At the first hearing he pleaded guilty. He was sent to us for observation on November 1, 1901. During his stay his behaviour was found to be unchanged. On admission he was very cheerful, composed, sure of himself, greeted his old acquaintances cordially, was very talkative and excitable, replying at great length to every question and tacking on remarks and stories showing flight of ideas. He recounted his life story in a coherent manner, keeping fairly well to the facts. At night he slept little, mostly lay awake in bed for hours worrying about "scientific" problems. He had theories about the origin of meteorites, about the transport of dead bodies to the moon, about airships, about the nature of the brain and mental processes, etc. He worked industriously and quickly, often talking to himself or keeping up an accompaniment of animal noises—miaowing, barking, cackling, crowing. When walking about the ward he sometimes went at the run, or even on all fours. At work in the fields he was talkative, enjoyed teasing others, adorned his hat with roots and leaves of vegetables. He conceived his ideas at night and put them down, elaborately and extensively, on paper. His compositions were closely written, looked clean and neat, and except for the copious use of foreign words the spelling was correct. They revealed an erudition of sorts, a very good memory, distinct flight of ideas, with great pressure of speech and forceful expressions. Prose pieces in literary style or in dialect

were jumbled together with quotations from Schiller, verses (his own and other people's), sentences in French, always with a connecting thread of meaning which, however, did not go very deep. No uniform, comprehensive idea could be found in any of his writings, except for an intense subjective feeling of his own value and an unbounded self-esteem. The language he used was sometimes full of deep pathos, sometimes deliberately paradoxical. He was ready to discuss his ideas, did not cling to them obstinately, but dropped them in order to turn to new problems. It was even possible to talk him out of his meteorite theory and to wring from him the admission that "even the greatest scholars have been mistaken." He would expatiate on all kinds of moral and religious questions, and displayed a lyrical and almost religious feeling—which did not prevent him, however, from blaspheming and making a laughing-stock of religious practices. Once, for example, he performed a gross travesty of the Mass. He said he was not born to work for his living, had better things to do, and must wait for the time when all his grand ideas would be realized, when he would create educational establishments for the young, a new system of world communications, etc. He had great hopes of the future, by comparison with which all thought of the actual present vanished. Despite this keen expectation he had no clear picture of the future in his mind, could only adumbrate vague and fabulous plans which were mostly concocted on the spur of the moment. But he was convinced that "all would come in good time," and hinted that he would perhaps live longer than other men in order to accomplish his work. His earlier statements that he was the Messiah, "the founder of God's new kingdom," he corrected as symbolisms; he was only comparing himself to the Messiah and not asserting that he had any more intimate connection with him or with God. In the same way he disclosed that what had previously been taken for delusional ideas were exaggerations or vivid comparisons.

²¹⁷   Occasionally there were angry moods, usually provoked by insignificant trifles which at another time would not have been followed by an angry reaction. For instance, he once created a great disturbance at 3 o'clock in the morning, shouting, cursing, and barking like a dog, so that he woke the whole ward. As usual, he had not slept properly after midnight and was annoyed

by the snoring of a patient. He justified the uproar by saying that if others were permitted to disturb him with their snoring, then he was permitted to make a noise at night too.

218   This patient came of an abnormal family, and at least two of his close relatives (father and brother) seem to have had the same mental constitution. The picture of manic mood disorder developed after puberty and had persisted with occasional exacerbations throughout his life. Here again we find a number of symptoms of psychic degeneracy apart from the specifically manic ones. The patient was only an occasional alcoholic, probably from lack of money and also because, being everlastingly occupied with his enormous afflux of ideas, he lacked real leisure for drinking. His ideas show certain affinities with "inventor's paranoia," but on the one hand he lacked the stability and toughness of the paranoiac, and on the other hand his ideas were not fixed and incorrigible, but were more in the nature of inspirations that came to him from his elation and exaggerated self-esteem. The hallucinatory episodes that are mentioned several times in his history cannot easily be related to any known clinical picture; one of them seems to have been an effect of exhaustion, another an effect of imprisonment, a third an effect of excitement. Magnan regards them as "syndromes épisodiques des dégénérés." Although we know that "prison complexes" [7] can occur in all sorts of degenerate subjects, we are unable to point to any particular underlying psychosis. Again, in our patient we see the delirious states passing quickly and without after-effects, for which reason they may best be regarded as syndromes of degeneracy.

219   Here too we find periodic mood disorders in the form of pathological irritability. Once (1885) there was a deeper depression, when the patient toyed with the idea of suicide. Despite careful investigation we were only able to discover this one depression, and it is not even certain whether it lasted for an appreciable time or whether it was a sudden change of mood, such as usually occurs with manics. Apart from these few features, which do not belong absolutely to the picture of mania, the case offers all that is necessary for a diagnosis of manic mood disorder. The patient showed distinct flight of ideas, a profusion of fanciful thoughts and words; his predominating mood

7 Rüdin, "Über die klinischen Formen der Gefängnisspsychosen" (1901), p. 458.

was not merely cheerful and carefree, but manically elated, expressing itself all the time in manic tricks and immense pressure of activity, which occasionally amounted to purposeless motor hyperactivity. His intelligence was good, and he was capable of judging his situation perfectly correctly, but the next moment his ideas of grandeur returned, and he was swung into them by the force of his overproductive pleasure feelings. He led the most miserable life as a vagabond, roaming about the countryside summer and winter, half starved, sleeping in barns and stables, yet in flagrant contrast with reality was forever brooding on lofty schemes of world reformation. Significantly, his non-recognition by the rest of humanity was of no concern to him, as it would be to a paranoiac. His continual pleasurable excitement helped him even over this adversity. From all this we see how very much the intellect was taken in tow by the emotions. He was not really convinced of his ideas, for he did not mind correcting them theoretically; but he hoped for their fulfilment, in contrast to the paranoiac, who hopes because he is convinced. This case reminds one forcibly of those miserable lives lived by poets and artists who, with small talent and indestructible optimism, eke out a hungry existence despite the fact that they possess quite enough intelligence to realize their social inadequacy in this form, and enough talent and energy, if applied in other directions, to do good and even outstanding work in an ordinary profession. The patient can also be compared, up to a point, with those individuals whom Lombroso describes as "graphomaniacs." They are psychopaths who, without being paranoid or feeble-minded, overestimate themselves and their ideas in the most absurd way, play about with philosophical or medical problems, write vast quantities of rubbish, and then ruin themselves by having their works published at their own expense. The defective critical faculty of such persons is often due not to feeble-mindedness, for they can sometimes detect the mistakes of their opponents very well indeed, but to an incomprehensible and exorbitant optimism which prevents them from seeing objective difficulties and fills them with invincible hopes of a better time to come, when they will be justified and rewarded. Our patient, however, reminds us also of numerous "higher imbeciles" and crackpot inventors whose feeble-mindedness is confined to lack of criticism of their own particular quirks, and whose intelligence and efficiency in other departments are at least average.

220   It should be emphasized that in the four cases we have reported the intelligence was good throughout, in the first and second cases even very good, in flagrant contrast to the outward conduct of life, which was extraordinarily inept. It is a contrast also met with in moral insanity. No doubt the majority of cases of moral insanity mentioned in the literature were more or less feeble-minded, but there can also be no doubt that in the majority of cases the feeble-mindedness is not sufficient to explain their social incapacity. One gets the impression that the intellectual defect is more or less irrelevant and that the main emphasis falls on emotional abnormality. And here it is not so much a lack of ethical feelings that seems to play the chief role as an excess of instinctual drives and positive inclinations. A simple lack of ethical feelings would be more likely to favour the development of a ruthless, coldly calculating "mauvais sujet" or criminal, rather than one of those pleasure-seeking individuals, instinctively up in arms against any form of social restriction, who unthinkingly fly off the rails at every point, often so brainlessly that the veriest imbecile could see the senselessness of it. Tiling [8] has recently pointed out that the main element in the picture of moral insanity is an excessively sanguine temperament,[9] which serves as too mercurial a basis for the intellectual process and fails to give it the necessary continuity of feeling-tone, lacking which there can be no arguments and no judgments capable of exerting any influence on the decisions reached by the will. A great deal has already been said and written about the relation between intellect and will. If there is any field of experience that teaches the dependence of action upon the emotions, that field is certainly psychiatry. The inferiority of the intellect as compared with instinctual impulses in regard to voluntary decisions is so striking that the daily experiences even of a psychologically minded, amateur psy-

8 "Die Moral Insanity beruht auf einem excessiv sanguinischen Temperament" (1901), pp. 205ff.
9 Schüle (Handbuch der Geisteskrankheiten, 1878) says that a middling or even a good intellectual capacity is still in the tow of perverse impulses and inclinations, and despite its abilities is incapable of producing countermotives.

chiatrist like Baumann [10] impel him to remark that the specific activity of thought is always preceded by something "primarily characterological," which provides the necessary disposition for this or that action. Here Baumann is simply voicing Schopenhauer's "operari sequitur esse" in other terms. What is "primarily characterological" is, in the wider sense, the feeling-tone, whether it be too little or too much or perverse; in the narrower sense it is the inclinations and drives, the basic psychological phenomena which make up man's empirical character, and this character is obviously the determining factor in the actions of the great majority of people. The role played by the intellect is mostly a subsidiary one, since all it does at best is to give the already existing characterological motive the appearance of a logically compelling sequence of ideas, and at worst (which is what usually happens) to construct intellectual motives afterwards. This view has been expressed in general and absolute terms by Schopenhauer,[11] as follows: "Man ever does what he wills, and does so by necessity; that is because he *is* what he wills; for from what he is there follows by necessity everything he will ever do."

221   Even if we admit the fact that numerous decisions are mediated or first considered by the intellect, we should still not forget that every link in a chain of ideas has a definite feeling-value, which is the one essential thing in coming to a decision and without which the idea is an empty shadow. But this feeling-value, as a partial phenomenon, underlies any changes in the whole sequence, which in the case of mania results in Wernicke's "levelling-down of ideas." Consequently, even the purest intellectual process can reach a decision simply through feeling-values. Hence the prime motive for any abnormal action, provided that the intellect is fairly well preserved, should be sought in the realm of affect.

222   Wernicke [12] regards moral insanity as a distant parallel to mania, supposing the elementary symptom to be a levelling-down of ideas. In most cases he finds an inner unrest and irritable moods, but omits all the other, equally important

10 "Über Willens- und Charakterbildung auf physiologisch-psychologischer Grundlage" (1897).
11 "Preisschrift über die Freiheit des Willens," *Werke*, II, pp. 231ff.
12 *Grundriss der Psychiatrie* (1894), p. 320.

manic symptoms like flight of ideas, pressure of talk, morbid euphoria, etc.

223   In surveying the literature on morally defective persons one cannot fail to be struck by the emotional excitability and lability so frequently reported.[13] It would perhaps be worth while, when investigating the morally defective, to direct attention mainly to this emotional abnormality, or rather lability, and to consider its incalculable effects on the intellectual processes. In this way it might be possible to shed new light on cases which till now have been judged only from the standpoint of moral defect, and to regard them rather as examples of emotional inferiority in the sense of a relatively mild or serious manic mood disorder. The greatest attention along the lines suggested would be claimed by the cases of moral insanity which follow a periodic or cyclic course with "lucid intervals" and paroxysmal exultations.

224   To sum up:

1. Manic mood disorder is a clinical condition that belongs to the field of psychopathic inferiority, and is characterized by a stable, hypomanic complex of symptoms generally dating back to youth.

2. Exacerbations of uncertain periodicity can be observed.

3. Alcoholism, criminality, moral insanity, and social instability or incapacity are, in these cases, symptoms dependent on the hypomanic state.

225   In conclusion, I would like to thank my chief, Professor Bleuler, for kindly allowing me to make use of the above material.

[13] Krafft-Ebing speaks of "abnormally increased emotional impressionability." *Text-Book of Insanity* (orig. 1879), p. 52. E. Müller ("Über Moral Insanity," 1899, p. 342) writes: "It is unanimously emphasized that the emotional reactivity is reduced or abolished, that there is emotional blunting or even complete loss of emotion." P. 344: "The restrictive checks which the patient's egotistic strivings meet with in the legal rights of other people lead to bad moods and affects, resulting in great emotional irritability." This contradiction is not the fault of the author but of his material. Its symptomatology is so extremely contradictory because under the term "moral insanity" are included cases of widely different provenance which merely happen to have the symptom of moral defect in common.

IV

A CASE OF HYSTERICAL STUPOR
IN A PRISONER IN DETENTION

A CASE OF HYSTERICAL STUPOR
IN A PRISONER IN DETENTION [1]

226   The following case of hysterical stupor in a prisoner in detention was referred to the Burghölzli Clinic for a medical opinion. Apart from the publications of Ganser and Raecke, the literature on cases of this kind is very scanty, and even their clinical status seems uncertain in view of Nissl's criticisms.[2] It therefore seems to me of interest to put such a case on record, particularly as the special clinical picture it presents is of considerable importance for the psychopathology of hysteria in general.

227   The patient, Godwina F., was born May 15, 1854. Her parents were stated to have been healthy. Two of her four sisters died of consumption, another died in a lunatic asylum, the fourth was normal. One brother was also normal and very steady-going. The second brother was Carl F., an habitual criminal. Her two illegitimate daughters were both healthy. Nothing was known of any previous major illnesses. The patient came of poor circumstances; she began work in a factory at the age of 14. At 17 she started a love affair, had her first illegitimate child at 18, her second at 28. She was entirely dependent on her lover, who provided her regularly with money. She alleged that

1 [First published as "Ein Fall von hysterischem Stupor bei einer Untersuchungs-gefangenen," *Journal für Psychologie und Neurologie* (Leipzig), I (1902) : 3, 110–22.—EDITORS.]
2 [See below, notes 3–5, for these citations.]

three years earlier she had received from him some 20,000 marks, which she quickly spent. Consequently she got into financial difficulties, let her hotel bills pile up, and then left the hotel, repeatedly promising the proprietor that she would pay as soon as she got the sum due—10,000 marks—from her lover. Suspected of theft, she was arrested on May 31, at 5 P.M. At the preliminary hearing on the same day, and on the following days, she conducted herself quite correctly, and her behaviour in custody was altogether quiet and respectable.

228   Her daughter stated that the patient had lately been irritable and depressed, which was understandable enough in view of her difficult situation. Otherwise nothing abnormal could be ascertained.

229   When, on the morning of June 4, 1902, the cell was opened at 6:30, the patient was standing "rigid" by the door, came up to the wardress "quite rigid" and furiously demanded that she should "give back the money she had stolen from her." She waved away the food that was put before her, remarking that there was "poison in it." She began to rage and shout, threw herself about in the cell, kept on asking for her money, saying that she wanted to see the judge at once, etc. At the call of the wardress, the jailer came with his wife and assistant, and together they tried to calm her down. Apparently there was a fairly lively scene; they held her by the hands and (according to the wardress) also "shook" her. They denied hitting her. The patient was then locked up again. When the cell was opened again at 11 o'clock the patient had torn the top half of her clothes to shreds. She was still very worked up, said the jailer had hit her on the head, they had taken the money she got from her husband, 10,000 marks, all in gold, which she had counted on the table, etc. She showed an acute fear of the jailer.

230   During the afternoon the patient was quieter. At 6 in the evening the District Medical Officer found her totally disoriented. The following symptoms are worth noting: almost complete lack of memory, easily provoked changes of mood, megalomaniac ideas, stumbling speech, complete insensibility to deep pin-pricks, strong tremor of the hands and head, her writing shaky and broken. She fancied she was in a luxury hotel, eating rich food, that the prison personnel were hotel guests. Said she was very wealthy, had millions; that during the night a man

138

attacked her, who felt cold. At times she was excitable, scream-
ing and shouting gibberish. She did not know her own name
and could say nothing about her past life and her family. She no
longer recognized money.

231   On the way to the asylum she was extremely nervous and
frightened, started at every little thing in an exaggerated way,
clung to the attendant. She was admitted at 8 P.M. on June 4.

232   The patient was of medium height, physically well nour-
ished. She looked exhausted and haggard. Expression of the
face was nervous and tearful, as if she felt utterly helpless and
hopeless.

233   Her head, tongue, and hands trembled. Depression in region of fontanelle; circumference of head 55 cm.; biparietal
15 cm.; occipitofrontal 18.5 cm. Pupils reacted normally to
light and to accommodation. Gait rather unsteady. No ataxia,
no Romberg sign. Reflexes of forearm and knee- and ankle-jerks
brisk; pharyngeal reflex present.

234   *June 5.* Patient passed a quiet night. Today she kept to
her bed, quiet and listless. Ate decently, was clean in her habits.
No spontaneous sign of affect; facial expression indicated a mood
of nervous discontent without any strong affects. She looked at
me with a helpless gaze, jumped at all sudden questions and
quick movements. Her mood was very unstable and depended
very much on the facial expression of her questioner. A serious
face made her cry at once, a laughing face made her laugh, too,
and to a stern face she reacted with instant fear, turned her head
away, buried her face in the pillows, saying: "Don't hit me."

235   There were no symptoms of any major restriction of the
field of vision. (Accurate tests were impossible owing to her
psychic condition.) Skin sensibility, or rather sensibility to pain,
exhibited peculiarities: at the first examination there was
total analgesia on the legs and feet for deep, unobserved pin-
pricks, with normal sensibility on the head and arms. After a
few minutes the picture changed completely: total analgesia on
the left arm and normal sensibility on the lower limbs—the very
places where the opposite condition had been observed shortly
before. The analgesic areas varied without rhyme or reason,
being apparently independent of suggestion (though this cannot
be ruled out with certainty). The striking thing was the patient's behaviour during this examination: she resisted it, but

did so in an impersonal way, not paying any attention to what I was doing, even when I intentionally administered the pricks quite openly, under her very eyes. *Rather, as if consciously denying the real situation, she looked for some unknown cause of the pain in her nightgown or in the bedclothes.*

236 The following conversation then took place:

Where are you? — *In Munich.*
Where are you staying? — *In a hotel.*
What time is it? — *I don't know.*
What's your name? — *Don't know.*
Christian name? — *Ida.* (This was the name of her second daughter.)
When were you born? — *I don't know.*
How long have you been here? — *Don't know.*
Is your name Meier or Müller? — *Ida Müller.*
Have you a daughter? — *No.*
Surely you have! — *Yes.*
Is she married? — *Yes.*
Whom to? — *To a man.*
What is he? — *Don't know.*
Isn't he the director of a factory? — *Yes, he is.* (Wrong answer.)
Do you know Godwina F.? — *Yes, she's in Munich.*
Are you Godwina F.? — *Yes.*
I thought your name was Ida Müller? — *Yes, my name's Ida.*
Have you ever been to Zurich? — *Never, but I've stopped with my son-in-law.*
Do you know Mr. Benz? (The son-in-law.) — *Don't know Mr. Benz, never spoken with him.*
But you've stopped with him, haven't you? — *Yes.*
Do you know Carl F.? (Her brother.) — *Don't know him.*
Who am I? — *The headwaiter.*
What is this? (A notebook.) — *The menu.*
Tell me the time. (I showed her my watch, which said 11.) — *One o'clock.*
What is three times four? — *Two.*
How many fingers is this (5)? — *Three.*
No, look carefully! — *Seven.*
Count them. — *1, 2, 3, 5, 7.*
Count up to 10. — *1, 2, 3, 4, 5, 6, 7, 10, 12.*

237 She couldn't say the alphabet or do simple multiplication. When she attempted to write, extremely strong tremors ap-

peared; she could not produce a single legible word with her right hand but managed a bit better with her left. She could read only with the utmost difficulty, and frequently misread the letters. With numbers it was even worse; she could not distinguish between 4 and 5. She recognized objects held before her. No symptoms of apraxia. She proved very suggestible. For instance, she was told when standing by the bed in her nightgown that she had a pretty silk dress on. "Yes, very pretty," she said, stroking the nightgown with her hand and looking down at herself. Then she wanted to lie down in bed again. "But you can't go to bed with your clothes on!" Silently she began unbuttoning her nightgown, then stopped suddenly: "But I'm not wearing a nightgown!"

238   *June 6.* The patient's condition was about the same, but she now knew her name was F., though she still gave "Ida" as her first name. She knew her age, but was otherwise totally disoriented.

239   *June 7.*

How long have you been here? — *A long time.*
Twenty years? — *Yes, a very long time.*
You've only been here a week, haven't you? — *Only a week?*
Where are you? — *In Munich. Must I always keep telling you?*
Where are you staying? — *In hospital. There are lots of sick people here, but I'm not sick.*
What's the matter with these sick people? — *Headache.*
Who am I? — *The doctor.*
Have you seen me before? — *No.*
So today is the first time? — *No, yesterday.*
What day of the week is it? — *Sunday.* (Wrong answer.)
Month? — *The second.*
Year? — *I don't know.*
1899? — *Yes.*
No, it's 1892! — *Yes, of course.*
Or is it 1902? — *Yes, yes, 1902!* (In an emphatic tone of voice.) *No, it's 1900, of course it's 1900, I was all muddled up.*
Weren't you in prison recently? — *No, I've never been in prison. A man with a beard hit me.*
Did that happen here? — *Yes.*
Have you any debts? — *No.*
Yes, you have! — *Well, I have a lot of money.*
Where from? — (No answer.)

How much? — *Quite a lot.*

How much, then? — *I don't know, I never counted it. It belongs to my daughter.*

Who was the father of your children? — *He died a long time ago.*

How old are you? — *Fifty.*

What year were you born? — *In May.*

What year were you born? — *I don't know.*

Is your daughter pregnant? (She was very near her time.) — *What's that mean?*

Is your daughter expecting a baby? — *No, it died.*

Have you only one daughter? — *Yes, only one.*

But you have two daughters! — *Yes.*

What is the name of your married daughter's husband? — *I don't know.*

240   The patient talked quite well today, only stumbling over the more difficult words. She was slow at reading, but didn't make too many mistakes. Comprehension of what she read was much hindered by a high degree of distractibility. Only quite short sentences of the simplest order were understood and reproduced. Longer sentences were neither understood nor reproduced, though the patient did everything she was asked. She recited the alphabet faultlessly. Her counting still had gaps: 10, 11, 12, 13, —, 15, 16, 17, 18, —, 20.

241   She still confused 4 and 5 when writing. Her writing was very much distorted by the tremor.

242   On the following days her condition remained essentially the same.

243   *June 9.* Better today, quick reaction, greeted me in a friendly manner. Orientation in space was correct, she knew her name was Godwina F. But had no idea when, how, or why she came here. Knew only of one daughter, Ida. Knew nothing of the existence of her brother, Carl F., nor of her arrest, her son-in-law, etc. No gross disturbances of sensibility ascertainable.

244   *June 10.* Received a visit from her daughter Ida this morning. Still remembered it in the evening. Orientation maintained. She asked the wardress about the date.

245   On being told that she was in detention, she exhibited strong affect, burst into tears, refused to believe it.

246   *June 11.* Again a little better than yesterday. She was oriented as to place and time, but complained of bad headache.

Lay quietly in bed, apparently very exhausted. Very distractible, and had to be prodded into answering. Her memory of events from June 6 back to several months before her arrest was grossly impaired. She had only the haziest ideas about her last stay in Zurich. She knew that she last stayed at a hotel run by a Mr. König, but could not remember the name of the hotel, despite my insistence. For the period immediately preceding her arrest, as also for the period of her detention, she had absolute amnesia. She could only remember that "a man hit her, not here, but somewhere else, probably in another hospital."

247 Her memory starts again from about June 10. She still remembered her daughter's visit yesterday, but not her painful agitation on being informed that she was in detention. She remembered from June 9 or even earlier that she thought at first she was in Munich (where she had in fact been six months previously). Despite insistent examination, nothing more could be ascertained.

248 Very nervous and frightened at the least thing. Easily fatigued, and several times wearily closed her eyes during the conversation.

249 *June 12.* Fully oriented. Had all sorts of ideas about her situation. Thought she came here because she was ill with bad headache and flickering before her eyes. Said she had been told the police brought her (she got this from the wardress), but that she knew absolutely nothing about it. Also that she had been in prison, but did not know how long, maybe a week. In prison she had been beaten because she said her money had been stolen. She thought she had put the money on the table and then it suddenly vanished.

250 She also remembered her large debts and the charge of stealing. She was extremely nervous and easily tired, rather unclear in the head, and had to think a long time before answering.

251 On the following days, no essential change.

252 *June 18.* Not so frightened or so easily fatigued. Gave a coherent anamnesis, but it still contained a fair number of errors due to distractibility, particularly in the dates. Her memory was fairly clear up to the day of her arrest (May 31); from then on, uncertain. She had to think a long time before remembering the place where she was arrested; said it was in the morning (instead of 5 P.M.). She knew she had been up for a

143

hearing, apparently only once, and said she'd been shut up in the cell for a week. She said the hearing took place on the first or second day of detention (June 2). (In reality it was immediately after her arrest, at 6 P.M., and on the following morning; she was also present at the examination of several witnesses.) She still vaguely remembered seeing her daughter there. (The daughter was arrested under the same charge.) She thought she had to sign something, but did not know what. On the second or third night "she was quite positive that she put the 10,000 marks which she'd been expecting on the table." The money was a great joy to her. Then it seemed as if the door suddenly opened and a black man came in, with bent head, who seized her by the shoulders with cold hands and pushed her into the pillows. Suddenly the thought came to her: "Christ, he's after my money!" She then came to herself from sheer fright, still feeling the cold hands on her shoulders; convinced herself that the door was shut, and looked round for her money on the table. It had vanished. She was in despair; she could not find her way about and no longer knew where she was. Next morning two men and two women came whom she did not know. One of the men seized her by the hair and hit her. She screamed and "must have lost consciousness." "It was just like being dead." When she came to herself again, she was lying here (in the asylum) in bed. She thought she was in Munich, but the wardress told her it was Zurich.

253   She now felt pretty well, except for the headache and for sleeping badly. Only at night she had bad dreams; for instance, of lying on kittens, or that swarms of cats were crawling over her.

254   The patient still exhibited marked torpor and considerably reduced power of attention. Comprehension good. Retention very bad; she failed altogether to remember stories of any length. She was good at short, simple sums, but could not solve more complicated ones such as 3×17, 7×17, $35 \div 6$, $112 + 73$, as she always forgot one part of the calculation. Rapid blunting of attention owing to high fatigability.

255   Precise sensibility tests showed poor discrimination between qualities of touch and temperature, particularly in the lower limbs. Perimetric examination showed normal field of vision. No analgesia.

256   In the evening the patient was put for a short time into hypnotic somnambulism by means of a few passes and closing of the eyes. Under suggestion, she drank wine and vinegar from an empty glass. On being told that it was an apple, she bit a pen wiper and pronounced it very sour.

257   Cautious questioning revealed that *the retrograde amnesia for the period from May 31 to the night of June 3 disappeared under hypnosis.* The patient related that she was arrested at 5 P.M. on the Bellevueplatz, where she was taking a walk with her daughter. The daughter was apprehended first, whereupon the patient, who was a few paces behind her, came up to see what was the matter. The hearing took place at 6 P.M. and continued on the following morning. (The details were confirmed by the daughter.) *The total amnesia for the period from the night of June 3 to June 10 resisted hypnosis.* No memory of this period could be awakened despite repeated attempts.

258   The headache disappeared under suggestion. Deep sleep was suggested for the night, also amnesia for the whole content of the hypnosis. The pains in the head were much better after she was wakened, and at night she slept uninterruptedly for eight hours.

259   On the following days she was hypnotized fairly regularly, with good results. In each hypnosis she showed continuity of memory with the previous ones.

260   *June 24.* The patient now spent the whole time out of bed, doing some kind of handiwork. Except for a certain dreaminess and distractibility, there were no more symptoms of note. *The retrograde partial amnesia and the total amnesia continued unaltered.* The patient proved very suggestible, so that post-hypnotic suggestions were realized too.

261   *June 27.* Today it was possible to penetrate the total amnesia by a trick.

262   The patient was put to sleep in the usual way. She at once became cataleptic and profoundly analgesic.

263   Are you hypnotized now? — *Yes.*
Are you asleep? — *Yes.*
But you can't be asleep, as you're talking to me! — *Yes, that's right, I'm not asleep.*
Look out, I'm now going to hypnotize you! (This procedure was

repeated several times. The patient lay quite slack; the slight twitching of the arms that always occurs under hypnosis stopped.)

Are you asleep now? — (No answer.)

Are you asleep? — (No answer.)

You will be able to speak presently! (Passes were made over the mouth.)

Are you asleep? — (Softly and hesitatingly:) *Yes.*

How did you get here? — *I don't know.*

You are now in the detention cell, aren't you? — *Yes.*

And now the door is opening? — *Yes, and a policeman comes in, he's taking me to the asylum.*

Then how did you get here? — *In a cab.*

You are now in the cab. — *Yes, I'm awfully afraid in the cab, there's thunder and lightning and pouring rain. I'm always afraid of the big fat man who beats me.*

Now the cab stops, you are in the asylum. What time is it? — *Eight o'clock. I'm sitting in a little room, a gentleman with a beard comes in and says I needn't be afraid, nobody's going to hit me. . . . then two women come and then another, they put me to bed.*

264   Here the memory broke off again. The patient's statements correspond exactly with reality. She was brought to the asylum in a cab, by a police sergeant, at 8 P.M., during a violent thunderstorm. On the way she clung frantically to the sergeant, saying in a terrified voice that she "was going to be beaten again." A doctor was present at her admission, also there were two senior wardresses, and the nurse came soon afterwards.

265   During the next fortnight the patient's general condition underwent considerable improvement with occasional use of hypnosis. The scope of the amnesias remained unaltered.

266   *June 21.* During the night the patient suddenly jumped out of bed, totally confused, in great terror, absolutely disoriented, and only after much persuasion could she be quieted down sufficiently to go back to bed. She stayed in bed this morning, trembling and starting violently when spoken to, expressing vague fears and complaining of dizziness and headache.

267   Immediate inquiries revealed that yesterday, at a concert given in the asylum, she met a male patient who, before being admitted here, had put her in a very unpleasant situation indeed by blurting out the whole story of her brother, the habitual criminal, in the hotel where she stayed before her arrest. She had already complained, at the concert and afterwards, about

the unpleasant impression the patient made upon her. After being ordered two hours' rest in bed, which had a very favourable effect, she was examined with the utmost care, and gave the following information:

268   On going to bed yesterday evening she had dizziness and "noises" in the head. But she slept very well and now felt quite clear. She could not remember anything unpleasant that happened yesterday. When asked whether she remembered yesterday's concert, she suddenly got very red and her eyes filled with tears, but she said in an indifferent tone of voice that she remembered the concert quite well—which she proved by mentioning various details. Nothing unpleasant had happened at the concert. All indirect questions remained without result, only the direct question whether she had seen the patient M. reminded her of the incident. She now related the affair in an indifferent tone of voice, without showing any noticeable affects.

269   *July 22.* Passed the night quietly. No deterioration.

270   *In today's hypnosis the amnesia for yesterday's twilight state disappeared.* She was put back into the state of the previous night on its being suggested to her that she was frightened and did not know where she was. She then showed how she jumped out of bed. The wardress called out: "Miss F., be quiet and go back to bed." But she did not go back, tried to hide herself, and felt terribly frightened; then a fellow patient came to comfort and soothe her. (Details of her account could be objectively confirmed.)

271   *July 24.* Still complained of headache and sleeping badly.

272   *It was suddenly discovered that even without double hypnosis the patient had a hypnotic recollection of the twilight state from June 4 to June 10.* Her memory now goes back to the morning of June 5, of which she reproduced the scenes of the visits and the examination with a wealth of detail. A fair amount was also elicited from the days following the 5th, but this could not be verified for lack of precise information. As a post-hypnotic suggestion she was told to remember the episode from the twilight state. In place of the short sleep, the hypnosis was followed by hysterical somnambulism, in which the patient mistook me for her lover and addressed tender words to "Ferdinand." By means of a few passes and energetic suggestions for sleeping, the twilight state was terminated and then converted

into simple sleep. Total amnesia after waking. The post-hypnotic suggestion that she would remember her admission to the asylum was not realized.

273   The patient was discharged on July 25 under police escort.

274   On August 8, 1902, she wrote in a letter to an acquaintance in the asylum: "Ever since I've been here [abroad] I've felt unwell, when I wake up at night I don't know where I am, and I get the feeling that I can't think any more. I have to jump up and run about the room until I know where I am again."

275   The patient wrote that she was in a difficult situation because of money.

*

276   This case has several interesting peculiarities to offer. It is undoubtedly a purely hysterical ailment.

277   While in detention, the patient suffered from a delirious twilight state, which after a short pause passed into a stuporous stage characterized by the symptom of the "senseless answer," strong disturbance of attention despite fairly good comprehension, high suggestibility, fatigability, disorientation, timidity, nervousness, absence of catatonic symptoms, and disturbances of sensibility.

278   In his lecture on a "remarkable example of an hysterical twilight state," Ganser,[3] in 1897, gave a cursory account of states which were mostly observed in prisoners in detention. The picture most of the patients present is one of hallucinatory confusion; many exhibit active fear, together with various disturbances of sensibility. Generally, after a few days, there is a striking change, sometimes an improvement, followed by amnesia for the attack. These states owe their characteristic features to the "symptom of the senseless answer," which consists in the patients' "inability to answer correctly the simplest questions put to them, although it was obvious from the kind of answers they gave that they had understood the meaning of the questions fairly well. Their answers revealed a positively astounding ignorance and a surprising lack of knowledge which they definitely must have possessed or must still possess."

[3] "Über einen eigenartigen hysterischen Dämmerzustand" (1898).

279   An alternating state of consciousness with defects of memory, in conjunction with other hysterical symptoms, provides the diagnostic basis for an hysterical twilight state. Raecke [4] has made a thorough study of such cases, and particularly of the symptom of the senseless answer. The cases he published in his first work were not all of the same kind and were not, perhaps, altogether unexceptional; consequently they provoked sharp criticism from Nissl,[5] who accused Raecke of faulty diagnosis and asserted that "Ganser's symptom of irrelevant talk is first and foremost a special manifestation of catatonic negativism." The irrelevant talk of hebephrenics and catatonics is a very well-known phenomenon, and I do not believe an observer with any experience could mistake it for the "senseless answers" of hysterics. The most he could do would be to overlook a catatonia masked by hysteriform symptoms. When the inadequate answers are the direct manifestation of catatonia, they are clearly characterized as catatonic by the significant absence of affectivity and by associations which seize on irrelevant points in the question, thus differing essentially from the deliberately senseless answers of the hysteric. The irrelevant talk of hebephrenics is often due merely to lack of interest, to the "don't care" attitude typical of such patients, perhaps also to negativistic compulsion. The senseless answer, on the other hand, is sometimes a product of semi-intentional negation, which opposes the effort to give an adequate answer, and sometimes a product of a deep restriction of consciousness, which prevents conscious association of the elements needed for an adequate answer. As an accompanying phenomenon very typical of these latter cases, we would emphasize the stuporous behaviour of the majority of the patients. Raecke, in his second publication,[6] describes several such cases of stupor, having already established stuporous behaviour in three of the five cases mentioned in his first publication.

280   Severe temporary loss of the intellectual faculties is a symptom not uncommonly met with in the field of hysteria. Here I would mention in passing the cases of alternating consciousness

4 "Beitrag zur Kenntnis des hysterischen Dämmerzustandes" (1901).
5 "Hysterische Symptome bei einfachen Seelenstörungen" (1902).
6 "Hysterischer Stupor bei Strafgefangenen" (1901).

described by Azam,[7] Weir Mitchell,[8] Schroeder van der Kolk,[9] MacNish,[10] etc. Some of the patients had, after a prodromal stage of sleep, lost all knowledge even of the simplest things. Weir Mitchell's case did not even know the meanings of words. Similar intellectual defects are also found in the moria states of young hysterics.

281   The phenomenon we are discussing has, however, a very different clinical setting in our case, and assumes a special aspect when combined with other symptoms. If we take Ganser's syndrome to mean a passing state of altered consciousness, amnesically separated from the normal state, in conjunction with exaggerated, negativistic senselessness, then its inner affinity with Raecke's description of stupor in convicts is unmistakable. This stupor is often found in criminals, generally soon after their arrest, and may be regarded as a consequence of the excitements and hardships they have undergone. An hallucinatory prodromal stage, preceding the stupor, is also found in Ganser's syndrome with the same clinical symptoms and can dominate the situation for a longer or shorter period. Similarly, disturbances of sensibility are common to both. The question as to the extent of amnesia is very obscure; like most hysterical amnesias, it is difficult and sometimes impossible to circumscribe. Course and prognosis are equally uncertain. One can only say that in this matter the same is true as in traumatic neuroses, where the illness stands in reciprocal relationship to the injuriousness of the cause.

282   Our case seems to me particularly suited to throw light on those aspects of the Ganser-Raecke picture which are still relatively unexplored because they are so difficult to observe, that is, on the still open question of amnesia and the psychological mechanism of the most characteristic symptoms.

283   In our patient, whose anamnesis had nothing special to offer, the picture described by Raecke developed in singularly pure form under the obvious influence of detention. In the loneliness of solitary confinement she naturally became intensely preoccupied with the misfortune that had suddenly befallen her; more-

[7] *Hypnotisme* (1887), case of Albert X.
[8] "Mary Reynolds" (1888).
[9] *Pathologie und Therapie der Geisteskrankheiten* (1863), p. 31.
[10] *The Philosophy of Sleep* (1830), cited in Binet, *Alterations of Personality.*

over, she was worried about her daughter, who was in the last stages of pregnancy, and on top of that there was the anxiety and agitation caused by the charge of theft (which later turned out to be false). All this led to the outbreak of a delirious state on the fourth night of her detention, with violent motor excitement. As chief content of the delirium we find a syndrome which "every prison psychosis can offer for a time." [11] It consists of that well-known mixture of hallucinatory wish-fulfilment and delusions of being wronged. We must regard as such a symptom of detention the episode which began like a vivid dream with a wish-fulfilling illusion and ended in a state of fearful perplexity and lack of judgment, where nothing could be corrected despite the fact that she was more or less awake. She dreamt that she received the expected 10,000 marks and put them on the table; a black figure suddenly comes in and gives her a violent fright; she leaps up; the hallucinations vanish, leaving behind them the delusions of being robbed, poisoned, etc. In the course of the next day the wish-fulfilling delusion gained the upper hand: the patient thought she was in a luxurious hotel, was very rich, had millions. At the same time she showed marked deficiency of intellect, which the prison doctor who was called in took for *dementia paralytica*.

284   This intensification of a wish-fulfilling delusion to a real delusion of grandeur may perhaps have been due to extreme restriction of the mental field of vision, since, as Wernicke points out,[12] delusions of grandeur may easily arise when there is a lack of orienting ideas and a predominance of egotistic thinking. Raecke noticed much the same thing in his cases.

285   On being admitted to the asylum, the patient presented a picture of the most profound restriction of consciousness, with marked anxiety and perplexity. A little later this state passed into a quieter phase characterized by absolute lack of psychic content; her consciousness was a *tabula rasa*. Continuity of all memories seems to have been broken; she fancied she was in a hotel, but this was rather a matter of guesswork, a faint echo of her previous life, than a real misinterpretation of her surroundings in delirium. She had lost all knowledge of the simplest things, even of her own name, and, as though it occurred

11 Rüdin, "Klinische Formen der Gefängnisspsychosen" (1901), p. 458.
12 *Grundriss der Psychiatrie* (1894), p. 316.

to her in a dream, gave her daughter's name as her own. In striking contrast to this marked deficiency of intellect was her good comprehension. She understood requests and questions well; only in her answers, or rather in her centrifugal psychic performance, was any disturbance evident. As might be expected, the power of attention was almost entirely absent, so that the whole psychic process was broken up into apparently disconnected elements. This picture was completed by her suggestibility; anything one told the patient or forced her to do supplied the only content in her mental void, and this behaviour was quite consistent with her behaviour under hypnosis.

286   This stuporous state is so far removed from catatonic stupor that the latter has no bearing whatever on a differential diagnosis of our case.

287   Despite this apparently absolute mental blank, we have a number of clues to support the hypothesis of a psychic process, though it is abnormal in not being illuminated by consciousness.

288   When asked her Christian name, the patient replied, "Ida." Ida was the name of the daughter who was arrested with her. Asked whether she knew anybody called Godwina F., she replied, "Yes, she is in Munich." The patient herself was formerly in Munich. The idea that she was now in Munich, a faint continuity of memory with her earlier personality, obviously gave her the shadowy idea of her former real stay in Munich, and hence a recollection of her real name.

289   Was she ever in Zurich? "Never, but I've stopped there with my son-in-law." The son-in-law did, in fact, live in Zurich, and the name "Zurich" stirred up memories of the unpleasant experiences she had there, which were also mainly connected with her son-in-law. This double connection thrust the memory of the son-in-law to the forefront, while the obvious answer—that she had been in Zurich—was rejected. We shall see more of this curious mechanism which is so characteristic of hysterical ailments.

290   Asked what was the matter with the patients in the asylum, she replied, "Headache." This answer shows that she was unconsciously oriented to her surroundings, but that her supraliminal consciousness could only produce a distant association to the right idea.

291   The psychology of the next answer is very similar. Asked whether she had recently been in prison, she replied, "No, I've never been in prison. A man with a beard hit me." Here again the right answer cannot be given, or rather it is flatly denied, and an idea closely associated with it is produced instead. The reverse, too, sometimes happens—an affirmative answer is given as a result of suggestibility, but must be denied immediately afterwards because of her peculiar negativism. Thus, when asked whether it was 1902, she answered, "Yes, yes, 1902—no, it's 1900, of course it's 1900. I was all muddled."

292   Her orientation was quite unmistakable, however, in the episode of the suggested silk dress. The suggestion that she was wearing a silk dress was realized at once, and lasted until she wanted to undress in order to go to bed. At that moment the unconscious orientation broke through; she stopped suddenly and said, "But I'm not wearing a nightgown!" She knew subconsciously that she was standing there in her nightgown and that she would be completely naked if she took it off. The feeling of shame was stronger than the suggestion and prevented her from undressing—not, however, with the right motivation, but because of a suggested association to the right idea.

293   With the improvement beginning June 9, despite fairly good orientation as to time and place, there was a striking defect of memory for all unpleasant events in the recent past, including all persons who were in any way associated with unpleasant memories for the patient. She remembered only her daughter Ida, but had no knowledge of her other daughter and of the son-in-law she quarrelled with, or of her brother the criminal. Although on June 10 she showed continuity of memory with the previous day, she no longer remembered the information which she received with such lively affect, concerning her arrest and detention. So once again something unpleasant was repressed out of the sphere of consciousness.

294   As can be seen from the patient's history, the scope of her consciousness gradually reconstituted itself, except for her defective memory of the whole period of the twilight state (which remained irreparable up till the end of observation). As already reported, elucidation of her summary memory from the moment of arrest to the outbreak of psychosis in the night of June 3 presented no difficulty at all. Much greater obstacles

153

stood in the way of hypnotic elucidation of the twilight state. However, I succeeded in the end, by making use of two tricks mentioned in the literature. The first was devised by Janet.[13] In order to put his well-known medium Lucie into a deeper sleep for a definite purpose, he would hypnotize Lucie II (that is, Lucie I, already hypnotized into somnambulism) by means of passes, just as if she were not yet hypnotized. By means of this procedure Janet discovered Lucie III, whose memory was like a large circle enclosing the two smaller circles of the memories of Lucie II and Lucie I; that is to say, it had at its disposal memories not accessible to either of them. As an inter-mediate state between Lucie II and Lucie III, Janet found a deep sleep in which Lucie was absolutely uninfluenceable.[14] The same thing was observed in our patient. The short sleeping state which followed the second dose of hypnotism, and from which it was rather difficult to get the patient to speak, prob-ably corresponds to the intermediate state mentioned by Janet.

295   The second trick I used was the method used by Forel in Naef's famous case.[15] This consists in putting the patient each time into the appropriate situation, thereby giving him *points d'appui* round which the other associations aggregate like crys-tals.

296   By means of these two procedures it was possible to demon-strate that our hypothesis of an unconscious but none the less certain orientation—even during the deepest twilight state—was correct. We therefore find the remarkable fact that the ap-parently severe disturbance of the psychic process in the Ganser-Raecke twilight state is merely a superficial one, affecting only the extent of consciousness, and that the unconscious mental activity is little affected, if at all.

297   The psychological mechanism whereby such a disturbance comes about is nicely illustrated in the story of the little relapse which was observed in the asylum, when the patient had that unpleasant encounter at the concert. In the evening she com-

---

13 *L'Automatisme psychologique* (orig. 1889), p. 87.
14 Ibid., p. 87: "This is that state of hypnotic syncope which I have already re-marked. I have frequently observed it since, and in the case of some patients it seems to constitute an unavoidable transition between the various psychological states."
15 Naef, "Ein Fall von temporärer, totaler, teilweise retrograder Amnesie" (1897).

plained of dizziness and noise in her ears, and that night she suddenly woke up, totally disoriented, confused, and frightened. The next day she had amnesia for the nocturnal interlude, and, when examined for its aetiology, displayed a systematic negativism that prevented her from saying what had really happened, although the words were almost put into her mouth. During this recital, she exhibited no adequate affect, but her sudden blushing and the tears in her eyes showed that the sore spot had been touched.

298   Here we have the primary phenomenon in the genesis of hysterical symptoms which Breuer and Freud have termed *hysterical conversion*.[16] According to them, every person has a certain threshold up to which he can tolerate "unabreacted" affects and allow them to pile up. Anything that exceeds that threshold leads—*cum grano salis!*—to hysteria. In the language of Breuer and Freud, our patient's threshold had been reached and exceeded as a result of her detention, and the unabreacted affect— the "excitement proceeding from the affective idea"—flowed off into abnormal channels and got "converted." Just how it will flow off is "determined" in most cases by chance or by the individual; that is to say, the line of least resistance is in one case the convulsion mechanism, in another sensibility, in a third the disturbance of consciousness, and so on. In our case, to judge from all the crucial points in the patient's history, the determining factor seems to have been the *idea of forgetting*. Her "not knowing" turns out to be partly an unconscious and partly a half-conscious *not wanting to know*. Raecke thinks that the not-knowing he found so remarkable in his patients may be due to fear, the fear of not knowing the simplest things, which, by auto-suggestion, leads to a real and effective not-knowing. This may often be true; but with our patient the semi-intentional repression of anything unpleasant from her consciousness was such a striking and dominant feature that Ganser's symptom seems to be altogether accessory. It may be regarded as a pathologically exaggerated consequence of the unconscious urge to forget, since her conscious mind drew back not only from feeling-toned ideas but from other zones of memory as well.

299   As to the clinical status of our case, we must define it as the "hysterical stupor of the convict" in the sense used by Raecke.

16 *Studies on Hysteria* (orig. 1895), p. 206.

This special form of hysterical illness—if we leave out of account the "prison complex" of hallucinations and delusions—may be described on the basis of the material at present available as a "prison psychosis," since, with few exceptions, the cases so far known have been observed only in prisoners.

300   In conclusion, I would like to thank my chief, Professor Bleuler, for his kindness in referring this case to me.

V

ON SIMULATED INSANITY

A MEDICAL OPINION ON A CASE
OF SIMULATED INSANITY

ON SIMULATED INSANITY [1]

301   Several cases of simulation have recently been published by
Bolte,[2] who in the course of his article remarks that the question
of simulation presents fewer difficulties in practice than it does
in theory. I would not like to go all the way with this statement.
As a matter of fact, cases do occasionally come up for observation which are extremely confusing and create any amount of
difficulty for the specialists who are asked to give a medical
opinion. It is precisely on the practical side that the art of the
diagnostician is sometimes taxed to the utmost. Generally speaking, simulation used to be suspected much more frequently and
injudiciously than it is now, yet in spite of this the older literature abounds in cases on which the observers were unable to
reach agreement. Today, through our knowledge of the various
clinical pictures of dementia praecox and hysteria, we have advanced a step further, and have also gained rather more insight
into the question of simulation, though this is not to say that
we have acquired greater certainty in regard to doubtful cases.
We possess no infallible method of unmasking the malingerer
and are as dependent as ever on the subjective impression he
makes on the observer. As Bolte rightly points out, it is always
a risky business to publish these cases at all, for it requires

1 [First published as "Über Simulation von Geistesstörung," *Journal für Psychologie und Neurologie* (Leipzig), II (1903): 5, 181–201.—EDITORS.]
2 "Über einige Fälle von Simulation" (1903).

159

considerable literary talent to lend an air of plausibility to subjective impressions. It is an unfortunate fact, as Fürstner says,[3] that the observer cannot convey to the reader all the detailed nuances of the picture—the changing facial expression, the attitude, verbal response, and so forth. Hence no author need be surprised if the reader doubts his cases of simulation or at least finds in them something to cavil at. In any conscientious appraisal of simulation there is so much to take into account and so much to investigate that, in reading a report that is the least bit summary, one is apt to regret the omission of this or that item which seems of importance.

302   Modern diagnostic requirements are far higher than formerly, when, strange as it seems, it was often simply a question of whether the case fitted into the purely theoretical scheme of the psychoses or not. The prolonged controversy over the famous case of Reiner Stockhausen [pars. 346ff. below] is particularly instructive in this respect. Since then, the theory of hysteria has brought us so much that is new and important that we are obliged to reckon with many more factors today than we were twenty years ago. Indeed, it is a well-known fact that the majority of malingerers are mentally abnormal and consist in the main of degenerates of various descriptions. How frequently hysteria occurs in such individuals it is difficult to say, but judging by other types of mental degeneracy the percentage must be very high, assuming, of course, that one takes as hysterical all "psychogenic" symptoms. The question of an hysterical disposition is of great importance in diagnosing simulation. The lying of hysterics is proverbial, and in the domain of psychiatry hysteria furnishes perhaps the most cases of simulation. We have reason to suppose that for simulated insanity, too, some importance attaches to hysteria, considering that a fairly large number of hysterical psychoses occur among persons in detention and among convicts, who are naturally greatly interested in simulating. Here I would refer the reader to the numerous studies of twilight states recently made by Ganser.

303   In judging a doubtful case of simulation, one must bear in mind that successful simulation is not a simple thing at all, but often makes the greatest demands in the matter of shamming, self-control, and psychic toughness. This cannot be achieved by

[3] "Die Zurechnungsfähigkeit der Hysterischen" (1899).

mere lying, for the deception must be kept up with consistency and unshakable will power for weeks or even months on end. All this requires an extraordinary amount of energy, coupled with an art of shamming that would do credit to the most accomplished actor. Such cases are rare, but they nevertheless exist. There can be no doubt that among the ranks of the degenerate and criminally minded there are persons who possess a quite unusual amount of energy and self-control, which apparently extends even to the vasomotor processes.[4] Exceptions of this kind are certainly uncommon, for the criminal is characterized, as a rule, by an impulsive energy that tires quickly, rather than by endurance. The art of shamming, however, seems to be a gift that is widely disseminated among criminals. It is found chiefly in thieves and poisoners. The mendacity of thieves is well known; Krauss[5] says of them: "All common criminals lie, but their lies are clumsy and palpable. Only thieves lie skilfully and naturally. They lie unthinkingly, without a moment's hesitation, as soon as they open their mouths. They no longer even know that they are lying. It has become so much second nature to them that they believe their own lies." In agreement with this we find a preponderance of thieves among malingerers. Of the ten malingerers investigated by Fritsch, seven were up for larceny, and two of the other three had previous convictions for theft. Among 8,430 admissions to this asylum, I found eleven malingerers.[6] Of these, six had been investigated for offences against property (larceny, embezzlement, swindling), two had previous convictions for theft, and one had been investigated for attempted poisoning.

304   Malingerers in this category of criminals therefore have a natural predisposition to deceive. If we discount the degree of intelligence and accidental factors which might assist simulation, then the one who plays his role best will be the one who lies most skilfully. The most confident of all liars are pathological swindlers, and the convincing thing about their lies is the fact that they believe them themselves, as they are no longer able to distinguish between truth and fiction. They differ from the actor in that the latter always knows when his role is

[4] Gross, *Criminal Psychology* (orig. 1898).
[5] *Die Psychologie des Verbrechens* (1884), p. 258.
[6] So far as listed in the records.

at an end, whereas the former allow themselves to be hypnotized by the game they are playing, and keep it up with a curious
intermingling of two mutually exclusive spheres of thought.
Delbrück even speaks of a real double consciousness.[7] The more
an actor enters into his role the more he loses himself in it,
and the more his acting is accompanied by unconscious emotional movements of the body,[8] which is just why he "acts" so
convincingly. The dramatic build-up of his role is certainly not
a pure act of volition, but is chiefly dependent on a special disposition whose essential ingredient seems to be a certain amount
of suggestibility. The greater this subjective suggestibility is,
the more likely it is that the role which began as a mere game
will falsify the reality, so captivating the subject as to replace
his original personality. Pick [9] has given us a beautiful example
of the way a daydream changes into a real twilight state. He
tells the story of a young girl who flirted with the idea that she
was an empress. She painted her role in ever more glowing
colours, got so absorbed in it that in the end it turned into an
hysterical twilight state with complete splitting of consciousness.
The second case reported by Pick concerns a girl who dreamt
herself into sexual situations and finally staged a rape on herself
by lying naked on the floor and tying herself to the table and
chairs. An interesting case of this kind is reported in a dissertation done under Wernicke: [10] A girl fantasized that she was engaged, and she received letters and flowers from her fiancé which
she had sent herself, with disguised handwriting. I observed a
case of the same type in a young girl who played an elaborately
contrived dream-role in her somnambulistic twilight states.[11]
Such phenomena are not so very rare and can be observed in
all gradations of intensity, from fanciful exaggerations to genuine twilight states. In all cases they begin with a feeling-toned
idea which develops on the basis of suggestibility into an automatism. These experiences must be taken into account in a
study of simulation. We should not forget that a large number

7 *Die pathologische Lüge und die psychisch abnormen Schwindler* (1891).
8 Cf. Lehmann's studies on the expression of emotion in an actor: *Die körperlichen Äusserungen psychischer Zustände* (1899), I, p. 182.
9 "Über pathologische Träumerei" (1896).
10 Bohn, *Ein Fall von doppeltem Bewusstsein* (1898).
11 [See the first paper in this volume, par. 116.—EDITORS.]

of malingerers are hysterical [12] and therefore provide favourable soil for auto-suggestions and disturbances of consciousness.

305   There is a Japanese proverb which says: "Thieving begins with lying." In the same way, congenital mendacity and an hysterical disposition are the beginning of simulation. The art of conscious shamming is a rare gift, so rare that it cannot be presumed in all malingerers, for sustained shamming requires an energy that exceeds the common measure both in quality and quantity. It ought not to be assumed so long as the commoner symptom of hysteria cannot be ruled out with certainty. We often find in hysteria all those mechanisms which make possible the most incredible toughness and a refinement of self-inflicted pain. When, for instance, a work-shy female hysteric can burn her feet in the most atrocious way with sulphuric acid, simply in order to get a free stay in a hospital, or another can kill off her entire dovecot so as to simulate haemoptysis with the blood, we may expect even more refined practices in individuals who are acting from feeling-toned motivations. In such cases we no longer have to reckon with the possibilities of normal psychology—which would be to credit them with the energy of a Mucius Scaevola [13]—but with subconscious mechanisms which far exceed the strength of the initial conscious impulse and, with the help of anaesthesias and other automatisms, bring about an auto-suggestion without further assistance from consciousness or even at its expense. The completely automatic nature of many hysterical symptoms explains their toughness and, in the case of histrionic performances, their perfection: since no reflective and deliberating conscious processes intervene, the subconscious complexes can reach full development. All doubtful cases of simulation should therefore be examined for possible hysterical symptoms, in the absence of suitable methods for investigating those disturbances of consciousness which unfortunately elude observation all too easily and, in general, form one of the darkest chapters of psychiatry.

306   If, then, we try to envisage the psychological mechanism of a twilight state on the basis described above, we shall not be surprised if the picture contains numerous elements which

[12] Hoche, *Handbuch der gerichtlichen Psychiatrie* (1901).
[13] [A legendary Roman who, when taken prisoner by the Etruscans, thrust his right hand into the fire to show his indifference to death.—TRANS.]

163

strike us as contrived and artificial, or even if certain symptoms are recognized as being wilfully produced. We should not, however, jump to the false conclusion that the other symptoms are being shammed as well. Similarly, technical tricks like the one recommended by Jacobi-Jenssen should be used with great caution, for if the subject takes over a symptom that has been suggested to him, this does not, in accordance with what we said above, decide anything for or against simulation. A confession of simulation at the end of the disturbance should be received with caution (especially when, as in one case, it followed a threat of a week's solitary confinement in darkness). Paradoxical as it may sound, certain experiences with hypnotized patients, who after an obvious hypnosis assert that they have not been hypnotized at all, make this caution necessary. On no account should one be satisfied in doubtful cases with a mere confession of simulation; a thorough catamnesis is needed for full elucidation, since only very rarely is objective insight into the inner state of the subject possible during the actual psychic disturbance. Despite confession there may easily be, in persons of a hysterical disposition, defects of memory that are unknown to the subject himself and can only be discovered by means of an accurate catamnesis.

307   We spoke above of feeling-toned ideas that may have a releasing effect on an hysterical disposition. How severe the consequences of violent emotion may sometimes be can be seen from disturbances following accident and shock neuroses. Besides the long-term consequences of the affect, we also find at the moment of the affect itself peculiar disturbances which outlast it for a longer or shorter period. I refer to the emotional confusion known as "examination fright," "stage fright," or "emotional paralysis." The latter term stems from Baetz,[14] who, during an earthquake in Japan, noticed in himself a general paralysis of movement and feeling, despite completely unimpaired apperception. This accords with numerous other phenomena observed during and immediately after violent affects.[15] We all know the tragicomic confusion exhibited by men during fires, when pillows and mattresses are carried downstairs and lamps and crockery thrown out of the window.

14 "Über Emotionslähmung" (1901).
15 Cf. the work done by Phleps, "Psychosen nach Erdbeben" (1903).

308   In accordance with these observations on normal persons, we should expect something similar in degenerate subjects, though with abnormalities both quantitative and qualitative. Our knowledge in this respect is unfortunately very defective and the case material scanty. I have put together a number of observations on this subject, drawn from mental defectives, but for the time being they should be regarded as case histories.

1

309   The first case concerns a mental defective who was sent to us for a medical opinion on a charge of rape. He had given perfectly reasonable answers at all the hearings, but, as the judge doubted whether the accused had the necessary power of discrimination to recognize the punishable nature of his action, a medical opinion was asked for. On admission the patient exhibited conspicuously stupid behaviour that made us suspect simulation. He spoke to nobody, walked up and down the room, his hands stuck impudently in his pockets, or stood apathetically in a corner and stared into space. When he was questioned, we had to repeat each question several times in a loud voice until the answer came. He stuttered, often did not answer at all but just gaped at the questioner. He was oriented as to time and place, but was unable to say why he was in the asylum. There were other striking peculiarities: when walking up and down the room he often made a sharp military turn, or would suddenly spin around himself where he stood (there was a catatonic in the room with him who made similar movements). After the fifth day his behaviour slowly began to change, he became freer in his movements, less rigid, demanded to know why he was here, since he was not mentally ill. Investigation now became possible, and we were immediately struck by the man's extraordinary dull-wittedness; all his reactions were very slow, he had to think a long time before giving particulars, the story of his life was a jumble of fragments in chronological disorder, made up of unintelligible contradictions. He could no longer remember dates and names he had been quite familiar with before, but described them in a clumsy, roundabout fashion. For instance, he had once been dismissed from a firm of lithographers because he could not stand the smell of acid. He told the story as follows: "There was a thing standing open where

the thing was in, a sort of little dish, and then I felt sick," etc. On the following days he grew more alert, and finally was able to give a clear and coherent account of his affairs. He had insight for his initial stupidity and explained that it was due to the great fright he got when he was sent to the asylum, saying that he always felt that way when he came to a new place.

310   Was the patient simulating? In my opinion not; he never tried to make capital out of this strange disturbance afterwards, although, with the stupid cunning of the mental defective, he sought every possible excuse for getting himself released. He seemed to regard this abnormal effect of emotion as a quite ordinary and regular thing. Moreover, it does not seem to me possible to simulate confusion and dull-wittedness, and particularly "examination fright," in so natural a way. Was his imitation of the catatonic intentional, unintentional, or merely accidental? I would prefer to reserve final judgment on this case.

2

311   The second case again has to do with a feeble-minded individual, a 17-year-old boy who was sent to us for a medical opinion, also on a charge of rape. He behaved very apathetically at first, had an extraordinarily stupid expression on his face, and gave hesitant answers brought out with great difficulty. During his stay of several weeks in the asylum his condition gradually improved; he became brighter, gave quicker and clearer answers, and it was noticed that he associated with the warders and patients in a natural and unconstrained way much sooner than he did with the doctors. In order to obtain a more accurate picture of the disturbance I took two series of association tests, amounting to 324 in all, at an interval of three weeks. The first series was taken the day after admission. The tests produced the result shown in Table I.

312   This list shows very clearly the change in the patient's mental state. The preponderance of meaningless reactions, clang reactions, and repetitions in the first series indicates a state of inhibited association which can best be described by the word "embarrassment." [16] With regard to the perseveration and its

16 In such a gross disturbance as this, practice is a factor that can be left out of account.

TABLE I *

Associations	May 6 1903	May 27 1903	Associations	May 6 1903	May 27 1903
Co-ordination, etc.	6.4	2.0			
Predicate relation	8.9	67.3 }Inner		15.3	69.3
Causal dependence	0.0	0.0			
Coexistence	14.1	15.3			
Identity	0.0	0.0 }Outer		16.6	27.5
Verbal-motor forms	2.5	12.2			
Word completion	0.0	0.0			
Clang	2.5	0.0 }Clang reactions		3.7	0.0
Rhyme	1.2	0.0			
Indirect	0.0	0.0			
Meaningless †	64.1	3.0			
Perseveration ‡	15.3	0.0			

Repetitions : ¶	19.1	13.0
Occurring 2 times	12.8	6.0
Occurring 3 times	5.1	1.0
Occurring 4 times	0.0	4.0
Occurring 5 times	0.0	0.0
Occurring 6 times	1.2	1.0
Occurring 7 times	0.0	1.0

* The classification follows Aschaffenburg's system; cf. Kraepelin, *Psychologische Arbeiten*, I, p. 231. The stimulus words were listed at random and not subordinated to any scheme based on number of syllables, grammatical qualities, or content. The figures are percentages.

† Meaningless reactions consisted in this case of names of objects that happened to be in the patient's field of vision. The second series includes a few "faults," where the patient failed to react.

‡ By perseveration I mean what Aschaffenburg calls "association to words that have occurred previously." I give here the percentage of associations to previous stimulus and reaction words.

¶ Repetitions = the number of reaction words that occur frequently, expressed in percentages.

comparatively large preponderance in the first series, I would not venture to say anything where the material is so limited. This syndrome may be regarded as analogous to the one described in Case 1.

313   The following two observations derive from investigations I am at present making with my colleague Dr. Riklin.

314   (1) Embarrassment is a state in which the attention cannot be concentrated, as it is fixed elsewhere by a strongly accentuated idea. I tried to reproduce this state by distracting the attention at the moment of association. This was done as follows: the subject (who was naturally a practised one) was asked to fix his attention on the visual ideas that presented themselves as the stimulus word was called, but, as in the ordinary test, to react as quickly as possible. He was therefore in a state that corresponds more or less to embarrassment, since his attention was fixed and only a fraction of it was left over for the reaction simultaneously taking place. The two experiments, made with two different people, each consisted of 300 separate tests (Table II).

315   (2) Similar results were obtained in experiments with outer distraction, where the subject associated while simultaneously making pencil strokes of a certain length in time to the beating of a metronome. A corresponding change is shown in Table III (page 170), based on 300 associations.

316   In this experiment, practice naturally plays an important part, but the change in the associations is nevertheless very striking. Later on,[17] I shall give a detailed report on the experiments and their significance for psychopathology. I think these examples suffice to throw an explanatory light on the association disturbances of our mental defective.

317   We see from these experiments that with inadequate investment of attention the quality of the associations shows a general deterioration; that is to say, there is a distinct tendency to produce outer and purely mechanical associations. A person who thinks in terms of such associations has very poor powers of comprehension and assimilation, and consequently comes very

[17] [Professor Jung was evidently contemplating a single paper at this time. As his subsequent publications show, however, he and his collaborators published several. Cf. "The Psychopathological Significance of the Association Experiment" and other papers grouped under "Studies in Word Association" in *Experimental Researches* (Coll. Works, 2); also "The Psychology of Dementia Praecox" (Coll. Works, 3).—EDITORS.]

TABLE II *

Associations	N	D	N	D	Associations	N	D	N	D
Co-ordination, etc.	15.5	4.0	13.5	19.0					
Predicate relation	25.5	19.0	31.5	12.0	Inner	42.5	23.0	46.5	33.0
Causal dependence	1.5	0.0	1.5	2.0					
Coexistence	7.5	6.0	7.5	4.0					
Identity	6.0	5.0	5.0	6.0	Outer	58.5	65.0	49.5	36.0
Verbal-motor forms	45.0	54.0	37.0	26.0					
Word completion	0.5	8.0	2.0	5.0					
Clang	0.0	2.0	0.5	15.0	Clang reactions	1.5	11.0	2.5	29.0
Rhyme	1.0	1.0	0.0	9.0					
Indirect	1.5	1.0	1.5	2.0					
Meaningless	0.0	0.0	0.0	0.0					
Perseveration	1.0	2.0	1.5	1.0					

* The figures are percentages. N = normal; D = distracted.

near to certain states of dementia. This may possibly be the reason for the feeble-mindedness heightened by emotionality observed in Case 2. The findings here throw some light on Case 1, which unfortunately was not subjected to detailed psychological investigation. In Case 2, simulation was quite out of the question, and yet the patient's behaviour ran much the same course as that of the first. Is it not possible that when feeble-minded and degenerate individuals are placed in an asylum the unwonted internment becomes associated with affects which are neutralized only gradually, in accordance with the poor adaptability of defectives? So far as it is possible to judge this

TABLE III *

Associations	N	D		Associations	N	D	
		Metronome rate per min.				Metronome rate per min.	
		60	100			60	100
Co-ordination, etc.	29.0	20.0	20.0				
Predicate relation	16.0	12.0	6.0	Inner	46.5	32.0	26.0
Causal dependence	1.5	0.0	0.0				
Coexistence	7.5	2.0	2.0				
Identity	6.0	0.0	2.0	Outer	33.5	36.0	36.0
Verbal-motor forms	20.0	34.0	32.0				
Word completion	0.5	0.0	2.0				
Clang	5.0	20.0	14.0	Clang reactions	5.5	20.0	16.0
Rhyme	0.0	0.0	0.0				
Indirect	4.5	12.0	12.0				
Meaningless	1.0	0.0	10.0				
Perseveration	0.5	2.0	2.0				
				Not understood	1.0	0.0	10.0

* The figures are percentages. N = normal; D = distracted.

matter at all, I should say it is not so much a question of mental defect as of a certain mental disposition, also found in other degenerate individuals, which puts abnormal obstacles in the way of an inner assimilation of affects and new impressions, and thus produces a state of continual perplexity and embarrassment.

318   How far this disposition to neutralize affects in a faulty or abnormal way coincides with hysteria is not easy to determine, but according to Freud's theory of hysteria the two are identical. Janet found that the influence of affects is seen most clearly in

hysterical persons, and that it produces a state of dissociation in which the will, attention, ability to concentrate are paralyzed and all the higher psychic phenomena are impaired in the interests of the lower; that is, there is a displacement towards the automatic side, where everything that was formerly under the control of the will is now set free. Speaking of the effect of emotion on hysterical subjects, Janet says:

Emotion has a decomposing action on the mind, reduces its synthesis and makes it, for the moment, wretched. Emotions, especially depressive ones such as fear, disorganize the mental syntheses; their action, so to speak, is analytic, as opposed to that of the will, of attention, of perception, which is synthetic.[18]

319   In his latest work, Janet extends his conception of the influence of affects to all possible kinds of psychopathic inferiority; he says, as earlier:

One of the marks of emotion is that it is accompanied by a decided lowering of the mental level. It brings about not only the loss of synthesis and the reduction to automatism which is so noticeable in the hysteric, but proportionately to its strength it gradually suppresses the higher phenomena and lowers tension to the level of the so-called inferior phenomena. Under the influence of emotion, mental synthesis, attention, the acquisition of new memories, are seen to disappear; with them diminish or disappear all the functions of reality, the feeling of and pleasure in reality, confidence and certitude. In place of these we observe automatic movements. . . .[19]

They have a particularly deleterious effect on the memory:

But this dissociative power which belongs to emotion is never more clearly displayed than in its effect on the memory. This dissociation can act on memories as they are produced, and constitute continuous amnesia; it can also act suddenly on a group of memories already formed.[20]

This effect is of special importance for us, as it explains the disturbance of memory in cases of emotional confusion and also

18 *L'Automatisme psychologique* (orig. 1889), p. 457.
19 *Les obsessions et la psychasthénie* (1903).
20 *Névroses et idées fixes* (1898) I, p. 144.

throws a remarkable light on the amnesias in Ganser's twilight states. In the Ganser syndrome which I analysed,[21] the most important feature was an anterograde amnesia which depended on affective elements. It was evident that the prolonged retrograde amnesia also present in this case covered all the unpleasant, powerfully affective events in the recent past. A relapse suffered by the patient while under observation was caused by a highly disagreeable affect. Phleps reports much the same thing in his above-mentioned study of the amnesia which, in his cases, was present for the causative affect (i.e., the Ljubljana earthquake).

320   The picture presented by the two patients mentioned above was one of gross feeble-mindedness, which obviously set in acutely and was not caused by any demonstrable illness. Further observation showed that the degree of feeble-mindedness actually present was not nearly so great. In many so-called malingerers who sham a high degree of stupidity we find the same outward behaviour, ranging from conscious, crassly nonsensical talk to the problematical borderline cases we have just been discussing. We find, however, in the twilight states described by Ganser, and recently by a number of other writers as well,[22] symptoms apparently indicating an almost impossibly high degree of feeble-mindedness, which in fact seems to be based on a purely functional deficiency that can be explained in terms of psychological motivations, as I have shown above. Ganser's "senseless answers" are of the same kind as those of the malingerer, only they arise from a twilight state that does not seem to me very far removed clinically from the cases of emotional stupidity reported earlier.[23] If we apply these remarks to the question of simulation, we can easily imagine that, in cases of emotional confusion following the excitements of

21 [See "A Case of Hysterical Stupor in a Prisoner in Detention," pp. 137ff., above. —EDITORS.]

22 Raecke, "Hysterischer Stupor bei Strafgefangenen" (1901); A. Westphal, "Über hysterische Dämmerzustände" (1903) ; and Lücke, "Über das Ganser'sche Symptom" (1903).

23 Of the 58 cases of simulation I collected, senseless answers corresponding to the Ganser complex were given in 29. The wide incidence of this symptom, which is the distinctive feature of the Ganser complex, is of importance in evaluating the state we are discussing.

arrest, interrogation, solitary confinement, etc.,[24] one person will hit on the idea of simulating insanity, while others will be inclined by the disposition I have described to lapse into a state of stupidity, in which, according to the mentality of the individual, conscious exaggeration, half-conscious play-acting, and hysterical automatisms will be fused in an impenetrable mixture, as in the picture of a traumatic neurosis, where the simulated and the hysterical are inseparably combined. I would even say that in my view it is but a step from simulation to Ganser's syndrome, and that Ganser's picture is simply a simulation that has slipped out of the conscious into the subconscious. That such a transposition is possible is proved by the cases of pathological swindling and pathological dreaminess. A contributory factor in all this is the abnormal influence of affects mentioned earlier. The literature on simulation leaves much to be desired in this respect, as very often in difficult cases the experts are only too delighted if they can succeed in unmasking one or the other symptom as simulated, and this leads to the false conclusion that everything else is "simulation" as well.

3

321   Here I would like to report on a case [25] which is instructive from several points of view.

322   J., born 1867, mill-hand. Heredity: father quick-tempered, mother's sister melancholic, committed suicide.

323   Nothing special is known of the patient's youth, except that his father early prophesied prison for him. At 16½, he ran away from home and began wandering, working in various textile-mills for about seven years. At 22 he married. The marriage was not happy, the fault being entirely his own. After two years he ran away from his wife, taking with him her savings, emi-

---

24 Schürmayer (*Lehrbuch der gerichtlichen Medicin,* orig. 1850, p. 378) says: "Very often a bad conscience has such a powerful effect on man's psychic life that it can feign the appearance of mental suffering. Dejection and irritable moods are found in practically all delinquents who are not professional criminals. Brooding is very common with them; for weeks on end they find no rest at night; they deteriorate physically, refuse nourishment, suffer from phobias, hallucinations, etc. Not only if they deny their crime do they become like this, but also if they confess it. They give quite absurd answers at the trial and are brought to the brink of despair under cross-examination."

25 [The case is detailed in the following paper.—EDITORS.]

grated to America, where he lived an adventurous and roving life. Came back after some years to Germany and tramped through it on foot. Arrived in Switzerland, he made it up again with his wife, who soon afterwards filed a petition for divorce. He ran away from her a second time, embezzled a sum of money entrusted to him by a fellow worker, spent the lot, and was arrested and sentenced to six months' hard labour (1892). After serving his sentence he resumed his roamings round Switzerland.

324   In 1894 he was sentenced to a month's imprisonment for theft. He is stated to have attempted suicide about this time (though not in connection with the punishment). After his release he took to the road again until 1896. From then on he worked uninterruptedly for four years in the same mill. In 1900 he married for the second time. This marriage, too, was unhappy. In 1901 he ran away from his wife, taking with him her savings to the value of 1200 francs. He went on a binge with it for a fortnight, then came back to his wife with 700 francs. Later (1902) he again took her money and ran away for good, committing two thefts when the money gave out. He was arrested soon afterwards and was sentenced to six months' hard labour for the first theft. It was not until the spring of 1903 that he was recognized and arrested for committing the second theft. At the first hearing he gave his particulars correctly, but denied the charge, involved himself in contradictions, and finally gave quite incoherent and confused answers. In solitary confinement he became restless at night, threw his shoes under the bed, covered the window with a blanket "because somebody was always trying to get in." The next day he refused food, saying it was poisoned. Gave no more answers, saw spiders on the wall. The second night, in a communal cell, he was restless, insisted that there was somebody under the bed. The third and fourth day he was apathetic, wouldn't answer, ate only when he saw the others eating, maintained that he had killed his wife and that there was a murderer under the bed with a knife. The prison doctor testified that the patient gave the impression of being a catatonic.

325   He was admitted on June 3, 1903, for a medical opinion.

326   The patient seemed listless, apathetic, his face rigid and stupid-looking. He could be made to answer only with difficulty.

Stated his name and address correctly, but appeared disoriented as to time and place. He gave five fingers held before him as four, ten as eight. Could not tell the time, named coins wrongly. He complied with requests correctly but carried them out in a senseless manner. When asked to lock the door he persistently tried to put the key in upside down. He opened a matchbox by breaking open the side. Strong suspicion of simulation. Was put in the observation room. Quiet at night, got up only once to move his bed, saying that the decoration on the ceiling would fall on top of him. Next day the same. At the examination he gave senseless answers and had to be pressed all the time. It was clear that he understood questions and requests quite well, but did his best to react to them in the most senseless way possible. Could not read or write. Took the pencil in his hand correctly, but held the book upside down, again opened the matchbox from the side, but lit a candle and put it out again correctly. He gave quite senseless names and values to coins.

327   Physical examination showed brisk reflexes of forearm and patella. Sensibility to pain seemed generally reduced, almost non-existent in some areas, so that there was only a scarcely perceptible reaction to really deep needle-pricks. The right pupil was somewhat larger than the left; reaction normal. The face was markedly asymmetrical.

328   This examination was carried out in a separate room on the same floor as the observation room in which the patient had been previously. When the examination was over we told him to find his way back to his room by himself. He went first in the opposite direction and rattled at a door he had not passed before, and was then told to go in the other direction. He now tried to open two more doors leading into rooms near the observation room. Finally he came to the right one, which was opened for him. He went in, but remained standing stiffly by the door. He was told to make his bed, but stood there without moving. His bed was in the corner facing him, clearly visible from where he stood. So we let him stand. He stood rigid on the same spot for an hour and a half, then suddenly turned pale, sweated profusely, asked the warder for some water, but fell unconscious to the floor before it arrived. After lying on the floor for ten minutes and recovering himself somewhat, he was put on his feet again, but rapidly went into another faint. He

was then put to bed. He didn't respond to questions at all, refused food. In the course of the afternoon he suddenly got up and threw himself against the door with considerable force, head foremost. When the warders tried to restrain him because of the danger of suicide, a hand-to-hand fight ensued, and it took several warders to subdue him. He was put in a strait-jacket, whereupon he quickly calmed down. On the night of June 4 he was quiet, turned his bed round only once. At the morning visit he suddenly seized hold of the doctor and tried to pull him into bed, then seized the warder. Hyoscine injection. On the following days he again showed dull and stupid behaviour with occasional attacks on doctors and warders, which however never came to dangerous blows. He seldom said anything, and what he said was always stupid and nonsensical, uttered in an unemotional, toneless voice. He refused all food for the first three days, but on the fourth day he began eating again, then better every day. On June 7 he suddenly demanded to have a vein opened because he had too much blood. When this was refused he sank back into a dull brooding. In contradiction to his apathetic behaviour, however, he seemed to take an interest in his surroundings; on seeing a patient in the bed next to him offering violent resistance to nasal feeding, he suddenly called out that they should tie the man's feet together, then it would go better. On June 8 he was given a strong dose of faradism. Poor reaction. He was told that this would happen daily from now on. On the morning of June 9 he was suddenly clear, demanded a private interview at which he made the following statement:

329   You know very well that there's not much the matter with me. When I was arrested I was so scared and upset thinking of my mother and sisters, they being so respectable, that I didn't know what to say, so I got the idea of making things look worse than they were. But I soon saw you weren't taken in, besides I felt such a fool playing the looney, also I got sick of always lying in bed. I'm sick of everything. I think all the time of killing myself. . . . I'm not crazy, yet I sometimes feel I'm not quite right in the head. I didn't do this to avoid going to jail, but for the sake of my family. I intended to go straight, and hadn't been in jail for nine years until last fall.

330   When asked how he came to simulate insanity, he said: "I was sorry for my old mother and regretted what I'd done. I was so frightened and upset that I thought, well, I'll make out I'm worse than I am. When I got back to the cell after the hearing I was at my wit's end. I would have done away with myself if I'd had a knife." He did not seem to be very clear about the purpose of the simulation, said he "just wanted to see what they would do with him." He gave adequate motives for his actions under simulated insanity. One striking thing was the statement that despite his four-day fast he had felt no appetite. A thorough anamnesis was now undertaken, a point of special interest being the patient's remark that he was always driven from place to place by an "inner unrest." As soon as he settled in one place for a time, the vague urge for freedom came over him again and drove him away. Throughout his story he showed a fair amount of uncertainty with regard to exact particulars (years and dates, etc.), but his uncertainty was quite surprising when it came to judging the time of recent happenings. Although otherwise properly oriented as to time, he maintained that he had been in the asylum for a fortnight (instead of six days). By the evening of the same day he had become uncertain again, and now wavered between ten and twelve days. He recounted the details of his stay in the asylum unclearly, and he no longer remembered many little incidents, trivial in themselves, that took place during his simulation; he also got various things muddled up in time. He had only a vague memory of his admission and the examination that followed; he knew that he had been told to put a key in the lock but thought he had done it correctly. He also remembered the examination on the next day, and said that the room had been full of doctors, about seven or eight of them (in reality there were five). He could still remember the details of the examination, but only when helped. With regard to the scene that took place afterwards, he made a statement to the following effect:

331   He remembered quite well how he came out from the examination; we had turned him loose and he lost his way in the big corridor. It seemed to him that in order to reach the examination room he had first gone up some steps. Then, when he found that he did not have to go down any steps, he thought we wanted to fool him and lead him to the wrong room. There-

fore, when we eventually took him to the sick room, he thought it was not the right room, nor did he recognize it again, especially when he saw that all the beds were occupied. (But his bed was empty and clearly visible.) That was why he remained standing by the door, then he felt queer and fell over. Only when he was put to bed did he notice that there was a bed unoccupied, that it was his bed and that he was in the right room.

332   He treated this intermezzo as if it were simply a misunderstanding, without the least suspicion that it was something pathological. The dangerous ruthlessness with which he banged his head against the door he explained as a deliberate attempt at suicide.

333   The next day, June 10, we got the patient to do simple additions based on Kraepelin's arithmetic tests. The average performance per minute was 28.1 additions, out of a total of 1,297 additions in 46 minutes. Increased practice produced an insignificant result: the difference between the average performance in the first and in the second halves amounted to only 1.5 in favour of the latter. So not only was the performance very poor, but the increased practice proved to be insufficient. In comparison with this relatively very easy work the number of errors was abnormally high: 11.2% of the additions were wrong; there were 1.5 errors per minute in the first half, 4.7 in the second half. These findings illustrate very well the rapid tiring of energy and attention despite the fact that there was no abnormal psychic fatigability. Optic perception was considerably reduced; the patient took a surprisingly long time to grasp the simple pictures in the Meggendorfer picture-book. His comprehension of things heard and read was likewise reduced. In reproducing a simple Aesop's fable, he left out important details and made up the rest. His retention, particularly for figures, was poor. As already indicated, his memory of events in the not so recent past was tolerably good, and he had retained a normal amount of school knowledge. No signs of mental defectiveness. No restriction of the field of vision. No other hysterical symptoms. Red-green blindness. Reflexes as at the first examination. No disturbances of sensibility other than general hypalgesia. About a week later (June 19) he was subjected to another thorough examination, having maintained correct behaviour in the meantime. No changes in his physical condition. Comprehen-

sion still not up to normal, but a decided improvement noticeable. No improvement in retention, but his work-curve showed a change for the better.

334   For the sake of clarity I give the results of the first and second tests side by side:

TABLE IV

	June 10	June 19
Average performance per minute	28.1	32.4
Average per minute for first half	27.4	31.9
Average per minute for second half	28.9	32.9
Error in total number of additions	11.2%	4.0%
Errors per minute for first half	1.5	1.1
Errors per minute for second half	4.7	1.5

335   The result of the second test shows an increase of 4.3 in the performance per minute as compared with the first series, and a very definite reduction in the number of errors. This result may be taken as confirming our clinical observations, in so far as a distinct improvement in the patient's energy and attention did in fact occur in the course of a week. Unfortunately, he was not given an association test. On June 23 he made an ostentatious attempt at suicide by slowly sawing through the skin of his left wrist with a sharp stone. Afterwards he put up a childish resistance to being bandaged.

336   The medical opinion stated that the patient must be assumed responsible for the theft, and therefore punishable, but only partially responsible for the offence of simulation.

337   There can be no doubt that the patient really did simulate. We have to admit that the simulation was excellent, so good, in fact, that, though we never lost sight of the possibility of simulation, we sometimes seriously thought of dementia praecox or of one of the deeper hysterical twilight states mentioned by Ganser. The consistent masklike rigidity of the face, the dangerous nature of his suicide attempt (banging his head against the door), the real fainting-fit, the—to all appearances—deep hypalgesia, are facts which cannot easily be explained as mere simulation. For these reasons we soon discarded the idea of pure simulation on the supposition that, if it really was a case of simulation, there must be some pathological factor in the

179

background which somehow lent a helping hand. Hence the sudden confession came as something of a surprise.

338   To judge by the material reported above, the patient was a degenerate. His forgetfulness and lack of concentration point to some form of hysterical inferiority, as grosser cerebral lesions seem ruled out by the anamnesis. Although we have no other direct indications of hysteria, this assumption nevertheless appears the most probable. (Hypalgesia is a mark of degeneracy which is also found elsewhere, particularly in criminals.) As we have seen, the patient got confused at the hearings, and explained that this was due to his state of desperation at the time, i.e., to a strong affect. The question of the logical motivation in this case still remains very obscure, and it looks as if he never came to a really clear decision to simulate. In his catamnesis he expressly emphasized and reiterated the strong affect he had experienced, and we have no grounds for not believing him in this point. It looks, rather, as if the affect played an important aetiological role. Although every feature of the resulting clinical picture is simulated (with the exception of the fainting-fit), almost every symptom is accompanied by phenomena that cannot be simulated. Lest I should lose my way in details, I shall confine myself solely to the fact, revealed by the catamnesis, that at least at times during his simulation the patient had a defective and faulty comprehension, as was borne out by the disturbance of attention noted on June 9. Accordingly, his memory of the critical period also proved strikingly vague. So, together with simulation, we find real and appreciable disturbances over the whole field of attention. These disturbances outlive the simulation and get very much better in the course of a week.

339   Earlier writers maintain that simulation has a deleterious effect on the mental state.[26] Allowing for diagnostic errors, the impairment will probably be confined to a disturbance of attention resembling hypnosis; this may offer a plausible explanation of our case.[27] It should not be forgotten, however, that an alteration of this kind never occurs as a result of a mere deci-

[26] Laurent, *Étude sur la simulation* (1866).
[27] As far back as 1856, Richarz, one of the experts in the Stockhausen case, expressed the view that outward behaviour exerts a great influence on mental activity. "Über psychische Untersuchungsmethoden" (1856).

sion: a certain predisposition is needed (what Forel would call a "dissociation"). And this is where, in my view, the decisive importance of affects comes in. As we have already explained at some length, affects have a dissociating (distracting) effect on consciousness, probably because they put a one-sided and excessive emphasis on a particular idea, so that too little attention is left over for investment in other conscious psychic activities. In this way all the more mechanical, more automatic processes are liberated and gradually attain to independence at the cost of consciousness. Here I would call attention to the beautiful experiments conducted by Binet [28] and Janet [29] on automatization in states of distractibility.

340   On this foundation Janet based his conception of the influence of affects, which holds that automatisms are one and all fostered by distractibility (i.e., feebleness of attention) and, as Binet expresses it, thrive chiefly on "the psychic shadow side." The assumption therefore is that certain ideas, which are present in consciousness at the same time as the affect but whose content need not be in any way related to it, become automatized. This assumption is amply confirmed by clinical experience, and particularly by the anamnesis of hysterical tics. Our case, showing a state of semi-simulation, has as its essential symptom a strong and stable disturbance of attention such as occurs in a hypnotized person, whose attention is likewise fixed in a certain direction. Any interesting object can so attract our attention that we are "transfixed" by it. Hysterical subjects go even further—they have a tendency to identify themselves more and more with the object of interest, so that not, as in normal persons, a limited, but an unlimited number of associations is produced with all their subconscious ties. Owing to the peculiar nature of hysteria, these ties can be severed only with the greatest difficulty. From this point of view I see our patient as a malingerer whose malingering worked only too well, in the sense that it slipped into the subconscious.

341   It would be desirable if more attention were paid to borderline cases of this kind. They might, perhaps, throw light on many things which at present are extremely difficult to explain. Here I am thinking of a case on which several medical opinions

[28] *Alterations of Personality* (orig. 1892).
[29] *L'Automatisme psychologique.*

have already been given by different German clinics. It concerns an accomplished swindler and thief who, the moment he is arrested, sinks into a catatonia-like stupor for months at a stretch. A medical opinion was also given on this case in our asylum. The moment he was released, the patient suddenly awoke from his profound, stuporous imbecility and took a polite and ceremonious farewell.

342   I have to thank my colleague Dr. Rüdin for the following case from the Heidelberg clinic, concerning an individual who had several previous convictions for theft and offences against decency. He had been epileptic for fourteen years. After his arrest for the second offence against decency in 1898, the patient could scarcely be made to answer at all, and a few days later became completely mutistic, remaining in a stuporous condition for seven months with unimpaired orientation. In 1901 he was caught *in flagrante* committing burglary with theft, became very excitable, then relapsed into his stuporous attitude for six weeks. In 1902 he was again arrested for theft, but this time he was very timid, silent, and gave only the briefest answers. Afterwards he became mutistic again, would not obey requests, but was otherwise quite orderly. A medical opinion was given on all three occasions and he was declared irresponsible on grounds of epileptic stupor.

343   Leppmann [30] reports the following case of "simulation": Mentally defective murderer, who, after making a full confession while in detention, lapsed into a stuporous condition ("depressive melancholia"). After the "depression" disappeared, he simulated imbecility with loss of memory for the recent past. Sentenced to fifteen years' imprisonment. After sentence was pronounced, the patient immediately relapsed into an apprehensive stupor.

344   Landgraf [31] reports a remarkable case of simulation in an habitual thief. In the second year of his ten-year prison sentence he became imbecilic, dumb, and kept his eyes closed. He spent eight years in this state, in the sick-ward, often not eating for weeks on end, usually sleepless, and playing at night with fruit-stones, buttons, etc. He put up a violent resistance to narcosis with chloroform. Afterwards he appeared paralysed for a fort-

[30] "Simulation von Geistesstörung" (1892).
[31] "Ein Simulant vor Gericht" (1884).

night, and was incontinent. On the expiry of his sentence he was sent home, imbecilic, blind, and dumb. Suddenly he left the house, committed a series of brilliant robberies. A fortnight later he was caught, and exhibited the same abnormal behaviour as before. Certified as a malingerer, he was sentenced to ten years' imprisonment. While in prison he was imbecilic, blind, deaf, and dumb for ten weeks, never once forgetting his role. Then he opened his eyes and began working, but remained deaf and dumb until his death.

345   Marandon de Montyel [32] reports on the following case: A menstruating, psychopathic woman tried to drown her four-year-old child, was arrested, made a full confession, and gave financial distress as the reason for her deed. A week later she recanted, shammed amnesia for the deed and its motive, acted like an imbecile, did not know either her surroundings or her past (anterograde amnesia). On account of simultaneous depression she was certified irresponsible and interned in a lunatic asylum, whereupon her condition improved. Several months later she came up before the public prosecutor, manifested violent fright, and the next day relapsed into "simulation."

346   The case of Reiner Stockhausen, on which monographs were written by Jacobi, Böcker, Hertz, and Richarz in 1855,[33] deserves mention. Stockhausen was a degenerate individual, many times convicted for theft and vagrancy. At one of the hearings he grew confused, gave strikingly senseless answers (Ganser), mostly negative in character: "It's all up, I must shoot myself, always in need of money, but there's nothing left, everything sold, everything gone," etc.[34] Later he was less informative, often irritable, muttering half-intelligible answers and repeating stereotyped phrases: "Haven't got nothing more, everything's sold, spent, gone on drink," etc. He was extremely unclean in his habits, slept little and fitfully.

347   Three of the medical opinions assumed simulation, one insanity. Thereupon he was sent to an asylum for a year for

32 "Folie simulée par une aliénée inculpée de tentative d'assassinat" (1882).

33 Cf. also Jessen's review of the study by Böcker, Hertz, and Richarz, *Reiner Stockhausen: ein actenmässiger Beitrag zur psychisch-gerichtlichen Medicin* (1855), and Richarz's reply, "Über psychische Untersuchungsmethoden" (1856). Also Snell, "Über Simulation von Geistesstörung" (1856).

34 It is surprising how often we find these negativisms in illnesses of this kind. Can it be due to emotional confusion, which inhibits the influx of associations?

observation. At first he was very excitable and inaccessible, then he "laid aside his stiffness and reserve more and more. He acted like a peaceable, fairly sociable, reasonable human being." But as soon as "the conversation turned to things which might be connected with the crime he was accused of, or as soon as his mental health or his emotional state was touched upon, he seemed to get violently indignant and at once began talking like a madman." A fourth medical opinion assumed simulation because the symptoms observed in the patient "did not accord with either melancholy, insanity, craziness, lunacy, or idiocy." He was sentenced to fifteen years' imprisonment, but it made no impression on him. Two years later he was still being examined off and on by the experts, and each time they found the logical continuation of symptoms that had already been in existence for three years.

348   Finally, I would like to mention a case published by Siemens [35] of a young day-labourer, who, falsely accused of murder, wept continuously while in detention, protested his innocence, then refused to answer any more, kept on lamenting his fate, would not eat, slept badly. When excited, he smashed things. Probably imbecilic (reading and writing very poor). On being admitted to the asylum he seemed very frightened, had to be questioned repeatedly before he would answer, said he was not ill but slept badly, refused food at first. Later he refused to answer at all, gazed at the doctors uncomprehendingly, but told the warder the story of his arrest. In spite of his apathetic behaviour he was provoked to laughter at the jokes of a maniac. Remained in this state for two months, until his release. Received the news of his release without moving a muscle. At home he was still taciturn for a time, indifferent, not working. Then he became normal again, complained about the wrong he had suffered, denied he was insane.

349   To our way of thinking, these cases can hardly be regarded as simulation. The characteristic feature of these disturbances is their dependence on external events, mostly of a highly affective nature; this, together with their clinical behaviour, brings them closer to the psychogenic ("hysterical") ailments described by Ganser and Raecke, and also (particularly the last case) to

[35] "Simulation von Seelenstörung" (1883), p. 41.

the kind of stupidity I would describe as "emotional." Freud has offered convincing proof that the chief aetiological role in psychogenic disturbances is played by affects. It would therefore be worth while to pay more attention than we have done hitherto to repressed affects in criminals who exhibit doubtful states. We already have a number of pertinent observations; for instance, the intercurrent Ganser syndrome noted by Westphal [36] can be traced back to emotion, and a similar case is reported by Lücke.[37] The recurrence of a Ganser syndrome observed by me [38] conformed absolutely to the Freudian mechanism of repressed affect. One may therefore, with some justification, regard these peculiar states as due to the prolonged influence of affects, and in psychogenic disorders it is not surprising if all kinds of "faked" symptoms creep in, depending on the environment.

350   It is impossible to discuss the question of simulation on the basis of the existing case material without making certain observations of a general nature.

351   First, as regards the material, one can scarcely imagine any that is more unequal and more difficult to evaluate. In many cases the method of description is at fault, since the main stress is laid on the obvious symptoms, while the other symptoms— the hysterical ones especially—come off very badly. The investigation and "unmasking" of symptoms often consist in technical tricks, if not in old-fashioned cruelties like cold showers, etc. The standpoint of the earlier writers (which has even been passed on to some of the books now in vogue)—namely, that anything which does not fit into the known clinical pictures or into a dogmatic system of ideas is not a disease but simulation— is depressing and highly unscientific. Particularly damaging to description and investigation alike is a diagnostic optimism,[39] that accords very ill with the facts. From time to time we meet with cases of simulation which can lead the most experienced doctors by the nose for a long time. There was, for instance,

36 "Über hysterische Dämmerzustände" (1903).

37 "Über das Ganser'sche Symptom" (1903).

38 [See "A Case of Hysterical Stupor in a Prisoner in Detention," pp. 137ff., above. —EDITORS.]

39 Cf. the following statements: "To unmask simulation, all that is needed is plain, sound common sense" (Claus, "Ein Fall von simulierter Geistesstörung," 1876, p. 153.) "So the question of simulation presents fewer difficulties in practice than it does in theory" (Bolte, "Über einige Fälle von Simulation," 1903, p. 47).

Billod's patient,[40] who simulated nine times with success; a case of Laurent's [41] simulated successfully for two years; and a case, "unmasked" on a second examination as a skilled malingerer, who had been declared incompetent on the authority of a very experienced doctor.[42] So we have every reason for caution.

352   Secondly, there is another point worth mentioning: the concept of simulation is not understood by all the authors in the same way. Fürstner [43] mentions the following case of "simulation" by seventeen-year-old Sabina S., who, spurred on by reading the life of Katharina Emmerich,[44] staged an enormous swindle by passing herself off as a saint. She abstained apparently from all food, twice drove nails through her insteps to the soles of her feet, and performed all sorts of miracles which fooled the doctors and officials and created a great sensation. When examined by Fürstner, she induced true-to-life tonic and clonic spasms of the eye-muscles and in the face and throat muscles. In the asylum, of course, her mystic abstention from food, etc., turned out to be the sheerest swindle, very cleverly done. The purpose of the whole undertaking, apparently, was that she wanted to stay with a relative, who functioned as a priest.

353   Such cases can hardly be described as simulation, for the means employed bear no relation to the ends but are merely symptoms of a known mental disorder of which history affords us hundreds of examples. When a criminal simulates insanity, that is a comparatively convenient and simple means of getting transferred to an asylum, from which he can escape more easily. Here the means are adapted to the ends. But when an hysterical girl tortures herself in order to appear interesting, both means and ends are the outcome of some morbid mental activity. An hysterical haemorrhage of the lung is something simulated, "faked," but that does not make the patient a simulant; she really is ill, only not ill with consumption. If the doctor calls her a simulant, he does so merely because he has not understood the symptom properly, i.e., has not recognized it as hysterical.

40 "Rapport medico-légal sur un cas de simulation de folie" (1868).
41 Emile Laurent, "Un Détenu simulant la folie pendant trois ans" (1888).
42 Wilbrand and Lotz, "Simulation von Geisteskrankheit bei einem schweren Verbrecher" (1889).
43 "Über Simulation geistiger Störungen" (1888).
44 [Cf. Jung, Symbols of Transformation, pars. 435ff.—EDITORS.]

When Sabina S. faked miracles she was not a simulant, if by this term we mean a person who is genuinely healthy and whose actions are intended to conceal his inner healthiness, whereas the abnormal actions of Sabina S. were precisely what revealed her inner morbidity. In the same way hysterics do not lie, even though what they say is not true in the objective sense. Wherever hysteria is involved, the term "simulation" should be used with caution in order to avoid misunderstandings.

354   I would like to sum up the results of my work in the form of the following conclusions:

    1. There are people in whom the after-effect of violent emotions shows itself in the form of a lasting confusion, which one could describe as "emotional stupidity."

    2. Affects, by acting specifically upon the attention, favour the appearance of psychic automatisms in the widest sense.

    3. A certain number of cases of simulation are probably due to the after-effect of violent emotions and their automatization (or to auto-hypnosis) and must therefore be termed pathological.

    4. Ganser's complex in prisoners can probably be explained in the same way and must be regarded as an automatized symptom closely related to simulation.

355   In conclusion, I would like to thank my chief, Professor Bleuler, for his kindness in allowing me to make use of the above material.

A MEDICAL OPINION ON A CASE
OF SIMULATED INSANITY [1]

356   Simulation of insanity is in general a rather rare phenomenon, being confined almost entirely to persons in detention
and convicts. For the ordinary public the fear of the lunatic
asylum is too great and this particular form of simulation too
inconvenient for it to be worth their while to seek illicit advantages in this way. The sort of people who take to simulation
have been found by experience to be composed for the most part
of individuals who show unmistakable signs of mental and physical degeneracy. Experience shows, therefore, that simulation
generally rests on a pathological foundation. This fact explains
why the recognition of simulated insanity is one of the most difficult tasks of the diagnostic art. If the simulation is recognized
and proved, it immediately raises the question of soundness or
unsoundness of mind, and the answer to this is beset with all
kinds of difficulties.

357   Apart from cases of exaggeration of real or imaginary symptoms, we also find a number of peculiar mental states in degenerate subjects whose cause can be traced back to the powerful affects produced by the arrest, trial, and solitary confinement.
Even among normal persons are many whose capacity to assimi-
late strong affects is much worse, and who are unduly depressed

1 [First published as "Ärztliches Gutachten über einen Fall von simulierter
geistiger Störung," *Schweizerische Zeitung für Strafrecht* (Zurich), XVII (1904),
55–75.—EDITORS.]

188

or irritated by unpleasant emotions and cannot recover their composure for a long time afterwards. In the domain of psychopathic inferiority, that broad and undefined zone separating the "healthy" from the "morbid," we find the various types of normality caricatured, and here the powerful affects manifested by normal individuals take on a character that is excessive and odd in every respect. The affective states are often abnormally prolonged or abnormally intense; they exert an influence on other parts of the psyche or on physical functions which are not directly touched by normal affects. Strange, sudden alterations of psychic behaviour may be produced in this way, and they are often so striking that they immediately make one think of simulation. Such emotional-changes are observed among feeble-minded persons especially, mostly in the form of extreme imbecility. The possibility that these states may occasionally be combined with conscious exaggeration makes the picture even more complicated. It is of some practical importance not only for the doctor, but also for the examining official, to be able to recognize psychological possibilities of this kind. The following case seems to me very instructive in this respect, as it concerns a prisoner who showed psychopathic inferiority with half-conscious simulation. The psychological and psychiatric side of this case has already been subjected to close study, and the findings were recently published in the *Journal für Psychologie und Neurologie*.[2] Here I am only putting the medical opinion on record. For the psychological discussion of this case I must refer the reader to the publication mentioned below.

358   The case was referred to us by the District Attorney, Zurich.

REPORT

359   We were asked to give an opinion on the mental state of I. G., of Rothrist, Canton Aargau, born March 24, 1867, mill-hand, and in particular to answer the following questions:

1. Is the respondent mentally ill?

2. If Dr. S. is correct in his suppositions, from what other mental illness might the respondent be suffering?

3. Since when is this condition presumed to have existed?

2 ["On Simulated Insanity," the foregoing paper in this volume.—EDITORS.]

360   The material on which our opinion is based consists of documents relating to the theft of a bicycle, of which the respondent is accused; documents of the criminal court, Schwyz, relating to theft in 1902; documents of the district court, Hinwil, relating to theft in 1894; documents of the district court, Baden, relating to embezzlement in 1892; a written statement by the respondent's brother; the deposition of police constable S.; and observations made in the asylum.

1. *Previous History*

361   The father of the respondent is stated to have been a respectable but rather quick-tempered man. The mother is alive and healthy. A brother of the father is alleged to be a religious crank. A sister of the mother committed suicide as a result of melancholia. Respondent has no children. His first wife had a still-birth.

362   Nothing special is known of the respondent's youth, except that he was a naughty boy who was often told by his father that he would end up in prison. He attended school for eight years. At fifteen he entered a textile mill, where he worked for a year and a half. One day he ran away from the mill and found similar work in Turgi. He remained there for sixteen months, and states that he occasionally sent money home to his parents. Then he wandered off again and found another job in a textile mill in Wollishofen, where he remained about five months. After that he wandered about for "many weeks" and came to Linthal, worked for a year and a half, wandered off again, came to Ziegelbrücke, where he stayed about three years. At 22 he married. The marriage was not happy; after two years he ran away from his wife, taking with him her hard-earned savings, and emigrated to America, where he lived a roving and adventurous life, and eventually, after many wanderings, found work as a stoker on a European steamer which took him to Germany. From Bremen he wandered on foot all through Germany into Switzerland, came to Wald, worked there for six months, and was also reconciled with his wife. The reconciliation did not last long, however. After a time the wife filed for a divorce, which was granted. To this end she made use of the opportunity afforded her by the respondent's first offence. Apparently, in

consequence of irregular employment, he had gone to Baden in Aargau, where he found work in a textile mill. He absconded on November 13, 1892, with 275 francs, which had been entrusted to him by his room-mate, as the respondent had at his disposal a lockable trunk. He travelled with his booty to Zurich, then to Mülhausen, Colmar, Strassburg, Belfort, Montbéliard, La Chaux-de-Fonds, Bern, and Glarus, where he was arrested on November 27, 1892, just as he was about to draw the dole. The money he embezzled had all been spent. He is also said to have had a previous conviction with ten days' imprisonment for fraud, some time in 1892. He received six months' "correctional punishment" and was deprived of his civil rights for three years. After serving his sentence he roamed round Switzerland aimlessly, working here and there for short periods in various jobs. On March 15, he was sentenced to one month's imprisonment by the district court at Hinwil, for having pocketed a pair of pruning shears to the value of fr. 4.50. From the certificate of good conduct applied for on this occasion it appears that he had been apprehended "shortly before" in a "totally destitute condition" in Canton Glarus and had been sent back to his home parish; also that he first attempted suicide and showed himself very refractory in transit, so that he had to be locked up in the local jail, from which he broke out during the night and escaped.

363   According to his own statement, he wandered or rather tramped round all the cantons of Switzerland until 1896, when he again found regular work in a textile mill in Schwanden. States that he remained there for four years and eight months, and married again in the autumn of 1900. The marriage was childless and not very happy.

364   In the summer of 1901 he ran away on the Monday following a Sunday night debauch, taking with him a savings book belonging to his wife, showing funds amounting to 1200 francs, which he unlawfully drew at the bank in Glarus. Accordingly a description of him was circulated in the police gazette in Zurich. After a fortnight he came back again and gave his wife 700 francs. The rest he kept for himself. Eight weeks later he again ran away, ostensibly to look for work, taking with him another 400 francs. When, after a little while, he returned, he pretended to his wife that he had no more money left. But

evidently he still had about 500 francs. After ten months he ran away again, always lodging in inns, and on September 15, 1902, stole a bicycle standing in front of a house, and on October 26 another bicycle from the corridor of a public-house in Siebnen, Canton Schwyz, valued at 200 francs, rode it to Lucerne, and was arrested on October 28, 1902, as he was about to sell it for 120 francs. He was sentenced to six months in the workhouse on November 22, 1902.

365   Later it was learned that he sold the first bicycle to a mechanic in Glarus for 70 francs, or rather for a pair of field-glasses valued at 45 francs and the rest in cash.

366   When questioned by the District Attorney on May 29, 1903, the respondent gave his particulars correctly, but denied the charge of theft and maintained that he had bought the bicycle from one Emil H. at the last church fête in Wädenswil. From then on his answers were unclear and inconsistent.

367   Previous to this the respondent is stated not to have given any impression of abnormality. Only in solitary confinement did he become restless at night. He threw his shoes under the bed, covered the window with a blanket "because somebody was always trying to get in." The next morning he refused nourishment, saying the food was poisoned. Henceforward he spoke only when pressed, said there was a spider on the wall, that spiders were poisonous, and that this was a sign that he was being poisoned. On the night of May 31 he slept in a cell for four persons. He was restless at night, repeatedly asserting that there was someone under the bed. On June 2 his behaviour was still the same; he was apathetic, did not speak to the other prisoners, but ate when he saw the others eating. The District Medical Officer testified that the respondent's remarks ("they wanted to do him in because he had killed his wife," "he had seen a murderer under the bed with a knife," etc.) and his general behaviour gave the impression of a catatonic state.

2. Observations Made in the Asylum

368   On his admission on June 3, 1903, the respondent sat there listlessly and could only with difficulty be made to answer. The expression of the face was dull and masklike. He gave his name and address correctly, knew he was in Zurich, but otherwise did

not appear to be oriented as to time and place, and could not state the year he was born. He persistently gave 5 fingers held before him as 4, 10 as 8. He could not tell the time, said 5:30 for 5:50, 3:30 for 7:30, and when shown 3:30 said "also 3:30." He recognized only 5-franc pieces; 1-franc pieces he called 20 cents. On being given a key and asked to lock the door, he put the key in upside down. He tried to open a matchbox sideways. He was then put to bed. During the night he was quiet, but moved his bed once, remarking that the plaster rose on the ceiling would fall on top of him.

369   At the examination next morning he gave scanty answers, had to be continually pressed. He seemed unclear about time and place, said he was in a hospital in Zurich. He evidently understood all the questions quite well but gave senseless answers, all very curt and confined to the fewest possible words.

370   Examples:

What is the name of this hospital? — *Zurich Hospital.*
What sort of people are in your room? — *Sick people.*
What is the matter with them? — *They can't walk.*
Aren't they wrong in the head? — *No, in the legs.*
How long have you been here? — *Two days.*
What day is it? — *Saturday.*
What day did you arrive? — *Wednesday.*
What day is it, then? — *Saturday.* (It was Thursday.)
What day is it? — *Sunday.*
What holiday was it last Sunday? (Whitsun.) — *Singing-festival in Zurich. I heard singing.*
Where were you last Sunday? — *In Zurich.*
What did you do? — *Nothing.*
Where do you live? — (No answer.)
Glarus? Wädenswil? — *Glarus.*
Where were you before you came here? — *Zurich.*
What did you do in Zurich? Did you go anywhere? — *Wandered around.*

371   Respondent gave no more answers, despite energetic pressing. He was then asked to do various things, and it was noted that he understood the requests correctly, as previously the questions, but carried them out in a deliberately senseless manner.

193

372 He was asked to write the word "Rothrist." He at once took the pen in his hand and made a zigzag line.

373 He was asked to read. He held the book upside down, tried to read from right to left. Called the letter O a "ring," a 9 (inverted) "5", a 1 a "line," a 6 (inverted) "3", a 4 (inverted) "2", a 3 (inverted) no answer, a 2 (inverted) "2", a 3 (inverted) "5".

374 Said spontaneously that he "couldn't read it."

375 He was told to hold the book properly. He turned over the pages. The book was then placed before him. Question: What's that? Reply: "What are you? Why are you here?" He could not be made to read.

376 He was asked to lock the door with a key. He turned the key to the right to lock, to the left to open, both times with a show of strength. (N.B.: Lock opens to the right.)

377 He was asked to open a matchbox. First he tried, as yesterday, to break it open from the side, but on being encouraged opened it properly, struck a match, also lighted a candle and put it out, both correctly.

378 He was asked to open the blade of a pocket-knife: opened the corkscrew.

379 He was asked to open a spectacles case and put on the spectacles. Spontaneous remark: "I don't want any. They aren't spectacles." Turned the case over in his fingers, then opened it correctly when shown how to. Tried to put the spectacles on upside down.

380 He was given a purse, with the question: What is that? "A little box." What's in it? "Cigars." Tried to open it by pulling off the clasp.

381 Some money (fr. 3.40) was put in front of him with the question: How much is that? "5 francs."

382 He was shown a gold piece (fr. 20) and asked: How much is that worth? "Nothing."

383 Physical examination showed brisk forearm and patellar reflexes.

384 Sensibility to pain seemed to be generally reduced, in places almost non-existent, e.g., on the right forearm. Pupils reacted to pain; right pupil somewhat larger than the left; both showed normal reaction. Face rather asymmetrical, the left eyebrow standing higher than the right. Badly swollen veins on the left leg. On the left side of the chest, over the second and third ribs,

there was a scar 5½ cm. long and almost 3 cm. broad (caused by the alleged attempt at suicide).

385   This examination was carried out in a separate room on the same floor as the observation room where the respondent had been since the previous evening. When the examination was over he was told to find his way back to his room by himself. He went first in the opposite direction and rattled at a door he had not passed before, and was then told to go in the other direction. He now tried to open two more doors leading into rooms near the observation room. Finally he came to the right one, which was opened for him. He went in, but remained standing by the door. He was told to make his bed, but stood there rigid, without moving. His bed was in the corner facing him, clearly visible from where he stood. We let him stand. He stood for 1½ hours on the same spot, turned pale, sweated profusely, asked the warder for some water, and suddenly toppled over before it arrived, slipping to the floor full-length by the stove. His face was pale purple and covered with sweat. He said nothing and did not react when spoken to, although he was conscious. After ten minutes he was put on his feet again, but hardly was he upright than he turned pale, his pulse very weak, soft, rather rapid. He was then put to bed, where he lay quiet and silent.

386   Towards four o'clock in the afternoon he suddenly got up, went to the door and banged it violently with his head, then took a run and threw himself head foremost against the door with considerable force. (According to the head warder, there was such a racket that he thought "everything was falling to bits" in the observation room.) When they tried to restrain him he struggled so much that he had to be straitjacketed, whereupon he calmed down at once.

387   On the night of June 4 he was quiet, turned his bed round only once, and then didn't want to go back again. At the morning visit he suddenly seized hold of the doctor and tried to pull him into bed, then seized the warder and fought with him. He was given a narcotic by injection. On the following days he exhibited the same dull, apathetic behaviour with occasional attacks on doctors and warders, though the attacks were confined to wrestling and never came to blows. He seldom said anything, and what he said was always stupid and nonsensical,

195

and was uttered in an unemotional, toneless voice. He ate nothing for the first three days. On the fourth day he began to eat a little, then better every day. On June 7 he suddenly announced to the doctor that he had too much blood, and would they please open a vein—a request which was naturally not granted. It was also observed that in contradiction to his apparent apathy he took a lively interest in what was going on around; for instance he suddenly called out that they ought to tie up the feet of a patient who was offering violent resistance to nasal feeding, then it would go better.

388   On June 8 he was given a strong dose of faradism, and was told that henceforth this would happen daily and would do a great deal to improve his condition, particularly his speech.

389   On the morning of June 9 he was suddenly clear, demanded an interview with the director. He was taken to a separate room, where he delivered the following oration:

390   "You know very well that there's not much the matter with me. When I was arrested I was so scared and upset thinking of my mother and sisters, they being so respectable, that I didn't know what to say, so I got the idea of making things look worse than they were. But I soon saw you weren't taken in, besides I felt such a fool playing the looney, also I got sick of always lying in bed. I'm sick of everything. I thought of killing myself. This week I asked to be bled and I planned to fight against being bandaged and so make the blood run. I'm not crazy, yet I sometimes feel I'm not quite right in the head. I didn't do this to avoid going to jail, but for the sake of my family. . . . I hadn't been in jail for nine years until last fall." (Wept.)

391   When asked how he came to simulate insanity, he said: "I was sorry for my old mother and regretted what I'd done. I was so frightened and upset that I thought, well, I'll make out I'm worse than I am. When I got back to the cell after the hearing I was at my wits' end. I'd have jumped out of the window but for the bars. I thought I can't bring any more disgrace on my mother and sisters. I'd have had a nice life if only I could have gone straight. I've always gone on the booze instead of working. My wife always told me I was wrong in the head—naturally, if your head's full of booze." He went on to say that he hadn't really known what would happen to him if he simulated, he just wanted to see what we would do. Other people had simulated and got

away with it. He didn't know he would be taken to Burghölzli, he thought it would be the cantonal hospital.

392   In this way he arrived at the idea of pretending to be mad. He hadn't eaten anything because he thought he would starve himself. (Another time he said he had lost his appetite.) He had been in despair and he still was; for all he cared we could open a vein today, the only reason why he had not killed himself before was that he did not want to bring more disgrace on his mother by committing suicide.

393   He said he feigned fear of poisoning because it gave him an excuse for not eating. He simulated hallucinations because he knew that mad people often saw such things. When he was moved to a communal cell he was obliged to start eating as soon as he saw the others eating. During this recital the respondent repeatedly burst into tears and was obviously in a very penitent mood.

394   On this and the following day (June 9–10) he was subjected to a thorough examination.

395   Pupillary, patellar, and other reflexes showed no change. When tested for sensibility to pain the respondent definitely reacted, but it was clear that sensibility in general was considerably reduced in a uniform way over the entire surface of the body (hypalgesia). The visual field showed no restriction, but he was found to have typical red-green blindness. Apperception was considerably reduced, so that simple pictures were perceived very slowly and faultily. If he was shown a picture long enough, he understood it and could describe it correctly. When Aesop's fable of the ass in the lion's skin was read out to him, he understood the meaning but reproduced the story very inaccurately:

396 An ass found a lion's skin with a dead lion inside it. [This passage was a spontaneous addition of the respondent's.] Then he took the skin and wrapped himself in it. He ran round roaring like a lion. Then the other animals tore him to pieces. The meaning is: Do not make yourself bigger than you are.

397   His retention was likewise reduced, and this was particularly apparent in reckoning, as he easily forgot one or the other component of a simple sum. For instance, he could not calculate 147 + 178; even simpler sums were difficult for him, e.g., "15 +

$17 = 42$—yes, 42, no, 37." He reckoned as follows: "$15 + 15 = 30 + 7 = 37$—no, 32." Division was the worst; he could not solve $92 \div 8$. Apart from poor aptitude for arithmetic, the fault lay chiefly with his reduced retention, i.e., a so-called bad memory.

398   Otherwise he showed medium intelligence and a knowledge that was sufficient and appropriate to his circumstances.

399   After this he composed an autobiography, running to five and a-half pages, in which he accepted the chief blame for his unsuccessful life and also for the unhappy outcome of his two marriages. In the same remorseful and contrite tone he gave an oral account of his life-history, emphasizing again and again that he alone was to blame for his criminal career, that he had drunk foolishly and neglected his work, that an inner unrest always drove him on his way and prevented him from settling down with his wife; he had never been able to "submit to the yoke." Every so often he had to run away, driven by a vague urge for freedom.

400   The story of his life was correct so far as it could be checked objectively. He was at fault only in the dates. He also told the story of his various thefts faithfully and without cover-up. He was surprisingly uncertain, however, with regard to the temporal location of recent happenings. He was unsure whether he had been three or four days in Selnau; on the morning of June 9 he was definite that he had been a fortnight in the asylum; later, towards afternoon, he thought it was certainly twelve days at least, and in the evening he hovered between ten and twelve days. Otherwise he was well oriented as to time. He recounted the details of his present stay in a confused manner, and he no longer remembered many little incidents that took place during his simulation; he also got various things muddled up in time. He had only a vague memory of his admission and the examination that followed; he knew that he had been told to put a key in the lock but thought he had done it correctly. He remembered also the examination on the next day, and said that the room had been full of doctors, about seven or eight of them (in reality there were five). He could still remember the details of the examination, but only when helped. With regard to the scene that took place afterwards, he made a statement to the following effect:

401   He knew quite well how he came out after the examination, we turned him loose and he lost his way in the big corridor. It seemed to him that in order to reach the examination room he had first gone up some steps. Then, when he found he did not have to go down any steps, he thought we wanted to fool him and lead him to the wrong room. Therefore, when we took him to the sick room, he thought it was not the right room, nor did he recognize it again, especially when he saw that all the beds were occupied. That was why he remained standing by the door. We let him stand there, and then he felt queer and fell over. Only when he was put to bed did he notice that there was a bed unoccupied, that it was his bed and that he was in the right room.

402   The fact that he banged his head against the door so forcefully was, he explained, due to his desperation; he was in such a state that he didn't care if he bashed his head in.

403   (Respondent would not admit the suicide attempt reported in the documents. He stated that he had merely been monkeying about with a revolver, that it had gone off, and that he had no intention of committing suicide.)

404   In order to obtain a more accurate picture of his condition at this time (June 10), we took what is known as his "work-curve." We put him to adding up single figures for 46 minutes and then plotted the results (performance and error) in a curve.[3] The striking thing is the low level of performance per minute despite increasing practice, and the large, rapidly increasing number of errors. This behaviour was not the result of fatigue; it reflected a state of peculiar psychic debility and uncertainty.

405   On the following days the respondent was left to his own devices. He passed the time in reading and playing cards, and

[3] The curve was so plotted that the number of additions carried out per minute was written down as one co-ordinate. Correlatively, the number of errors was also plotted in a curve. The curves were appended to the medical opinion. In place of the curves I give here only the average figures as a guide:

	June 10	June 19
Average performance per minute	28.1	32.4
Average per minute for 1st half of total number	27.4	31.9
Average per minute for 2nd half of total number	28.9	32.9
Error in total number of additions	11.2%	4.0%
Errors per minute for 1st half of additions	1.5	1.1
Errors per minute for 2nd half of additions	4.7	1.5

complained off and on of vague ailments ("weak back," etc.), grumbled about the warders and the asylum, saying that there was nothing whatever the matter with half the so-called patients here, etc.

406   On June 19 he was subjected to another thorough examination.

407   His physical condition showed no change.

408   In his comprehension there was a distinct improvement, for although his perception was still uncertain and not quick enough, it was quicker and more accurate than before.

409   No change could be demonstrated in his retention. Memory and calculation were just as uncertain as on June 9.

410   On the other hand, the work-curve (taken on June 17) showed a distinct improvement. Not only was the average performance higher, there was also a considerable drop in the number of errors.

411   Respondent now exhibited a continual mood of mild depression and often asked when he could go away.

412   On June 23 he suddenly made an attempt at suicide by slowly sawing through the skin of his left wrist with a sharp stone, near the artery. On beginning to bleed he asked the warder for a knife, because he hadn't "finished it off properly," whereupon, of course, the attempt was discovered. At first he resisted when we tried to stitch and bandage the wound, but gave way at once when we threatened to have him held down by four warders.

3. *Opinion*

413   The following points are clear from the material set forth under sections 1 and 2:

414   Respondent has always inclined to lead a work-shy, vagrant existence. He never remained anywhere for long, was continually moving about and changing his job; he could not endure the settled life of marriage, quarrelled with his wife, embezzled her money, and squandered it. If opportunity were favourable, he several times resorted to stealing. His characteristic instability was, in his opinion, due to an inner unrest which drove him forth again and again, even from jobs that might have suited him. He himself was aware of this peculiarity,

and realized also that he had only himself to blame for his unfortunate career.

415   Investigation shows that even apart from this peculiarity the respondent is not quite normal. He exhibits a number of deviations from the norm which, if not exactly pathological, must nevertheless be described as signs of degeneracy; for instance, general reduction of sensibility to pain (hypalgesia), red-green blindness (Daltonism), reduced attention, poor comprehension of things seen and heard, characterized by retardation and lack of accuracy.

416   This abnormal condition comes nearer to congenital degeneracy than to any known mental illness. Owing to our meagre knowledge of the family circumstances no strong hereditary influences could be proved, but they may nevertheless exist.

417   One can, if necessary, distinguish certain groups among hereditarily tainted persons which correspond to definite clinical pictures, according to the way the symptoms are constellated. The respondent comes closest to hysteria, since his chief symptoms—instability of character and forgetfulness—play a particularly prominent role in hysteria. Red-green blindness, dulling of the senses in general, are symptoms that are found in various forms of degeneracy (or "psychopathic inferiority"). His easy emotional excitability, his inquisitive interest in the asylum's affairs, and his rash judgments, though they cannot with certainty be described as hysterical, nevertheless give that impression. On the other hand, the attempt at suicide, which stopped just at the point where it began to be dangerous, has a definitely hysterical character. (This is not to say that a depression cannot sometimes reach such a pitch that the attempt has a more than merely theatrical outcome.)

418   In view of the fact that the respondent comes of an otherwise reputable family and is not just a moral degenerate, but was prevented from leading a steady and useful life mainly on account of his abnormal psychic disposition, we must assume that the reasons he gave for simulation, particularly the powerful feeling of remorse, were in fact sufficient, although the psychology of it is not altogether clear. Indeed, it is remarkable how vague he was in this connection, for he had no very clear idea of what he really wanted to gain by simulation, and of what would happen to him if he simulated. It is probable that

the thought uppermost in his mind was that his offence would be forgiven him; but, judging by what he told us, he had at the time absolutely no conception of the consequences of his actions. It looks very much as if he were following an inexplicable urge to extricate himself from his simulation rather than a clear train of thought.

119   With regard to the outward appearance of his condition at that time, it must be emphasized that apart from a number of minor inconsistencies and improbabilities which always kept us on the watch for simulation, the respondent acted the part of a madman extremely well on the whole—so well, in fact, that there could be no mistaking a distinct affinity with certain hysterical twilight states on the one hand and with certain forms of dementia praecox (tension neurosis) on the other. The dull facial expression, the ruthlessness with which he banged his head against the door, his real fainting-fit, all these are facts which it would be difficult to explain as pure simulation. So even at this stage we had the impression that, if simulation were present at all, there must still be some pathological factor in the background which enabled the respondent to play his strenuous role. Further observation fully confirmed this conjecture. According to his own subsequent confession, it was an intentionally simulated insanity, but, without his either knowing it or willing it, it succeeded so well that it almost turned into real insanity—that is to say, it began to take on pathological features, because the meticulous imitation of a semi-imbecilic state had an effect on the normal activity of the mind, and this showed itself in various symptoms which could no longer be simulated. What the respondent said about the scene in the observation room is proof of this. His bad memory, which moreover was particularly defective for the whole period of simulation, cannot be held responsible for the above report of the incident, since it was a quite positive memory of a falsification of perception which cannot be regarded as normal and which sufficiently explains the oddity of the situation at the time. We see from this that the respondent already had a pathologically indistinct and definitely falsified perception of his environment. Further proof of the supposed disturbance of consciousness is furnished by the respondent's obvious helplessness, which led to

his fainting-fit. He could easily have altered his position or done something to avoid fainting from discomfort, without necessarily stepping outside his role. The remark that he had no appetite at the beginning of his hunger-strike is also significant. All this suggests that the intention to simulate insanity became a powerful auto-suggestion which blurred his consciousness and in this way influenced his actions regardless of his conscious will. This also gives us the key to his histrionic feats. There are numerous cases known to science of deceptions which started off as conscious and became, by auto-suggestion, involuntary and unconscious, and also much more convincing and consistent. Into this category fall, in particular, all cases of pathological lying (*pseudologia phantastica*).

420   These phenomena are observed as a rule in hysterically disposed persons, which is an additional reason for suspecting the respondent of some hysterical degeneracy.

421   Although certain episodes doubtless came about only as a result of the restriction and blurring of consciousness, it is not surprising that the respondent occasionally dropped the mask and showed an interest in his surroundings that contradicted his apparent apathy.

422   The most probable hypothesis is that he acted the greater part of his seeming insanity with conscious intent, but that certain elements in the simulation worked on him so convincingly that they acquired the force of an overmastering suggestion and so induced a genuine auto-hypnosis. That these abnormal psychic processes had an injurious effect on his mental activity in other ways is shown by the difference between the work-curve on the second day after simulation ceased and nine days later.

423   As is clear from the respondent's own statements, the development of simulation was attended by strong affects. Affects always have a disturbing influence on consciousness, as they place undue emphasis on feeling-toned thought-processes and thus obscure any others that may be present. Hence it is understandable that the respondent was not very clear as to what he wanted to gain by simulation. In our opinion, the initial affects were the source of the overmastering suggestion to simulate that later ensued. That this phenomenon of partly conscious, partly

unconscious simulation could come about at all was evidently due to the respondent's hysterical disposition, and the most outstanding feature of this disposition is an abnormal dissociability of consciousness, which, the moment a strong affect appears, can easily lead to mental confusion and the formation of suggestions which are very difficult to combat. Altogether, the psychological mechanism of his simulation seems to us to suggest that the initial psychic weakness was the final cause of the idea of simulation. The respondent was probably aware of the confusion wrought by his emotions, and he may have converted it into the wish to go mad rather than bring more disgrace on his mother through another penal conviction.

424 However that may be, it is sufficient to show that his simulation had pathological features and that it appears to have been influenced, even in origin, by causes that were not quite normal.

425 We have no reason to suppose that the same or a similar disturbance of consciousness existed before his imprisonment, that is to say, at the time the offence was committed; moreover, it is very improbable there was any pathological disturbance at that time—unless, of course, one chooses to regard his ordinary state of congenital degeneracy as such a disturbance. Degenerative symptoms of this kind are, however, found in a large number of habitual criminals who must be considered fully responsible in the eyes of the law. On the other hand, we are of the opinion that the psychological state in which the decision to simulate was taken is not quite the same as the one designated by the term "responsibility," because in the former case there was an undeniable predisposition which underlay the wish to simulate and fostered it in such a manner that we must suppose the respondent was acting under abnormal influences which considerably restricted his freedom of will.

426 We therefore conclude that insanity within the meaning of the law was not present at the time the theft was committed, but that partial responsibility must be assumed for the simulation.

427 Further, having regard to the fact that the simulation was for the most part conscious, and that a spontaneous twilight state is in consequence precluded, the respondent must also be deemed punishable.

428 We therefore answer the questions put to us as follows:

429 1. The respondent is not at the moment mentally ill.

2. He is, on the other hand, in a condition of psychopathic inferiority with hysterical features.

3. This condition has existed presumably since birth. It does not preclude responsibility for theft; but partial responsibility must be assumed for simulation.

VI

A THIRD AND FINAL OPINION
ON TWO CONTRADICTORY
PSYCHIATRIC DIAGNOSES

———

ON THE PSYCHOLOGICAL
DIAGNOSIS OF FACTS

A THIRD AND FINAL OPINION ON TWO CONTRADICTORY PSYCHIATRIC DIAGNOSES [1]

430   It is not so very uncommon for two psychiatric diagnoses to reach contradictory conclusions, especially when, as in the present case, it is a question of the very elastic borderline between complete irresponsibility and partial responsibility. The peculiarity of this case consists firstly in the fact that the medical expert was confronted, not with the defendant herself, but merely with the reports that had previously been passed on her. In adopting this procedure, the authorities were swayed by the reflection that the material already amassed in these reports was so exhaustive that further observation would be superfluous. The medical expert was able to concur with this view. Secondly, the case is of interest inasmuch as it gave rise to a discussion of principle concerning the relation—a very important one in practice—of moral defect to hysteria. The medical expert would like to submit the views expressed in the final opinion for the consideration of his professional colleagues.

431   Our opinion is based on the existing records, etc., the legal records being specified under "Documents."

432   At the same time we have tried to form our own judgment on the basis of two consultations with the defendant in prison.

1 [First published as "Obergutachten über zwei sich widersprechende psychiatrische Gutachten," *Monatsschrift für Kriminalpsychologie und Strafrechtsreform* (Heidelberg), II : 11/12 (Feb.–Mar., 1906), 691–98.—EDITORS.]

Questions Asked by the Examining Magistrate

433   (*i*). May one assume, from the psychiatric reports (Opinions A and B) that Mrs. Z. is totally irresponsible, or is it a case of partial responsibility only?

(*ii*). Was the material at the disposal of the Governors of Asylum B. complete?

Opinion A: November 17, 1904

434   THE FACTS: Mrs. Z. defrauded two women of 200 marks by telling them she had a ticket in the Hungarian state lottery, and had drawn a high prize (38,000 or 180,000 marks). She now needed the money to pay for her ticket, so that she could collect the winnings.

435   EXAMINATION: To the examining magistrate the defendant stated that in November 1903 a certain August Baumann had offered her further lottery tickets to the value of 2000 francs. In order to buy them, she had tried to raise the money.

436   The examination showed, however, that in 1900 and 1901 she had relieved a certain B. [another person] of 4000 francs by telling the same story. Nevertheless, the defendant maintained the existence of Mr. Baumann with such obstinacy that it was at first conjectured she might perhaps be his victim.

437   Despite exhaustive inquiries, Baumann's existence could not be proved. But as the defendant stuck to her story, and the evidence of several witnesses raised the question of her mental health, the examining magistrate considered it possible that she was suffering from pathological self-deception. For these reasons she was recommended for a medical opinion.

438   DOCUMENTS: The Opinion was based on the documents then in existence, the following being of special interest: The records of the Cantonal Court of G.; a report from the penitentiary in G., which states: "Z. is a pleasure-seeking, dissolute person and a first-class impostor. Her behaviour in the penitentiary was entirely normal, there was never any sign of a psychic defect"; and, finally, a report from the District Medical Officer of K., September 1904, which assumed an abnormal mental condition and limited responsibility on the grounds of various nervous troubles, such as the unshakable "self-suggestion" of Baumann's

existence and the incomplete correction of an anxiety dream she had in prison. In addition, there were a number of important testimonies representing the defendant as mentally abnormal.

439 Observation began on September 28, 1904, and the Opinion was delivered on November 17. The observation established the presence of hysterical symptoms, and that the belief in Baumann's existence was a pathological self-deception in which the defendant herself believed. She admitted that she obtained the money by fraud, but insisted that she meant to pay it back as soon as she received her winnings.

440 There were no other disturbances of intelligence and consciousness.

441 CONCLUSION DRAWN BY THE OPINION: The most important finding is the presence of hysteria. Basic to all hysteria is an hysterical character, which is generally congenital. "Experience shows that persons of this kind habitually lie even when there is no need to, and invent whole stories," which, however, have reality value for the person concerned. "It goes without saying that with constitutionally hysterical persons lying and fraud cannot be judged in the same way as with normal people; they succumb more easily to an already existing tendency to deceive, their lies readily suggest themselves, and many of the checks which prevent normal people from lying and cheating do not operate in these persons."

442 The Opinion assumed partial responsibility.

443 CRITICISM OF THE OPINION: The previous history is incomplete, as it is based almost entirely on the documents. That, however, is not the fault of Asylum A., but of its distance from Switzerland, which prevented a personal examination. Examination by letter would have been impossible. The discovery of hysterical symptoms is not particularly difficult, hence the risk of deception is small. Moreover the examining doctors X. and Y. are professionals of good repute. Although greater completeness would have been desirable, the findings are nevertheless not only reliable but sufficient to warrant the above conclusion.

444 The important question of how far the belief in Baumann's existence influenced her actions is not discussed. If she really believed in Baumann and his lottery tickets, her fraudulent manipulations would be bound to appear much less reprehen-

sible to her, as she could always exculpate herself in her own eyes by telling herself that she would pay the money back again. This kind of reasoning would appeal very much to the weak character of an hysteric, a fact which ought to have played a considerable part in determining the degree of responsibility. Opinion A seems to assume that the defendant did believe in Baumann. In that case there is an omission in the Opinion which makes the whole conclusion appear doubtful. But if the defendant was lying, if she purposely put the blame on somebody unknown, then the conclusion reached by the Opinion could still be correct, even though it takes no stand on this question.

Opinion B: March 23, 1905

445 THE FACTS: Mrs. Z. defrauded a certain H. of 700 francs. She told the injured party that she had a ticket in the Budapest lottery, which had won—first 135,000 and then 270,000 francs. On various pretexts of secondary importance she induced H. to give her considerable sums of money from time to time, thus repeating the game as before.

446 EXAMINATION: At the hearing the defendant again insisted that she had received a lottery ticket from the agent Baumann. In view of the fact that one medical opinion had already been submitted, the examining magistrate thought it advisable to obtain a second.

447 DOCUMENTS: The Opinion was based on the documents then available (list of documents followed). Private inquiries concerning the defendant were also initiated by the asylum.

448 This material is much more complete than in Opinion A. We refrain from giving in detail all the valuable points of view arising out of the above material, and refer the reader to the "Conclusions" below. They confirm at some length that the defendant was from the beginning a morally defective psychopath, who already had a variegated record of offences behind her.

449 Observation began on January 19, 1905, and the Opinion was delivered on March 23, 1905. The period of observation was therefore sufficiently long to warrant a very thorough appreciation of her psychic state. The main finding was again a number of undoubted hysterical symptoms. (The fact that other physical

disturbances of a different nature were found in Opinion B is of no special importance: hysterical symptoms can change very rapidly.) As in Opinion A, no pathological defect of intelligence and no disturbance of consciousness could be demonstrated. The far more thorough investigation of her mental state proved, first and foremost, the existence of an hysterical character with all its subsidiary symptoms—unsociableness, irritability, tendency to lie and to intrigue, bad memory, etc.

450   Here too the belief in the existence of Baumann proved unshakable (at least to all appearances). The defendant maintained that she had spent the best part of the money on Baumann's tickets. In her relations with those about her she showed her sly and rebellious nature.

451   CONCLUSIONS DRAWN BY THE OPINION: From the life and behaviour of the defendant, who has an hereditary taint, it is abundantly clear that she suffers from hysteria. Her hysterical character expresses itself in the form of crass egotism. She manifests an extraordinary lack of feeling towards her relatives, her former husband, and her fiancé, both of whom she swindled without scruple. In the sexual sphere she knows no moral restraints. She is pleasure-seeking and extravagant. Her extreme instability and moodiness are characteristic. Her feelings vary inordinately.

452   She knows what is permitted and what is not, but is totally wanting in moral feeling.

453   The belief in the existence of Baumann must be regarded as a pathological fraud which she has gradually talked herself into believing.

454   Her unlawful actions must be regarded as symptoms of her hysterical aberration. She is therefore totally irresponsible. Her illness has developed with her personality. She is therefore incurable.

455   The defendant is a danger to the community, and it is necessary to protect society from her machinations. Considering the craftiness of her procedure, this would seem best accomplished by permanent internment in a closed institution.

456   CRITICISM OF THE OPINION: The material leaves nothing to be desired; it is more than sufficient to establish constitutional hysteria. In our view, however, the Opinion goes decidedly too far in its conclusions.

157   It establishes quite correctly that there is a total lack of moral feelings, but that is not an hysterical symptom and does not belong in any way to the hysterical character. There are thousands of severe hysterics who have very sensitive moral feelings, and there are just as many hardened criminals who show no signs of hysteria. Moral defect and hysteria are two completely different things, which occur independently of one another, as everyday experience shows.

458   As may be elicited from the Opinion, the defendant is a morally defective person who, besides that, is hysterical. Only her moral defect can lead to criminality, not her hysteria; otherwise all hysterics would be criminals, which is contrary to all experience.

459   Consequently, the conclusion that the unlawful actions are symptoms of hysteria falls to the ground, and the question of responsibility appears in quite another light, a point to which we shall return later on.

460   Despite thorough discussion, the question of belief in Baumann does not find a satisfactory solution in this Opinion either. Nevertheless, thanks to its greater thoroughness, one can see much more clearly here that this question is of no particular significance as regards her freedom of action. Before she ever got this idea, the defendant lied, defrauded, indulged in sexual activity to excess, and, in the case of the offence mentioned in Opinion B, acted with full consciousness of defrauding. It therefore seems completely out of the question that any pathological compulsion emanated from this idea.

461   One could perhaps say that the general idea of fraudulent action depended on belief in the existence of Baumann, supposing that this belief was really present. Be that as it may, it is at any rate certain that the defendant carried out the details of her frauds with clear consciousness. For instance, she journeyed to K., ostensibly to pay for the tickets, but returned after a few days loaded with new clothes and presents.

462   The correct conclusion to be drawn from Opinion B, therefore, is that she acted unlawfully in consequence of her moral defect. One must, however, agree with the Opinion in so far as the undoubted existence of hysteria had a considerable influence on her actions.

214

Final Opinion

463   From the material collected under Opinions A and B, it seems to us proven beyond a doubt that Z. is a morally defective and hysterical person.

464   Moral defect (moral insanity) is a congenital condition characterized by the absence of moral feelings. Hysteria never causes a moral defect; it can at most mask the existence of such, or exaggerate its pre-existing influence on a person's actions. Hysteria is a morbid condition, congenital or acquired, in which the affects are exceedingly powerful. Hence the patients are more or less the continual victims of their affects. At the same time, however, hysteria generally determines only the *quantity*, not the *quality*, of the affects. The quality is given by the patient's character. A soft-hearted person, if she becomes hysterical, will simply burst into tears more easily, a ruthless person will become harder, and one who is inclined to excess will fall victim to her inclinations even more unresistingly than before. It is in this manner that we have to envisage the influence of hysteria on criminal actions.

465   A person who is morally defective from the beginning and who is or becomes hysterical therefore has even less power of resistance than one who is only morally defective. This behaviour is brought out very nicely in Opinion B. No sooner is she released from prison than the defendant immediately succumbs again to the temptation of fraud. She brings off her coups with consummate skill and has, so far as one can judge, a positively uncanny influence over her victims. As Opinion B rightly remarks, these artful powers of persuasion must be put down to hysteria, for in hysteria there is always so much feeling and such a natural gift for play-acting that, however much they lie and exaggerate, hysterics will always find people gullible enough to believe them. Even doctors are often taken in by their wiles.

466   Neither of the Opinions has proved that the defendant was acting under the compulsion of a pathological conviction, a delusional idea (Baumann), or a pathological and irresistible instinct. Both stress that she knew her actions were immoral. A clouding of consciousness at the moment of the deed is likewise out of the question.

467   The defendant simply gives way to her evil inclinations. She acts exactly like any common criminal. Her hysteria fosters her actions and prevents any resolutions to the contrary. It does this because only evil inclinations are present. If good ones were there too, the hysteria would occasionally foster them as well, as happens in hysterical persons who are not morally defective. This shows that the essential thing can only be the moral defect.

468   Is the defendant legally irresponsible on account of her moral defect?

469   Every habitual criminal is morally defective, and is thus ill in a scientific sense. The law, however, as it stands at present, claims all individuals who recognize the punishable nature of their actions and who are not acting under an irresistible compulsion.

470   The juridical conception of irresponsibility therefore includes all psychic abnormalities with the exception of moral defect. So if we adhere to the meaning of the law, moral defect should logically not be taken into account in adjudging the question of responsibility.

471   In the present case, is the hysteria by itself strong enough to cause total irresponsibility?

472   As the Münsterling Opinion [B] makes clear, the defendant is morally defective. If such a defect is present and offences are committed, they must naturally be connected first of all with the moral defect, since they are two things that go together unconditionally. If the offences are to arise from hysteria, it must be shown from the character of the offences that they have their roots in hysteria and not in moral defect.

473   Are the defendant's offences specifically hysterical?

474   No proof of this has been furnished. To all appearances it is a question of conscious and intentional fraud, of a kind common among skilled impostors. Its roots lie in evil inclinations and lack of resistance to them. But that is not hysterical. The only point where one might surmise a specifically hysterical motive is the question of Baumann. But it is precisely here that the greatest mistrust is to be recommended. The Baumann swindle served a purpose, and on one occasion it very nearly came off (in K.). Opinion B emphasizes that the defendant once said she would not let herself be hypnotized, as she was "not obliged to tell the doctors the whole truth." In view of this re-

mark it may be supposed that she had more insight into her swindles than she was credited with. It therefore behoves us to exercise the greatest caution in regard to the Baumann swindle. On the occasion of the present offence, the undersigned had a lengthy talk with the defendant on this point and ascertained that this time she swindled on purpose, in order to obtain money. Baumann played no part in it at all. She also assured me that she did not possess any tickets, but she still maintains the existence of Baumann to this day with the greatest positiveness and many tears, so that it is extremely difficult to resist the impression of his reality. However, the only point of practical importance here is that in the present instance she swindled on her own account, quite clearly and without beating about the bush, as once before in 1900. It is also clear that no hysterical motivation may be inferred for her offences.

475   These offences, and particularly their remarkably sure results, must be understood as the co-operative action of moral defect and hysteria, the hysteria being merely an accessory influence in respect of the offence. Owing to the strength of their affects, hysterical persons are always their own victims; they do not belong to themselves, as it were, but to the momentary affect. Consequently, their actions are always being compromised by passing moods. We all know how much these can obscure our judgment and hinder reflection. With a higher degree of hysteria, such as the defendant exhibits, the decisions of the will are always influenced by abnormal affects, which is not the case with normal people, who can calmly weigh the pros and cons of their actions. Hysteria therefore limits the subject's responsibility.

476   Accordingly, we answer your questions thus, to the best of our knowledge and conscience:

(i). On the basis of Opinions A and B, only a diminished or partial responsibility can be assumed.

(ii). The material collected under Opinion B is put together with so much care and thoroughness that one could hardly add anything more than subsidiary details to its completeness.

477   The standpoint of the Opinion [B] means nothing less, in practice, than an abandonment of the scientific conception of moral defect. The logical conclusion to be drawn would be the

exclusion of moral defectives from the legal conception of insanity. In theory this might be described as a retrograde step or concession to the lay psychologist's interpretation of criminal law, and in practice as a lack of consideration for society. We, as doctors of the mentally ill, should pay no attention to either reproach, for our first charge is to watch over the welfare of the state institutions committed to our care. If we, too, now put into practice our theory of the mental sickness of moral defectives, we find that with increasing psychological education of the judiciary our institutions are getting choked with criminals, thanks to our altruistic medical reports. Conditions in an asylum will rapidly become untenable. (Just now in Burghölzli, only one more criminal is needed to make the situation quite impossible.) In this way we ruin the character and reputation of an asylum completely, and no one could blame a respectable family if it did everything in its power not to send an unfortunate mentally sick relative into the villainous hubbub of a criminal ward. The presence of criminals completely poisons the tone of the place, and its spirit as a hospital. In addition, only a very few asylums have the equipment for confining criminals. The more the legal experts realize the futility of the existing criminal practice, the more they will insist upon getting rid of their permanently incorrigible clients by interning them in a lunatic asylum, on the increasingly popular plea that society must be protected. Naturally criminal justice wants that, but why must the asylum suffer for it? The asylum should never become the executive organ of criminal law. By relieving criminal justice of inconvenient elements we do not make them better, we merely ruin our asylums. So long as society is unwilling to alter the laws relating to criminal justice, it must also discover to its cost that, as a result of the rapidly increasing number of partially responsible persons, the most dangerous criminals are turned loose against it at ever shorter intervals. Only in this way can the pressing need for reforms be demonstrated to the public.

ON THE PSYCHOLOGICAL DIAGNOSIS OF FACTS [1]

478   As readers of the *Centralblatt* may be aware, the "psychological diagnosis of facts" has recently been the object of some discussion. The essence of psychological diagnosis consists in bringing to light, by means of associations, the complex of ideas relating to a crime. In our work on "The Associations of Normal Subjects," [2] Riklin and I put forward the concept of the "feeling-toned complex" and described its effects on the associations; these effects were examined in greater detail in my inaugural paper on "Reaction-Time in the Association Experiment." The discovery of feeling-toned complexes in the associations of insane persons has been of great help to us in our diagnostic work for the past two years, as is apparent from a number of publications by Riklin and myself.

479   After the publication of my studies in word-association, an article by Wertheimer and Klein appeared in Volume XV of the *Archiv für Kriminalanthropologie und Kriminalistik*, on the psychological diagnosis of facts.[3] The authors discuss, in the main, the possibility of finding, through the associations, the

1 [First published as "Zur psychologischen Tatbestandsdiagnostik," *Zentralblatt für Nervenheilkunde und Psychiatrie* (Leipzig), XXVIII (N.S. XVI) (November, 1905), 813–15.—EDITORS.]

2 [This and the other works of Jung's mentioned in this paper are in *Experimental Researches*, Vol. 2 of the *Collected Works.*—EDITORS.]

3 "Psychologische Tatbestandsdiagnostik" (1904).

feeling-toned complex relating to a crime committed in the past. As Messrs. Wertheimer and Klein are erroneously described as the "discoverers" of this idea, I would like to clarify the situation by taking this opportunity to remark that, so far as the experiment is concerned, the honour of the title of discoverer belongs to Galton or Wundt. The concept of feeling-toned complexes, however, and the determination of their specific effects on association, derive from the Zurich Clinic, and more particularly from the "Diagnostische Assoziationsstudien" published in the *Journal für Psychologie und Neurologie*, 1904–5. If Wertheimer and Klein had had a little more respect for the workers before them in this field, and had cited the source from which they appropriated their seemingly original ideas, they could have spared themselves sundry unpleasant discussions (cf. Weygandt's criticism in the latest issue of Aschaffenburg's *Monatsschrift* [4]).

480   Wertheimer's merit is confined at present to having emphasized a special instance of the feeling-toned complex—crime—and the possibility of discovering it from the associations. I am privately informed that experiments in this direction are in progress, though as yet they do not seem to have advanced much beyond the laboratory stage.

481   Readers may be interested to know that today I succeeded for the first time in testing out, on a delinquent, our method of discovering complexes, and with excellent results.

482   A detailed account of the case will appear in a forthcoming issue of the *Schweizerische Zeitschrift für Strafrecht*.[5] I permit myself only a brief report on the case now:

483   Yesterday evening an elderly gentleman came to see me, obviously in a state of great agitation. He told me that he had staying with him a young man of eighteen, whose guardian he was. Some weeks ago he noticed from time to time that small sums of money were missing from his cashbox, now amounting to over 100 francs. He at once informed the police, but was unable to bring proofs against any one person. He rather suspected

[4] "Zur psychologischen Tatbestandsdiagnostik" (1905).
[5] [In section II of "Die psychologische Diagnose des Tatbestandes," XVIII (1905), 369–408; republished under same title in *Juristisch-psychiatrische Grenzfragen* (Halle, 1906), IV:2, 3–47; also published as a pamphlet (Halle, 1906; Zurich and Leipzig, 1941). For translation, see "The Psychological Diagnosis of Evidence," *Experimental Researches*.—EDITORS.]

his ward, but had no absolute proof of this. If he knew that his ward was the thief, he would prefer to settle the matter on the quiet, so as to spare the feelings of the boy's highly respectable family. But first he wanted to know for certain whether his ward was really a thief. He now asked me to hypnotize the young man and question him under hypnosis. As can readily be understood, I declined this strange request, but proposed instead an association test, which could be rendered plausible enough in the form of a consultation (the suspected delinquent had wanted to consult me once before on account of mild nervous troubles). His guardian agreed to the plan and this morning the young man turned up for the consultation. I had, of course, previously equipped my list of one hundred stimulus words with the critical words designed to hit the complex. The experiment went off smoothly; but in order to determine the critical reactions still more precisely I decided to employ my reproduction procedure as well. The complex for the theft was then revealed so plainly by the associations that I was able to tell the young man with quiet assurance: "You have been stealing." He paled, was completely nonplussed for a moment, and after a little hesitation broke down and tearfully admitted to the theft.

484   I would merely like to add, in this provisional report, that the effects of a theft complex on the associations are naturally exactly the same as in the case of any other complex of similar emotional intensity. For further details I must refer the reader to the forthcoming publication.

BIBLIOGRAPHY

BIBLIOGRAPHY

The items of the bibliography are arranged alphabetically under two headings: *A.* List of periodicals cited, with abbreviations; *B.* General bibliography, including both books and articles. It has not been possible to establish the full names of some medical writers cited in the early literature.

A. LIST OF PERIODICALS CITED, WITH ABBREVIATIONS

Allg Z f Psych = Allgemeine Zeitschrift für Psychiatrie und psychisch-gerichtliche Medicin. Berlin.

Ann méd-psych = Annales médico-psychologiques. Paris.

Arch f d ges Psych = Archiv für die gesamte Psychologie. Leipzig.

Arch f Krim u Krim = Archiv für Kriminalanthropologie und Kriminalstatistik. Leipzig.

Arch f Psych und Nerv = Archiv für Psychiatrie und Nervenkrankheiten. Berlin.

Arch de neur = Archives de neurologie. Paris.

Brain. A Journal of Neurology. London.

Centralbl f Nerv und Psych = Centralblatt für Nervenheilkunde und Psychiatrie. Berlin and Leipzig.

L'Encéphale. Journal des Maladies mentales et nerveuses. Paris.

Friedrich's Blätter für gerichtliche Medizin und Sanitätspolizei. Nuremberg.

Harper's Magazine. New York.

Jahrb f Psych = Jahrbuch für Psychiatrie und Neurologie. Leipzig and Vienna.

Journ f Psych u Neur = Journal für Psychologie und Neurologie. Leipzig. (A continuation of the *Zeitschrift für Hypnotismus,* q.v.)

Juristisch-psychiatrische Grenzfragen. Halle.

Mind. A quarterly review of psychology and philosophy. London.

Monatsschrift = Monatsschrift für Kriminalpsychologie und Strafrechtsreform. Edited by Gustav Aschaffenburg. Heidelberg.

Münch med Wochenschr = Münchener Medicinische Wochenschrift. Munich.

Neur Centralbl = Neurologisches Centralblatt. Berlin.

Proc Soc Psych Res = Proceedings of the Society for Psychical Research. London.

Prog méd = Progrès médical. Paris.

Rév de l'hyp = Revue de l'hypnotisme. Paris.

Rev phil = Revue philosophique de France et de l'Étranger. Paris.

Samml der päd Psych = Sammlung von Abhandlungen aus dem Gebiete der pädogogischen Psychologie und Physiologie. Berlin.

Trans Coll Phys Philadelphia = Transactions of the College of Physicians of Philadelphia.

Trib méd = Tribune médicale. Paris.

Union méd = Union médicale. Paris.

Wiener med Presse = Wiener medizinische Presse. Vienna.

Z f Hyp = Zeitschrift für Hypnotismus, Psychotherapie, etc. Leipzig. (Continued as the *Journal für Psychologie und Neurologie,* q.v.)

Z f Straf = Zeitschrift für Strafrecht. Switzerland.

Zukunft, Die. Berlin.

B . GENERAL BIBLIOGRAPHY

AZAM, C. M. ÉTIENNE EUGÈNE. *Hypnotisme, double conscience, et altérations de la personnalité.* Paris, 1887.

BAETZ, E. VON. "Über Emotionslähmung," *Allg Z f Psych,* LVIII (1901), 717ff.

BAIN, ALEXANDER. *The Senses and the Intellect.* London, 1855.

BALLET, GILBERT. *Le Langage intérieur et les diverse formes de l'aphasie.* Paris. 1886.

BAUMANN, JULIUS. "Über Willens- und Charakterbildung auf physiologisch-psychologisches Grundlage," *Samml d päd Psych,* I (1897) : 3.

BEHR, ALBERT. "Bemerkungen über Erinnerungsfälschungen und pathologische Traumzustände," *Allg Z f Psych,* LVI (1899), 918ff.

BILLOD, E. "Rapport médico-légal sur un cas de simulation de folie," *Ann méd-psych,* 4th ser., XII, 26th year (1868), 53–82.

BINET, ALFRED. *Alterations of Personality.* Translated by Helen Green Baldwin. London, 1896. (Original: *Les Altérations de la personnalité.* Paris, 1892.)

BÖCKER, F. W., HERTZ, CARL, and RICHARZ, FRANZ. *Reiner Stockhausen, ein actenmässiger Beitrag zur psychisch-gerichtlichen Medicin.* Elberfeld, 1855.

BOETEAU, M. "Automatisme somnambulique avec dédoublement de la personnalité," *Ann méd-psych,* 7th ser., V, 50th year (1892), 63–79.

BOHN, WOLFGANG. *Ein Fall von doppeltem Bewusstsein.* Dissertation, Breslau, 1898.

BOLTE, AUGUST. "Über einige Fälle von Simulation," *Allg Z f Psych,* LX (1903), 47–59.

BONAMAISON, L. "Un Cas remarquable d'hypnose spontanée, etc.," *Rév de l'hyp,* 4th year (Feb., 1890), 234–43.

BOURRU, HENRI, and BUROT, FERDINAND. *Variations de la personnalité.* Paris, 1888.

BRESLER, JOHANN. "Kulturhistorischer Beitrag zur Hysterie," *Allg Z f Psych,* LIII (1896), 333ff.

BREUER, JOSEF, and FREUD, SIGMUND. *Studies on Hysteria*. Translated under the editorship of James Strachey. (Standard Edition of the Complete Psychological Works of Sigmund Freud, 2.) London and New York, 1955. (Original: *Studien über Hysterie*. Leipzig and Vienna, 1895.)

CARDAN, JEROME (Girolamo Cardano *or* Hieronymus Cardanus). *De subtilitate libri III*. Nuremberg, 1550. (Other editions: Paris, 1550, 1551; Basel, 1554, 1560, 1582, 1611; Lyons, 1580.)

[CELLINI, BENVENUTO.] *The Life of Benvenuto Cellini, Written by Himself*. Translated by John Addington Symonds. London (Phaidon Press), 1949.

CLAUS, ——. "Ein Fall von simulierter Geistesstörung," *Allg Z f Psych*, XXXIII (1877), 153–70.

CULLERRE, A. "Un Cas de somnambulisme hystérique," *Ann méd-psych*, 7th ser., VII, 46th year (1888), 354–70. (Reviewed by H. Kurella in *Allg Z f Psych*, XLVI (1890), p. 356* [Litteratur-bericht].)

DELBRÜCK, ANTON. *Die pathologische Lüge und die psychisch abnormen Schwindler*. Stuttgart, 1891.

DESSOIR, MAX. *Das Doppel-Ich*. Berlin, 1890. (2nd edition, Berlin, 1896.)

DIEHL, AUGUST. "Neurasthenische Krisen," *Münch med Wochenschr*, 49th year, no. 9 (March, 1902), 363–66.

DONATH, JULIUS. "Über Suggestibilität," *Wiener med Presse*, 1892, no. 31, cols. 1244–46. (Cited in the next work.)

——. "Der epileptische Wandertrieb (Poriomanie)," *Arch f Psych und Nerv*, XXXII (1899), 335–55.

ECKERMANN, J. P. *Conversations with Goethe*. Translated by R. O. Moon. London, n.d. [1951].

EMMINGHAUS, H. *Allgemeine Psychopathologie zur Einführung in das Studium der Geistesstörungen*. Leipzig, 1878.

ERLER, ——. "Hysterisches und hystero-epileptisches Irresein," *Allg Z f Psych*, XXXV (1879), 16–45.

FLAUBERT, GUSTAVE. *Salammbô*. Translated by J. S. Chartres. London (Everyman's Library), 1931. (Original: Paris, 1862.)

FLOURNOY, THÉODORE. *From India to the Planet Mars*. Translated by D. B. Vermilye. New York and London, 1900. (Original: *Des*

Indes à la Planète Mars. Étude sur un cas de somnambulisme avec glossolalie. Paris and Geneva, 1900.)

FOREL, AUGUSTE. *Hypnotism, or Suggestion and Psychotherapy.* Translated from the 5th German edition by H. W. Armit. London and New York, 1906. (Original: *Der Hypnotismus, seine . . . Bedeutung und . . . Handhabung.* Stuttgart, 1889. Later editions, 1891, 1911, 1918, etc.)

FREUD, SIGMUND. *The Interpretation of Dreams.* Translated by James Strachey. (Standard Edition, 4 and 5.) London and New York, 1953. 2 vols. (Original: *Die Traumdeutung.* Leipzig and Vienna, 1900.)

———. See also BREUER.

FÜRSTNER, C. "Die Zurechnungsfähigkeit der Hysterischen," *Arch f Psych und Nerv,* XXXI (1899), 627–39.

———. "Über Simulation geistiger Störungen," *Arch f Psych und Nerv,* XIX (1888), 601ff.

GANSER, SIGBERT. "Über einen eigenartigen hysterischen Dämmerzustand," *Arch f Psych und Nerv,* XXX (1898), 633ff.

GOETHE, J. W. VON. *Elective Affinities.* A translation of *Die Wahlverwandtschaften.* With an introduction by Victoria C. Woodhull. Boston, 1872.

———. *Zur Naturwissenschaft. Allgemeine Naturlehre.* Stuttgart and Tübingen, 1817–23.

GÖRRES, JOHANN JOSEPH VON. *Die christliche Mystik.* Regensburg and Landshut, 1836–42. 4 vols.

GRAETER, C. "Ein Fall von epileptischer Amnesie durch Hypermnesie beseitigt," *Z f Hyp,* VIII (1899), 129–63.

GROSS, HANS. *Criminal Psychology. A Manual for Judges, Practitioners and Students.* Translated from the 4th German edition by Horace M. Kallen. London, 1911. (Original: *Criminalpsychologie.* Graz, 1898.)

GUINON, GEORGES. "Documents pour servir à l'histoire des somnambulismes," *Prog méd,* 1891, XIII, 401–4, 425–29, 460–66, 513–17; XIV, 41–49, 137–41.

——— and WOLTKE, SOPHIE. "De l'influence des excitations des organes des sens sur les hallucinations de la phase passionnelle de l'attaque hystérique," *Arch de neur*, XXI: 63 (May, 1891), 346–65.

HAGEN, F. W. "Zur Theorie der Hallucination," *Allg Z f Psych*, XXV (1868), 1–113.

——. Review of J. F. C. Hecker, *Über Visionen* (q.v.), *Allg Z f Psych*, VI (1849), 285–95.

HAHN, R. Review of Jung's *Zur Psychologie und Pathologie sogenannter occulter Phänomene, Archiv f d ges Psych*, III (1904), Literaturbericht, p. 26.

[HARDEN, MAXIMILIAN.] "Der kleine Jacobsohn," *Die Zukunft*, XLIX (1904), 370–78.

HAUPTMANN, CARL. *Die Bergschmiede*. Munich, 1902.

HECKER, JUSTUS FRIEDRICH CARL. *Über Visionen. Eine Vorlesung*, etc. Berlin, 1848.

HOCHE, ALFRED ERICH. *Handbuch der gerichtlichen Psychiatrie*. Berlin, 1901.

HÖFELT, J. A. "Ein Fall von spontanem Somnambulismus," *Allg Z f Psych*, XLIX (1893), 250ff.

JAMES, WILLIAM. *The Principles of Psychology*. New York and London, 1890. 2 vols.

JANET, PIERRE. "L'Anesthésie hystérique," *Arch de neur*, XXIII : 69 (May, 1892), 323–52.

——. *L'Automatisme psychologique*. 7th edition, Paris, 1913.

——. *Névroses et idées fixes*. Paris, 1898. 2 vols.

——. *Les Obsessions et la psychasthénie*. Paris, 1903.

——. *The Mental State of Hystericals*. Translated by Caroline Rollin Corson. New York and London, 1901. (Original: *État mental des hystériques*. Paris, [1893].)

JESSEN, W. Review of F. W. Böcker et al., *Reiner Stockhausen* (q.v.), *Allg Z f Psych*, XII (1855), 618–32.

——. "Doppeltes Bewusstsein," *Allg Z f Psych*, XXII (1865), 407. (Report of address at Naturforscherversammlung zu Hannover, Psychiatrische Section, Sept. 18–23, 1865.)

JUNG, C. G. *Collected Papers on Analytical Psychology*. Edited by Constance E. Long; translated by various hands.   London and New York, 1916; 2nd edn., 1917.

——. *Contributions to Analytical Psychology.* Translated by C. F. and H. G. Baynes. London and New York, 1928.

——. "The Psychological Diagnosis of Evidence." In: *Collected Works,* Vol. 2.

——. "The Psychology of Dementia Praecox." In: *Collected Works,* Vol. 3.

——. "The Reaction-Time Ratio in the Association Experiment." In: *Collected Works,* Vol. 2.

——. *Symbols of Transformation. Collected Works,* Vol. 5.

——, and Riklin, Franz. "The Associations of Normal Subjects." In: *Collected Works,* Vol. 2.

[KANT, IMMANUEL.] *Kant's Cosmogony as in His "Essay on the Retardation of the Rotation of the Earth" and His "Natural History and Theory of the Heavens."* Edited and Translated by W. Hastie. Glasgow, 1900.

KARPLUS, J. P. "Über Pupillenstarre im hysterischen Anfalle," *Jahrb f Psych,* XVIII (1898), 1–53.

KERNER, JUSTINUS. *Blätter aus Prevorst.* Karlsruhe, 1831–39.

——. *Die Seherin von Prevorst.* Stuttgart and Tübingen, 1829. 2 vols. (Translation, not cited herein, by Mrs. [Catherine] Crowe: *The Seeress of Prevorst.* New York, 1859.)

KRAEPELIN, EMIL. *Psychologische Arbeiten.* Leipzig, 1895–1927. 9 vols.

KRAFFT-EBING, RICHARD VON. *Text-Book of Insanity based on Clinical Observations.* Authorized translation from the last German edition by C. G. Chaddock. Philadelphia, 1904. (Original: *Lehrbuch der Psychiatrie auf klinischer Grundlage,* Stuttgart, 1879. 7th edition, 1903.)

KRAUSS, A. *Die Psychologie des Verbrechens. Ein Beitrag zur Erfahrungsseelenkunde.* Tübingen, 1884.

LADD, C. TRUMBULL. "Contribution to the Psychology of Visual Dreams," *Mind,* XVII (April, 1892), 299–304.

LANDGRAF, KARL. "Ein Simulant vor Gericht," *Friedrich's Blätter,* 35th year, 6 (1884), 411–33. (Summary in *Allg Z f Psych,* XLII (1886), 60 [Literaturbericht].)

LAURENT, ARMAND. *Étude sur la simulation.* Paris, 1866.

LAURENT, EMILE. "Un Détenu simulant la folie pendant trois ans," *Ann méd-psych,* 7th ser., VIII, 46th year (Sept., 1888), 225–34.

LEHMANN, ALFRED GEORG LUDWIG. *Aberglaube und Zauberei von den ältesten Zeiten an bis in die Gegenwart.* Translated from Danish by Dr. Petersen. Stuttgart, 1898.

———. *Die körperlichen Äusserungen psychischer Zustände.* Translated from Danish by F. Bendixen. Leipzig, 1899–1905. 3 parts.

LEPPMANN, A. "Simulation von Geistesstörung umgrenzt von Störungsanfall und Rückfall," *Allg Z f Psych,* XLVIII (1892), 530–32.

LOEWENFELD, LEOPOLD. *Der Hypnotismus: Handbuch der Lehre von der Hypnose und der Suggestion.* Wiesbaden, 1901.

———. "Über hysterische Schlafzustände, deren Beziehungen zur Hypnose und zur Grande Hystérie," *Arch f Psych und Nerv,* XXII (1891), 715–38; XXIII (1892), 40–69.

LÜCKE, ROBERT. "Über das Ganser'sche Symptom mit Berücksichtigung seiner forensischen Bedeutung," *Allg Z f Psych,* LX (1903), 1–35.

MACARIO, M. M. A. "Des Hallucinations," *Ann méd-psych,* VI (1845), 317–49; VII (1846), 13–45. (Reviewed in *Allg Z f Psych,* IV [1848], 137ff.)

MACNISH, ROBERT. *The Philosophy of Sleep.* Glasgow, 1830.

MARANDON DE MONTYEL, E. "Folie simulée par une aliénée inculpée de tentative d'assassinat," *L'Encéphale,* II (1882), 47–61. (Reviewed in *Allg Z f Psych,* XL [1884], 337–38.)

MAURY, LOUIS FERDINAND ALFRED. *Le Sommeil et les rêves.* Paris, 1861. (3rd edition, Paris, 1865.)

MENDEL, EMANUEL. *Die Manie.* Vienna and Leipzig, 1881.

MESNET, ERNEST. "De l'automatisme de la mémoire et du souvenir dans la somnambulisme pathologique," *Union méd,* 3rd ser., XVIII : 87 (July 21, 1874), 105–112.

———. "Somnambulisme spontané dans ses rapports avec l'hystérie," *Arch de neur,* no. 69 (1892), 289–304.

MITCHELL, SILAS WEIR. "Mary Reynolds: A Case of Double Consciousness," *Trans Coll Phys Philadelphia,* 3rd ser., X (April 4, 1888), 366–89.

MOLL, ALBERT. "Die Bewusstseinsspaltung in Paul Lindau's neuem Schauspiel," *Z f Hyp,* I (1893), 306ff.

MÖRCHEN, FRIEDRICH. *Über Dämmerzustände.* Medical dissertation, Warburg, 1901.

MÜLLER, ERDMANN. "Über Moral Insanity," *Arch f Psych und Nerv*, XXXI (1899), 325–77.

MÜLLER, JOHANNES. *Über die phantastischen Gesichtserscheinungen.* Coblenz, 1826. (Cited in Hagen, "Zur Theorie der Hallucination," q.v.)

MYERS, FREDERIC W. H. "Automatic Writing," *Proc Soc Psych Res*, III (1885), 1–63.

NAEF, M. "Ein Fall von temporärer, totaler, theilweise retrograder Amnesie," *Z f Hyp*, VI (1897), 321–54.

NIETZSCHE, FRIEDRICH. *Thus Spake Zarathustra.* Translated by Thomas Common, revised by Oscar Levy and John L. Beevers. 6th edition, London, 1932. (Original: *Also Sprach Zarathustra.* 1883–91.)

——. *Ecce Homo.* Translated by A. M. Ludovici. London, 1927. (Original: 1888.)

NISSL, F. "Hysterische Symptome bei einfachen Seelenstörungen," *Centralbl f Nerv und Psych*, 25th year, XIII (1902), 2–38.

PELMAN, C. "Über das Verhalten des Gedächtnisses bei den verschiedenen Formen des Irreseins," *Allg Z f Psych*, XXI (1864), 63–121.

PHLEPS, EDUARD. "Psychosen nach Erdbeben," *Jahrb f Psych*, XXIII (1903), 382–406.

PICK, ARNOLD. "Über pathologische Träumerei und ihre Beziehung zur Hysterie," *Jahrb f Psych*, XIV (1896), 280–330.

——. "Vom Bewusstsein in Zuständen sogenannter Bewusstlosigkeit," *Arch f Psych und Nerv*, XV (1884), 202–23.

PINEL, PHILIPPE. *A Treatise on Insanity.* Translated by D. D. Davis. London, 1806. (Original: *Traité médico-philosophique sur l'aliénation mentale, ou la manie.* Paris, an IX [1801]. 2nd edition, (1809).

PLUMER, REV. WILLIAM S. "Mary Reynolds: A Case of Double Consciousness," *Harper's*, XX : 120 (May, 1860), 807–12.

PREYER, WILLIAM THIERRY. *Die Erklärung des Gedankenlesens.* Leipzig, 1886.

PRINCE, MORTON. "An Experimental Study of Visions," *Brain*, XXI (1898), 528ff.

PROUST, A. A. "Cas curieux d'automatisme ambulatoire chez un hystérique," *Trib méd*, 23rd year (March, 1890), 202–3.

QUICHERAT, JULES. *Procès de condamnation et de réhabilitation de Jeanne d'Arc, dite la Pucelle,* etc. Paris, 1841–49. 5 vols.

RAECKE, JULIUS. "Beitrag zur Kenntnis des hysterischen Dämmerzustandes," *Allg Z f Psych,* LVIII (1901), 115–63.

———. "Hysterischer Stupor bei Strafgefangenen," *Allg Z f Paych,* LVIII (1901), 409–46.

REDLICH, JOHANN. "Ein Beitrag zur Kenntnis der Pseudologia phantastica," *Allg Z f Psych,* LVI (1900), 65ff.

RIBOT, THÉODULE ARMAND. *Die Persönlichkeit.* Translated from French by F. T. F. Pabst. Berlin, 1894.

RICHARZ, FRANZ. "Über psychische Untersuchungsmethoden," *Allg Z f Psych,* XIII (1856), 256–314.

———. See also BÖCKER.

RICHER, PAUL. *Études cliniques sur l'hystéro-epilepsie.* Paris, 1881.

RICHET, CHARLES. "La Suggestion mentale et le calcul des probabilités," *Rev phil,* XVIII (1884), II, 609–74.

RIEGER, CONRAD. *Der Hypnotismus.* Jena, 1884.

RÜDIN, ERNST. "Über die klinischen Formen der Gefängnisspsychosen," *Allg Z f Psych,* LVIII (1901), 447–62.

SCHNITZLER, ARTHUR. "Der Fall Jacobsohn," *Die Zukunft,* XLIX (1904), 401–4.

SCHOPENHAUER, ARTHUR. "Preisschrift über die Freiheit des Willens." In: *Arthur Schopenhauers Werke.* Edited by Moritz Brasch. 3rd edition, Leipzig, n.d. [1891]. (Vol. II, pp. 231–317.)

SCHROEDER VAN DER KOLK, JACOBUS LUDOVICUS CONRADUS. *Die Pathologie und Therapie der Geisteskrankheiten auf anatomisch-physiologischer Grundlage.* Translated from Dutch by F. W. Theile. Brunswick, 1863. (Quoted in *Allg Z f Psych,* XXII [1865], 406–7.)

SCHÜLE, HEINRICH. *Handbuch der Geisteskrankheiten.* (Ziemssens Handbuch der speciellen Pathologie, etc., 16.) Leipzig, 1878.

SCHÜRMAYER, IGNAZ HEINRICH. *Theoretisch-practisches Lehrbuch der gerichtlichen Medicin.* Erlangen, 1850. (4th edition, 1874.)

SIEFERT, ERNST. "Über chronische Manie," *Allg Z f Psych,* LIX (1902), 261–70.

SIEMENS, FRITZ. "Zur Frage der Simulation von Seelenstörung," *Arch f Psych und Nerv,* XIV (1883), 40–86.

SNELL, L. "Über Simulation von Geistesstörung," *Allg Z f Psych*, XIII (1856), 1–32.

STEFFENS, PAUL. "Über drei Fälle von 'Hysteria magna,'" *Arch f Psych und Nerv*, XXXIII (1900), 892–928.

TILING, T. "Die Moral Insanity beruht auf einem excessiv sanguinischen Temperament," *Allg Z f Psych*, LVII (1901), 205–40.

VAN DEVENTER, J. "Ein Fall von sanguinischer Minderwerthigkeit," *Allg Z f Psych*, LI (1894), 550–78.

WERNICKE, CARL. *Grundriss der Psychiatrie in klinischen Vorlesungen.* Leipzig, 1894.

WERTHEIMER, MAX, and KLEIN, JULIUS. "Psychologische Tatbestandsdiagnostik," *Arch f Krim u Krim*, XV (1904), 72–113.

WESTPHAL, A. "Über hysterische Dämmerzustände und das Symptom des 'Vorbeiredens,'" *Neur Centralbl*, XXI (1903), 7–16, 64–72.

WESTPHAL, C. "Die Agoraphobie, eine neuropathische Erscheinung," *Arch f Psych und Nerv*, III (1872), 138–61.

WEYGANDT, WILHELM. "Zur psychologischen Tatbestandsdiagnostik," *Monatsschrift*, II (1905), 435–38.

WILBRAND, ——, and LOTZ, ——. "Simulation von Geisteskrankheit bei einem schweren Verbrecher," *Allg Z f Psych*, XLV (1889), 472–90.

WINSLOW, BENIGNUS FORBES. *Obscure Diseases of the Brain and Mind.* London, 1863. (Cited in *Allg Z f Psych*, XXII [1865], 405.)

WOLTKE, SOPHIE. See GUINON.

ZSCHOKKE, JOHANN HEINRICH DANIEL. *Eine Selbstschau.* 3rd edition, Aarau, 1843.

ZÜNDEL, FRIEDRICH. *Pfarrer J. C. Blumhardt: Ein Lebensbild.* Zurich and Heilbronn, 1880.

INDEX

A

abnormality, emotional, 119, 134

accident, and affect, 164

accusation, false, effect of, 184

acoustic control: defective, and misreading, 90

Acta Sanctorum, glossolalia in, 84

acting: excellence of performance in simulation, 179, 202; skill of hysterics at, 215; submersion of self in assumed role, 66, 69, 162

action (s) : automatic, 69, 92; dependence on emotions, 132*f;* symptomatic, 98, 100

activity: mental, 110*f,* 180*n,* 202*f;* motor, *see* motor; pressure of, 131

Adam, 38

adaptability: poor, of mental defectives, 169*f*

adolescent: character of, 63; *see also* puberty

Aesop's fable, patient's reproduction of, 197

affect(s): and abnormal action, 133; aetiological role of, 180; *re* detention, 142; dissociating effect of, 181; effect of, on hysterical persons, 170*f,* 217; and hysteria, 215; influence on consciousness, 203; lack of control of, 21; pleasure/pain, 120; produced by arrest, trial, and confinement, 188*f;* and psychic automatisms, 187; and psychogenic disturbances, 184*f;* repressed, 185; unabreacted, 155; violent, effect of, 164

aggression, 176, 195

alcohol, use of, 6, 13, 16; *see also* alcoholism

alcoholism, 90, 111, 112*f,* 124; dependent on emotional lability, 119; and manic behaviour, 120; resulting from depression and despair, 115*ff*

amnesia: anterograde, 172, 183; for automatic phenomena during ecstasy, 33; caused by affects, 171; difficulty of determining extent of, 150; disappearance under hypnosis, 147; in lethargy, 72; penetrated by trick, 145*f;* periodic, 3, 10*ff;* retrograde, 10, 143*f,* 172; and somnambulistic states, 20, 61*ff;* for unpleasant episode, 155

anaesthesia: cerebral, 49; of entire body surface, 63*f;* hysterical, 44; systematic, 64

analgesia, 145; total, for pinpricks, 139; *see also* hypalgesia

anamnesis, in simulated insanity, 177*f*

anger: reaction to censure, 118*f;* at trifles, 129

animal noises, made by manic patient, 128, 129

animals, life-forces of, 41

answers: irrelevant, 92; senseless, 140*ff,* 148*f,* 172, 173*n,* 174, 183, 193

anxiety: effect of, 151; precordial, 100

apathy, 166, 174*f,* 184, 192, 195; behaviour contradictory to, 196, 203

apperception, reduced, 197

appetite, lack of, after 4-day fast, 177

arm, motor area isolated from consciousness by auto-suggestion, 51

artist(s), 16, 106, 131

Aschaffenburg, Gustav, 167n, 220
assimilation: of affects, 188f; and association, 168f
association(s): without aid of consciousness, 96; automatic substitution of, 46; concord of, 86; conscious, and senseless answers, 149; and distraction of attention, 168; effect of attention on quality of, 168; feeling-toned, as creative force, 105f; inhibited, as embarrassment, 166; law of, and memory-image, 95; minimum of, and cryptomnesic idea, 81, 83f; in psychological diagnosis, 219; repression of, and perception, 45; restriction of, 86n; and songs or tunes, 97; substitutions of, 46; and supraliminal consciousness, 152; and suggestion, 52; unlimited, in hysterical subjects, 181
association tests, 166–70; in discovery of theft, 221
astronomy, as source of names in S. W.'s mystic system, 85
asylum: fear of, 188; as institution for mentally ill and not for criminals, 218
attention: concentration of, and new ideas, 86n; —, and automatic actions, 69; distracted by fixed idea, 168; disturbances of, 21ff, 44, 148, 180f; and fatigability, 144; subliminal, 68n; and train of thought, 69n; see also distractibility
auditory hallucinations, and silence, 58
authority, reaction to, 113, 116, 120
auto-hypnosis: in cases of simulation, 187; induced by simulation, 203
automatic phenomena, see phenomena, automatic
automatic writing, see writing, automatic
automatism(s): and auto-suggestion, 58; creation of, by feeling-toned idea, 162; creative force of, 105f; feeling of strangeness invoked by, 52, 53; fostered by distractibility, 181; in hysteria, 171; in minor somnambulistic attacks, 21; motor, as hypnotist, 74f; and partial hypnosis, 49; in semi-somnambulism, 48–61; subconscious, hypnotic influence of, 70; and submersion in dream role, 69; in visual sphere, 57f; waking and somnambulistic, 14
automatisme ambulatoire, 3, 10
auto-suggestibility, 12f
auto-suggestion, 49; and automatisms, 58; and daydreaming, 66f; deeper hypnosis through, 55; and development of automatic motor phenomena, 51; and loss of knowledge, 155; malingerers and, 163; and self-deception, 210ff; and simulated insanity, 203
Azam, C. M. É. E.: on periodic amnesia, 10ff; on spontaneous somnambulism, 62f, 79, 150

B

Baetz, E. von, 71n, 164
Bain, Alexander, 51n
Ballet, Gilbert, 51n
"Baumann, August," in hysterical patient's fantasy, 210ff, 215, 216f
Baumann, Julius, 133
Baynes, H. G., and Cary F. Baynes, on "emotionally toned complex," 97n
behaviour: aggressive, 176; apathetic, 192, 195; boisterous, 116f; in detention, 138; manic, 118ff; outward, and mental activity, 180n; psychic, sudden alterations in, 189; social, in manic mood disorder, 115ff; in solitary confinement, 174, 191; in somnambulistic

states, 19*f;* stupid, in simulation
of insanity, 165, 174; stuporous,
149*ff*
Behr, Albert, 67*n*
Beyond, the, trance journeys to, 33–
35, 42
Billod, E., 186
Binet, Alfred, 11*n*, 12*n;* on automatic actions, 69; on automatization, 181; experiments with patient's anaesthetic hand, 57*f*, 80,
91; on hysterical patients, 67*n;* on
influence of darkness, 56; on Janet's experiment in unconscious
personality, 53; on substitution of
associations, 46; on semi-somnambulism, 48; on somnambulism, 5
—, and Féré, 13*f*, 55*n*
blaspheming, 129
Bleuler, Eugen, 3*n*, 88, 134, 156,
187; on case of attempted suicide,
15
blindness, hysterical, 22
bliss: facial expression of, 28; feeling of, 22, 27
Blumhardt, J. C., 84
Böcker, F. W., 183*f*
Böcklin, Arnold, 100
Boeteau, M., 11
Bohn, Wolfgang, 67
Bolte, August, 159*f*, 185*n*
Bonamaison, L., 71*f*
Bourne, Ansel, 11
Bourru, Henri, 63
brain, physiology of, and reproduction of impressions, 103*f*
Brentano, Bettina, 71
Bresler, Johann, 84
Breuer, Josef (with Sigmund Freud),
78*n;* on hysterical conversion, 155
brightness, hypnagogic, 22
Broca's convolution, 106
brooch, lost and found, 85
brooding, 173*n*
Burghölzli Mental Hospital (Zu-
rich), 113, 117*f*, 125, 126, 127, 137,
218, 220
Burot, Ferdinand, 63

C

Camuset, Louis, 63
Cardan, Jerome, 59*n*
CASES IN SUMMARY, *listed alphabet-*
ically by reporting physician:
Azam: boy, 12½, illustrating periodic amnesia, 10*ff*, 150*n;*
Felida, somnambulistic girl
whose second state became dominant, 62*f*
Bleuler: male, middle aged, suddenly attempting suicide without prodromal symptoms, 15
Boeteau: widow, 22, with somnambulism and amnesia, 11
Bourru and Burot: Louis V., male
hysteric with amnesic alternating character, 63
Flournoy, *see* Smith, Hélène
Guinon and Woltke: hysterical
female, illustrating associations
with colour, 12
James: male, 30, of "ambulatory
sort," a psychopath with amnesia, 11
Janet: hystero-epileptic, male,
whose attacks were associated
with vision of fire, 76; Léonie,
63–65
Jung: *see s.v.*
Landgraf: male, habitual thief,
who simulated imbecility, 182*f*
Leppmann: mentally defective
murderer who simulated imbecility, 182
MacNish: young female showing
sleep disorder followed by amnesia, 12, 150
Marandon de Montyel: psychopathic woman who drowned
her child and shammed am-
nesia, 183
Mesnet: soldier, 27, with somnambulistic attacks with restriction of consciousness, 11*f*
Mitchell: Mary Reynolds, young
woman with character change

CASES IN SUMMARY (*cont.*)
after deep sleep of 20 hours, 61*f*, 79, 150*n*
Nael: male, 32, illustrating retrograde amnesia, 10
Pick: young girl whose daydream passed into twilight state, 162
Proust: male, 30, with *automatisme ambulatoire*, 10*f*
Renaudin: character change in young man with periodic anaesthesia of entire body surface, 63*f*
Richer: woman, 30, a hysteric with hallucinations of children being devoured, 9; hysterical girl, 17, with hallucinations of dead mother, 9
Rüdin: male, convicted of theft and offences against decency and declared irresponsible because of epileptic stupor, 182
Schroeder van der Kolk: girl, 15, exhibiting change of character in periods separated by amnesia, 62, 150
Siefert: male, 36, illustrating chronic manic state, 109
Siemens: young male, day-labourer, falsely accused of murder, 184
Van Deventer: male, with hereditary taint, illustrating sanguine inferiority, 110
catalepsy, 19*f*, 28, 145
catamnesis, 180; in doubtful cases of simulation, 164
catatonia: imitation of, 165; impression of, 192; masked by hysteriform symptoms, 149
Cellini, Benvenuto, sun vision of, 60
cemetery: Miss E.'s behaviour in, 6*ff*; walk in, 13
censure, angry reaction to, 118*f*
chain of ideas, 133
character: and actions, 133; development at puberty, 92; psychological

fluctuations of, 44; quality of affects determined by, 215
character, change in, 47, 61–70; without amnesic split, 63*f*; literary use of amnesic, 63; in somnambulistic state, 87*n*; second state, 61*f*
Charcot, Jean Martin: on somnambulism, 9*f*; scheme for word-picture composition, 51*n*
cheating, pathological, 66
Chevreul, Michel Eugène, 48
childhood: and later abnormal emotional state, 123; *see also* puberty
children: dead, hallucinations of, 6*f*, 13; gibberish of, 85*n*; hallucinations of devouring of, 9
Clairvoyante of Prevorst (Frau Hauffe), 27, 34, 36, 42, 44, 66, 84, 85, 87
clang-reaction, 166*ff*
Claus, —— (Sachsenberg), 185*n*
collecting, mania for, 11
colour, associations in hysterical attacks, 12
communications: automatic, 19, 25*ff*, 31, 44; trance, origin of, 31
complex(es): associated, objectivation of, 77*n*; feeling-toned, 97*n*, 219; psychic, 53
composition, literary: of manic patient, 126, 128*f*; patient's, autobiographical, 198
comprehension: and association, 168; and distractibility, 142; faulty, 180; reduced, 178*f*; retention of, despite loss of knowledge, 152; and senseless answers, 193*f*
compulsion: negativistic, 149; pathological, 214
concepts, and feelings, 87
concert, unpleasant episode at, 146*f*, 154*f*
confession: and forgiveness, trance pantomime of, 30; of simulation, 176, 196*f*
conflagration, vision of, 76
confusion: emotional, 204; —, disturbance of memory in, 171*f*; —,

as motivation for simulating insanity, 172*f;* —, and "stage fright," etc., 164; hallucinatory, 148*ff;* mental, 165*f,* 174, 177, 204
conscience, effect on psychic life, 173
conscious mind: and associations, 98*f;* tyrannized by memories, 100
consciousness: alternating states of, 12, 149; amnesic split, 76; dissociability of, 204; dissociated, and memory, 63; disturbances of, 163; division of, 69; double, *see* double consciousness; entry of cryptomnesic image, 81–87, 96; and feeling-toned memory complexes, 98; and fraud, 215*f;* hysterical splits of, 76; identity of, in somnambulistic attacks, 9; loss of previous impressions, 104; rare states of, 3*ff;* reconstitution of scope of, 153*f;* restriction of, 11*f,* 45*f,* 151*f,* 203; —, and cryptomnesia, 86; —, and the senseless answer, 149; secondary complexes, 72*f;* in semi-somnambulism, 47*f;* in severe hysteria, 9; split, in misreading, 91; supraliminal, 71, 152; threshold of, 14, 45; tyrannized by unconsciousness, 105
consideration for others, lack of, 131
control, mediumistic, 30*ff*
Conventi, Italian murderer, somnambulistic personality, 35
conversation, trance, 20*f,* 28, 29; impression of wilful deception, 43; by means of intended tremors, 54; memory of, 27; with somnambulist personality, 31*f*
convulsions, hysterical attacks of, 115
Cook, Florence, medium, 36
counter-suggestion: and prevention of automatisms, 54; *see also* suggestion
creation, original, 41, 82
creativity: and ecstasy, 104*f;* of hallucinations, 12; and memory complex, 100*f;* and wish-fulfilment, 99; *see also* originality
crime: psychological diagnosis of, 219*ff; see also* fraud; murder; rape; suicide; swindling; theft; vagrancy
criminal(s): energy and self-control in deception, 161; influence of hysteria on actions of, 215; reason for simulated insanity, 186; stuporous behaviour of, 150; unjustifiable presence of, in asylums, 218; *see also* prisoners
Crookes, Sir William, 36
cryptomnesia, 81–87, 95–106; defined, 101; enrichment of conscious memory, 86
Cullerre, A., 9*n*

D

Daltonism, 201
dark, powers of, 41*f*
darkness, 22; automatic writing in, 27*f,* 55; effect of, 26, 56; solitary confinement in, 164; and suggestibility, 57
David, Jacques Louis, 37
daydream(ing): passing into twilight state, 162; pathological, 66*f*
dead, the: hallucinations of, 6*ff,* 26; spirits of, 47
death, thoughts of, 20
deathbed, and cryptomnesic reproduction, 84, 104
deception: in hallucinatory phenomena, 78; *see also* malingering; self-deception
decisions: and feeling-values, 133; voluntary, and feeling-tone, 132*f*
degeneracy: congenital, 204; effect of detention on, 169*f;* and hypalgesia, 180; hysteria as mark of, 99*f;* inherited, 64; and malingering, 160; psychic, symptoms of, 130; signs of, 201; and simulation, 188; symptoms of, 111
degenerate(s): case of simulation,

degenerate(s) (*cont.*)
183*f*; energy and self-control of, 161
dejection, 173*n*
Delbrück, Anton, 66&*n*, 68*n*, 162
delirium: delusions of grandeur in, 125; hysterical, 7, 8*f*, 67; with motor excitement, 151; syndromes of degeneracy, 130
delirium tremens, 117, 118
delusion(s): of being wronged, 151; in hysterical delirium, 8*f*; of grandeur, 125, 126*f*, 151; *see also* self-deception
dementia, and outer associations, 169
dementia paralytica, and intellectual deficiency, 151
dementia praecox, 159, 202
depression, 115, 117, 119; epileptic, 15*n*; source of, 123
"depressive melancholia," 182
Dessoir, Max, 76*n*, 80
detention: characteristic states of prisoners in, 148*ff*; fear of, 188; and hysterical psychoses, 160; hysterical stupor of prisoner in, 137–56; influence of, 150*f*; patient's affect *re*, 142, 169*f*
diagnoses: contradictory psychiatric, 209–18; difficulty of differentiation in certain states of epilepsy, somnambulism, and hysteria, 15; modern requirements for, 160; optimistic, in cases of simulation, 185*f*; psychological, of facts, 219–21; of rare states of consciousness, 3*f*
dialect word, *see* word substitution
Diehl, August, 15
diphtheria, in case history, 112, 114
disorientation: following unpleasant episode, 146*f*; patient's, as to location of room, 195, 199; in senseless answers, 140*ff*; *see also* orientation
disposition: hysterical, 161; —, outstanding feature of, 204; —, subsidiary symptoms, 213; mental, and assimilation of affects, 170; —, and simulation, 173; pleasure-seeking, 132, 210
dissociation: and affect, 171, 181; of consciousness, 204
distractibility, 111, 120; and automatizations, 181; effect on comprehension, 142; and faulty memory, 143; hysterical, 45; and interest, 82; and lethargy, 72; low-grade states of, 46*f*; and misreading, 45, 90
distraction, outer: experiments with, 168
disturbance(s): of attention, 44*f*; of emotions, 8*f*; of memory, 8; psychogenic, 184*f*; of sensibility, 150; of thinking, 110; of writing, 140*f*
dizziness, 146*f*; *see also* fainting-fits; giddiness
Donath, Julius, 62*n*
double consciousness, 3, 12, 149; and amnesia, 76; and new character formations, 79; and submersion in role, 162
"double life," S. W.'s, 25
dream(s): of black and white figures, 23*f*; hysterical thinking in, 67; of kittens and cats, 144; level, consciousness and, in severe hysteria, 9; objectivation of, 68; origin of, 69; pictures, somnambulistic, 13*f*; realization of ideal state, 66; somnambulistic, 32, 46, 66*f*; symbolism in, 57; symbols, and memories, 100; uninhibited by conscious mind, 99; visual, and light sensations of retina, 59
dreaminess: lapses into, 21*f*; pathological, 3, 16, 68*f*, 173
dream-state: pathological, 46; somnambulistic, 13
dream-world, reality of, 23
drowsiness, and darkness, 56
drunkenness, *see* alcohol; alcoholism
dualism, derivation of idea of, 87

dull-wittedness, 165*f*
Dyce, ——, 79

E

E., Miss, case of spontaneous somnambulism, 5–17; hallucinations
of dead children, 6*f*, 13
earthquake: and amnesia, 172; paralysis of movement and feeling
caused by, 164
Eckermann, J. P., 84*n;* on deathbed
memories, 104
ecstasy: and creativity, 104; fantasy
activity in, 32*f;* and glossolalia,
84; and intellectual exaltation,
87; in manic mood disorder, 126;
Nietzsche on, 84*n;* poetic, 84; in
somnambulistic states, 19*f;* and
table-turning experiments, 25
Eder, M. D., 3*n*
Edmond, Laura, daughter of judge,
84
educational level, improvement of,
in somnambulistic states, 18, 19,
88
ego: pubertal changes in constitution of, 64; somnambulist, 24, 32,
36, 80; —, and patient's distractibility, 72; —, *see also* Ivenes
ego-complex: and cryptomnesic
idea, 81; link between twilight
and waking states, 76, 78; splitting
off of psychic functions from, 91
egotism, extreme, 213; *see also*
megalomania
Einfall, word, 96
elation, 120, 124*ff;* in chronic mania,
110*f;* continuous state of, 125*f*
embarrassment: and attention, 168;
and inhibited association, 166
Emmerich, Katharina, 186
Emminghaus, H., 62*n*
emotion(s): changes in, in feeble-
mindedness, 189; disturbances of,
and hysterical delirium, 8*f;* domi-
nation over intellect, 131*f;* influence on actions, 132*f;* and paralysis, 164; and psychogenic disturbances, 185; repressed, 56; violent,
after-effect of, 187; *see also* affect
employment, frequent change of,
121, 123, 124*f*, 173*ff*
enchantment of spirits, S. W.'s attempts at, 34
energy, impulsive, of criminals, 191
entoptic phenomena, 58
environment, falsified perception
of, 202*f*
epilepsy, 3; depression in, 15*n;* diagnostic difficulty in certain states
of, 4*f*, 15; epileptic stupor, 182;
and hysteria, 4; *see also* hystero-
epilepsy
epileptoid, term, 15
Erler, —— (Eberswalde), 9*n*, 67
eroticism, 118; in manic mood disorders, 121*f*
ethical feelings: effect of lack of,
132; *see also* moral defect
exaggeration, conscious: in abnormal affective states, 189
examination, fear of, 165*f*
excitability, 122*f;* and alcoholism,
125; emotional, 117, 138, 201; —,
in morally defective persons, 134
exhaustion, 14*f;* after ecstasy, 22;
and manifestation of hysteria, 16;
temporary, and protracted hysterical delirium, 8
expectation, feeling of, 56, 59
external world: isolation of ego-
consciousness from, 73; orientation to, 24; relation of subconscious personality to, 64

F

facial expression: blissful, 28; rigidity of, 175, 179, 192; stupid, 166
facts, psychological diagnosis of,
218–21
fainting-fits, 5, 17, 175, 179, 202*f*

fantasy(ies): pathological, 67; and romance, 162; in somnambulistic states, 32f, 36ff, 68
fatigue, 143; see also exhaustion
fear: of detention, 183f, 188; of examination, 165f; and rage, 138f; and simulation, 165f
feeble-mindedness, 110; and compulsive talking, 105; and doubtful simulation, 166ff; and defective critical faculty, 131; heightened by emotionality, 169; imbecility induced by emotional changes, 189; and social incapacity, 132
feelings, and concepts, 87
feeling-tone(d), 97f; associations, 105f; and decisions reached by the will, 132; ideas, 68, 162, 219; memory, 146f, 155; motivation, 163; relationship to character and actions, 133; thought-processes, 203f; train of thought, 97f
feeling-values, influence on decisions, 133
feet, burned with sulphuric acid, 163
Felida (Azam's case), 62f, 79, 150
Féré, Charles, 13f, 55n
figures: black and white, 22, 42; hallucinatory, 144, 151; white, 26
Flaubert, Gustave, 71n
flexibilitas cerea, 20
flight of ideas, 111, 113, 118, 122f, 125, 128, 130f
Flournoy, Théodore, 55n, 57n, 71n; case, see Smith, Hélène; on cryptomnesia, 101; on glossolalia, 84; on somnambulistic dreams, 66n; on speech automatisms, 73n
flower: Goethe's image of, 14; in visions, 26, 60
food: delusion of poisoning of, 138; refusal of, 174f, 192, 196f, 203
forces, attractive and repulsive, 39ff
foreign words, manic patient's use of, 126, 129
Forel, Auguste: on dissociation, 181;

on pathological cheating and daydreaming, 66
forgetfulness, hysterical, 68f; see also amnesia
forgetting, idea of, 155
forgiveness, trance pantomime of, 30
Förster-Nietzsche, Elisabeth, 83, 103
fraud: case of, 209–18; conscious and intentional, 216ff; and self-deception, 214
French language, words derived from, 85
Freud, Sigmund: dream investigations of, 56, 78, 99; on hysterical identification, 67; on psychogenic disturbances, 185; on symptomatic actions, 98; theory of hysteria, 92, 155, 170; on train of thought and attention, 69n; see also Breuer, Josef
Fritsch, ——, 161
Fürstner, C., 160, 186
future: adventurous plans for, 123; optimism re, 117, 123, 126, 129

G

Galton, Francis, 220
Ganser, Sigbert, 137, 154; on hysterical ailments, 184f; on "senseless answer," 149; on states observed in prisoners in detention, 148ff; studies of twilight states, 160, 172f, 179; syndrome, 185, 187
"Geiss," see "Ziege"
genius: creative, and wish-fulfilment, 99; and degeneracy, 99n; "possessed" nature of, 82; psychology of, 4; and sensibility, 99; symptomatic actions of, 100; work of, 105
Gerbenstein, Ulrich von (somnambulistic personality), 29, 32, 36, 37, 43; gay-hilarious type, 77; increased influence of, 78
gibberish, 85n

giddiness, 5; *see also* fainting-fits
Gilles de la Tourette, Georges, 87*n*
glass tumbler, as "psychograph," 25, 27
Gley, M. E. E., 48
glossolalia, 84*f*
gnostic system, parallels in S. W.'s mystic science, 88
Godwina F.: case of hysterical stupor, 137–56; peculiarities of case, 148*ff;* physical examination, 139; tests, 144
Goethe, J. W. von, 59*n;* and Bettina Brentano, 71; conjuration of flower image, 14; in S. W.'s trance fantasies, 37; *see also* Eckermann, J. P.
Görres, J. J. von, 67*n*, 84*n*
Graeter, C., 76*n*
grande hystérie, symptoms of, 10*f*
grandeur, delusion of, 125, 126*f*, 151
grandfather: Jung's, 26, 56; S. W.'s, as spiritualistic control, 19, 26, 31, 73, 74*f*, 77
"graphomaniacs," 131
Greek: deathbed memory of, 104; mystic terms derived from, 85
Gross, Hans, 161*n*
Guinon, Georges, 9*n;* and Sophie Woltke, experiments with hysterics, 12, 46

H

haemoptysis, simulation of, 163
Hagen, F. W., 56*n*, 59*n*, 60*n*, 71*n*
Hahn, R., 89*ff*
hallucinations: auditory, *see* auditory hallucinations; complex, in partial waking state, 61; creative, 12; of dead people and skeletons, 6*f;* in *grande hystérie,* 9; habitual, 16; hypnagogic, 14, 23, 59; induced, 11*f;* intuitive, 61; and passage from night-dreams to waking state, 23; in prodromal stage, 150; psychogenic, 14; reasons for appearance of, 58*f;* of the senses, in

hysterical delirium, 8*f;* in solitary confinement, 192; systematic nature of, 22*f;* teleological, 79; of theft of money, 144; transition to somnambulism, 55*f;* voices, 125, 127, 128, 130; waking, 17
hand: anaesthetic, 57, 80, 91; thrust into fire, 163*n*
Harden, Maximilian, 106
Hauffe, Frau, *see* Clairvoyante of Prevorst
Hauptmann, Carl, 77*n*
head, patient's banging of, against door, 176*ff*, 195, 199
headache, 5, 7*f*, 14, 16, 29; cured by suggestion, 145; in hysterical stupor, 142*ff;* self-magnetization to dispel, 27
hebephrenics, irrelevant talk of, 149
Hebrew, deathbed memory of, 104
Hecker, J. F. C., 59*n*, 61
Heidelberg Clinic, 182
heightened unconscious performance, *see* unconscious performance
Hélène Smith, *see* Smith
hell, journey to, 82*f*, 101*ff*
heredity: and degeneracy, 64, 201; in case of fraud, 213; and hysterical stupor, 137; manic mood disorder and, 112, 115, 120, 124, 130; and psychopathic inferiority, 5; and simulated insanity, 173, 190
Hertz, Carl, 183*f*
Hoche, A. E., 163*n*
Höfelt, J. A., 62
hunch, cryptomnesic image as, 81
hydrotherapy, 5
hypalgesia, 178, 179, 197; and degeneracy, 180
hyperactivity, motor, 131
hypermnesia, 81*n*, 86
hypnosis: continuity of memory under, 145*f;* deepening of, 55, 56; double, 145*f*, 147, 154; effect on amnesia, 145; hystero-, 74; partial, *see below;* patients' denial of being hypnotized, 164; self-, partial,

hypnosis (*cont.*)
73; treatment by, 8; word, derivation of mystic terms from, 85
hypnosis, partial, 49; and automatic writing, 54*f;* influence of, 70*f;* penetration into speech area, 51*f;* and response to suggestion, 54; self-, 73
hypnotist, automatism as, 74*f*
hypomanic: behaviour, chronic, 109; complex of symptoms, 134; state, chronic, 111
hysteria, 3*ff;* and affects, 215; and assimilation of affects, 170; associations with colour in attacks of, 12; automatization of psychic functions, 91; diagnosis of, 14; and epilepsy, relationship between clinical pictures of, 4; and feeling-toned memory complex, 98; and genius, 99*f;* and memory, 152; modern theory of, 160; and moral defect, 214*ff;* periodic changes in personality in, 63; psychopathology of, 137*ff;* severe, 9; and simulation, 187; and somnambulism, 5*ff;* strength-producing mechanisms of, 163; symptoms, 180, 201; *see also grande hystérie*
hysterical conversion, 155
hysterical misreading, *see* misreading
hysterical subjects: constitutional lying and fraud, 211; and forgetfulness, 68*n;* identification of, with object of interest, 181; influence of affects on, 171, 217; influence of darkness on, 56; irrelevant answers of, 92; lying of, 160; phenomena observed in, 203; self-torture by, 186; sensibility of, 80*f;* systematic anaesthesia among, 64; young, moria states of, 150
hystero-epilepsy: attacks induced by open fire or lighted match, 76; visions in, 9
hystero-hypnosis, 74

I

idea(s): affective, 155; associations with ego-complex, 81; automatization of, 181; chain of, and feeling-value, 133; combinations of, 100*f;* delusional, 215; feeling-toned, 68, 162, 219; "levelling-down" of, 133; motor components of, 73; new, development of, in somnambulism, 86*n;* new combinations of, 99; original, 81; predominating, influence of, on intended tremors, 49*n;* —, and retinal phenomena, 60; —, surrender to, 67*f; see also* flight of ideas
ideal, subconscious personality as, 65*f,* 77*f*
identification, hysterical, 67
image(s): combination of, *vs.* new formation, 96; cryptomnesic, intrapsychic entry into consciousness, 81–86; hypnagogic, and dream-images, 59; formed from spots of light, 58*ff;* visual, and cutaneous stimuli, 13
imagination: and fantastic figures, 58*f;* and visions, 61
imbecility, simulation of, 182*f*
impostors, intentional fraud of, 216
impressions: forgotten, reappearance of, in cryptomnesia, 103; subjective, of the malingerer, 159*f*
impulse, unexpected, 12, 13
incarnation of Parisian poisoner, 38
inclinations, evil: and hysteria, 216
inferiority: hysterical, 180; intellectual and emotional, 4; neurasthenic, diagnostic difficulty, 15
inferiority, psychopathic, 3*ff;* borderlines between clinical pictures of, 111; character of affects, 189; classification of cases, 4*f,* 15; and hysteria and epilepsy, 4*ff;* influence of affects on, 171; phenomena related to other clinical pictures, 16
influence, magnetic, 41

inhibition(s): of association, 166; imposed by conscious mind, 98f

insanity: cyclic, 63; feeling-toned complexes of associations in, 219; legal conception of, 218; and legal responsibility, 204; simulated, case of, 159–205; —, medical opinion on, 188–205

insight: of defendant, as to her swindling, 217; during psychic disturbance, 164; increased, in question of simulation, 159; patient's, as to illness, 106, 113, 118, 119, 123, 126, 176

inspiration, Nietzsche on, 82n, 105

instability: and inner unrest, 200f; psychopathic, 112ff; social, in patient with manic mood disorder, 120ff

instinct, pathological, 215

instinctual drives, excess of, 132

instructions, response to, in case of simulated insanity, 175ff

intellect: and action, 133; effect of emotional lability on, 134; exaltation of, in ecstasy, 87; under sway of emotions, 131f; and will, 132

intelligence, 128; defective, in hysterical stupor, 149f; in manic mood disorder, 112ff, 115, 120, 124, 132

interest, and object, 81f

internment: in case of fraud, 213; and simulation, 182f; see also detention

inventors: crackpot, 131f; "paranoia" of, 130

irreparabile damnum, 76

irresponsibility, legal, see responsibility

irritability, 109, 122f, 125, 130, 133, 173n; in chronic mania, 110f

Ivenes (S. W.'s somnambulistic ego), 32, 36; character and reincarnations of, 36ff; deterioration of, 78f; improvement over normal

personality of S. W., 65; mental products grouped around grandfather, 74f; study of, 64ff; subconscious personalities' knowledge of, 74

J

Jacobi, ——, 183

Jacobi-Jenssen, ——, 164

Jacobsohn, Siegfried, 106

James, William, 61n; on case of psychopath with amnesia, 11

Janet, Pierre: on disturbance of attention, 44f; on hystero-epilepsy, 76; on influence of affects, 170f, 181; Léonie, case of, 63, 65; on lies of hysterical subjects, 68n; on unconscious personality of subject, 53, 54n; use of double hypnosis, 154; whispered suggestions, experiment with, 51n, 70f

Japan: earthquake, 164; proverb, 163

Jessen, W., 79n, 183n

Joan of Arc, 60, 79

journeys, trance, 22, 27, 29, 33f

Jung, C. G.: on "feeling-tone," 97n; his grandfather in S. W.'s séances, 26, 56; inaugural dissertation, 3n, 219; professional career, v–viii; S. W. and, 21; in S. W.'s trance fantasies, 35, 37ff

CASES IN SUMMARY (in order of presentation, numbered for reference):

[1] Miss E., 40, showing hallucinations of skeletons and dead children. Illustrates concept of spontaneous somnambulism based on hysterical psychopathic inferiority. — 5ff

[2] Miss S. W., 15½, somnambulistic girl (spiritualistic medium) with poor inheritance. — 17–88; see also S. W., Miss

Jung (cont.)

[3] Hysterical young woman, illustrating feeling-toned memory complex. — 98

[4] Business man, 27, illustrating mild form of manic mood disorder. — 112–15

[5] Woman, 44, with manic mood disorder, illustrating alcoholism dependent on emotional abnormality. — 115–20

[6] Nurse, 26, exhibiting manic mood disorder with social instability. — 120–24

[7] Male, 55, painter, charged with theft, whose intense manic symptoms ruled out even "partial responsibility." — 124–32

[8] Godwina F., 48, illustrating hysterical stupor in a prisoner in detention. — 137–56

[9] Doubtful simulation in male mental defective charged with rape. — 165f

[10] Doubtful simulation in boy, 17, charged with rape. — 166ff

[11] Male, 35, mill-hand, degenerate, illustrating simulation of insanity. — 173–80, 189–205

[12] Youth, 18, whose theft was discovered through the associations of a feeling-toned complex relating to the crime. — 220f

WORKS: "A Review of the Complex Theory," 97n; Collected Papers on Analytical Psychology, 3n; Experimental Researches, 168n, 219n; "On Psychical Energy," 97n; "The Reaction-Time Ratio in the Association Experiment," 219; Symbols of Transformation, 186n; "The Psychology of Dementia Praecox," 168n; and Riklin, "The Associations of Normal Subjects," 219ff; for account of works, see v–x

K

Kant, Immanuel, 39f
Karplus, J. P., 77n
Kerner, Justinus, 27, 34, 44, 66; Blätter aus Prevorst passage paralleled by Nietzsche, 82f, 102ff; and Frau Hauffe, 87; see also Clairvoyante of Prevorst
Klein, Julius, 219ff
knowledge: cosmic, plane of, 42; intuitive, of somnambulists, 86; loss of, 12, 61, 140ff, 148, 151; —, and not wanting to know, 155; retention of, 178; see also educational level; quality of being known
Koch, ——, 110
Kraepelin, Emil, 167n; arithmetic tests, 178
Krafft-Ebing, Richard von, vi, 86n, 110, 134n; on hysterical ecstasy and memory, 104; on protracted states of hysterical delirium, 8f
Krauss, A., 161

L

lability, emotional, 111ff, 116, 119, 123ff, 213; see also instability
Ladd, C., 59
Landgraf, Karl, 182f
language, 101; exaggerated, in manic mood disorder, 118; French, 85; Greek, 85, 104; Hebrew, 104; idiom used by S. W., 20, 28, 35; Latin, 85; loftiness of, 126; Martian, 85; of the spirits, 33f; Swiss dialect, 18, 89ff; see also glossolalia
lapses, 65; see also preoccupation
Latin, mystic terms derived from, 85
Laurent, Armand, 180n; on patient who simulated, 186
Legrand du Saule, Henri, 63
Lehmann, A. G. L., 48, 49n, 73n, 162n

Léonie (Janet's case), 63, 65
Leppmann, A., 182
lethargy, 3, 70*f;* changed into hypnosis, 72; hallucinations in, 72; hysterical, induced by hypnosis, 71*f*
letters, transposed or reversed, 25*f,* 52; *see also* love letters
liar, pathological, 67; *see also* lying
light: entoptic perceptions of, 58*f;* formless, vision of, 59*n;* powers of, 41*f*
Lindau, Paul, 63
Ljubljana earthquake, 172
Loewenfeld, Leopold, 87*n;* on development of new ideas, 86*n;* on lethargy, 70–72; on sleepwalking, 10*n*
Lombroso, Cesare: on genius, 99; "graphomaniacs," 131
lottery tickets, case involving, 209–18
Lotz, —— (Frankfurt a. M.), 186*n*
love letters, from imaginary fiancé, 67, 162
Lücke, Robert, 172*n,* 185
lung, hysterical haemorrhage of, 186
lying, 3; hysterical, 160; pathological, 16, 67, 68, 203, 211; of thieves, 161; and self-deception, 212

M

Macario, M. M. A., 61
MacNish, Robert, 12, 150
Magnan, Valentin, 111, 130
magnetism, derivation of mystic term from, 85
magnetization: and cerebral anaesthesia, 49; self-, 27
malingerer(ing): character of, 160*f;* difficulty of unmasking, 159*f;* passage into subconscious, 181; use of feeble-minded behaviour, 172; *see also* shamming; simulation
mania, 90; chronic, cardinal symptoms, 111; ——, Wernicke on, 110; periodic, diagnosis of, 126
manic mood disorder, 109–34; periodic exacerbations of, 134; summary, 134; symptoms, 111*f*
manie sans délire, 110
Marandon de Montyel, E., 183
marriage: effect on patient of breakup of, 116; unhappy, 190*ff*
Mars: S. W.'s description of, 34; visions of, 60
Martian language, 85
Mary Reynolds, *see* Reynolds
materialization: as origin of Adam, 38; trance, 29, 42
Maury, L. F. A., 59
megalomania, 111, 124*ff,* 126, 130; *see also* egotism
Meggendorfer picture-book, 178
melancholia, 109; depressive, 182
memory(ies): auto-suggestive falsification of, 67; blocking of unpleasant events in, 153; conscious, enrichment in cryptomnesia, 86; continuity of, in hypnosis, 145; defective; in hysterical subjects, 164; ——, for period of simulation, 202; direct and indirect, 95*ff;* and dissociated consciousness, 63; disturbed, 8; effect of affects on, 171; feeling-toned, 100, 146*f,* 155; fragmentary, reproduction of, 105; gaps of, and acquisition of content through auto-suggestion, 13; hysteriform lapses of, 12; loss of, 138 (*see also* amnesia); medium's, at disposal of somnambulist personalities, 32*f;* old, re-emergence of, 103*f; see also* cryptomnesia
memory-image: in cryptomnesia, 81; and the law of association, 95; and unconscious perception, 96
Mendel, Emanuel, 110
menstruation: and abnormal emotional state, 123; in case of spontaneous somnambulism, 5, 7
mental: activity, in chronic mania, 110*f;* ——, effect of simulation on,

mental *(cont.)*
202*f;* content, intrusion of, in motor phenomena, 51; defectives, simulation of insanity among, 165*ff;* disease, and epileptoid attacks, 15; phenomena, in automatic table-turning, 51*f;* productivity, in chronic mania, 110*f*
Mesnet, Ernest, 11*f*
Messiah, manic patient's delusions of self as, 126, 128
Michelangelo Buonarroti, 100
miracles, faked, 186
mirror-writing, 52, 55
misreading, hysterical, 18, 44, 45–47, 89–92; essential difference from all other types, 91; as prodromal symptom, 46; psychology of, 45*f*
Mitchell, S. Weir, 150; case of Mary Reynolds, 61*f,* 79
Moll, Albert, 63*n*
money: attitude toward, 121; delusion of theft of, 138*ff,* 143*ff,* 151
moods: actions affected by, 217; unstable, 139; *see also* lability, emotional; manic mood disorder
moral defect (moral insanity), 111, 114, 119, 124, 132, 134, 212; and alcoholism, 116; congenital condition, 215; and emotional abnormality, 134; explanation of, 115; and hysteria, 214*ff;* periodic or cyclic, 134; scientific conception of, 217*f*
moral insanity, *see* moral defect
Mörchen, Friedrich, 15, 68*n*
motion, forces of, 41
motivation: in case of simulated insanity, 180; characterological, 133; feeling-toned, and subconscious mechanisms, 163; psychological, 172
motor: area, deeper hypnosis of, by auto-suggestion, 55; automatism, 74*f,* 86; centres, excitation limited to, 73; hyperactivity, 131; impulses, barring of perception of, 51

motor phenomena: automatic, intrusion of mental content into, 51; in automatic writing, 55; suggestion and, 48*f;* unconscious, 48*ff*
Müller, Erdmann, 134*n*
Müller, Johannes, 59*n*
Muralt, Ludwig von, 88
murder, impulse toward, 64
murderer, case of simulated imbecility, 182
muscles, tonic and clonic spasms of, 186
mutism, simulated, 182*f*
Myers, F. W. H., 52, 59
mystic science, 39–42; derivation of names in, 85; diagram of forces, 40; groups of forces, 41*f;* as heightened unconscious performance, 87

N

Naef, M., 10*f*
narcolepsy, 3, 70
needlepricks, *see* pricks
negativism, 183; catatonic, 149
nervous system, psychopathic disposition of, 79
neurasthenia, 3*ff;* crises, 14*f;* and psychopathic inferiority, 4*ff,* 16
neuropathies, and epileptoid attacks, 15
neuroses: shock, 164; traumatic, 150
New Testament, glossolalia in, 84
Nietzsche, Friedrich: cryptomnesic parallel of passage from Kerner, 82*f,* 101*ff;* on ecstasy, 84*n;* on inspiration, 82*n;* on inspiration and revelation, 105; interest in Kerner, 83; mental state when writing *Zarathustra,* 104*f*
Nissl, F., 137, 149
noises: animal, 128, 129; hallucinatory, 147; *see also* voices
Nordau, Max Simon, 99*f*
normal state, linked with pathological dreaming, 68*f*

number: experiments with, 57f, 86, 91; gaps in counting, 142f; patient's confusion re, 141; tests with, 193, 197f

O

object: cryptomnesic reproduction, 84; and interest, 81f, 181
objectivation: of associated complexes, 77n; of dreams, 68; of visual images, 57
obnubilation, 61
occultism: and heightened unconscious performance, 80; so-called, Jung's case of, see S. W.
Oehler, Pastor, Nietzsche's grandfather, 83
offences, criminal: moral defect vs. hysteria as source of, 216
optic impression, and misreading, 90
optimism, 117, 123, 126, 129; exorbitant, 131
oracular sayings, in séances, 35
orientation: as to place, 152; as to space, 142; as to time, 177; as to time and place, 153, 165, 175, 193; unconscious, 152f, 154; see also disorientation
originality: of ideas, 81; source of, 96
over-activity, 111, 117f, 120

P

pain: self-inflicted, 163, 186; sensibility to, 139, 175, 194, 197
painting, patient's, 127
pallor, in somnambulistic states, 19, 26, 28, 29, 71
paralysis, 90; emotional, 71n, 164
paranoia, 130
Pelman, C., 15n, 79n
pendulum, experiments with, and intended tremors, 49n

penitentiary, manic patient's behaviour in, 127
perception: activated by association, 95; along verbal-motor route, 45; and reproduction, in misreading, 91f; unconscious, 87; —, related association activated by, 96; —, via anaesthesic skin, 80
performance tests, 178ff, 199f; see also unconscious performance
perseveration, 166f
personality: alteration of, in semi-somnambulistic states, 24; automatic splitting of, 52; change of, in somnambulistic states, 19, 24; future, and double consciousness, 79; and hysterical twilight states, 16f; somnambulistic dissociation of, 67; see also character
personality(ies), unconscious: automatic expression of, 56; continuity of, 64f; development of, through suggestion, 53; distinct from automata, 78; gay-hilarious, 73; hypnosis of, 154; hypnotic effect of, 72; Janet's Lucie and Léonie, 63; origin of, 77f; range of knowledge, 73f; relation to somnambulistic ego, 74ff; relationship of, 37f; serio-religious, 73; somnambulistic, in S. W.'s trances, 30–36, 37f; split off, 72f; split off from dream-ego, 78; splitting of, 56f; two types of, 72f; unity of, 76f
persuasion, powers of, and hysteria, 215
pessimism, 112
phenomena, automatic: memory of, 33; misreading as, 90
Phleps, Eduard, 164n, 172
physical examination, 6, 139; in case of simulated insanity, 178f, 194f, 197, 200
Pick, Arnold, 15n, 66f, 162
Pinel, Philippe, 109f
pinpricks, see pricks
plagiarism, and cryptomnesia, 81, 101ff

plants, life-forces of, 41
playing cards, experiment with hypnotized subject, 76
pleasure/pain affects, 120
pleasure-seeking, 132, 210
pneumatological school, 16
poets, 16; lives of, 131; and wish fulfilment, 99
poisoner(s): Parisian incarnation of, 38; art of shamming among, 161
poisoning of food, delusion *re*, 174, 192, 197
pope, manic patient's delusions of himself as, 125
possibility, psychological: and success of suggestion, 53
powers, light and dark (good and evil), 41*f*
practice, effect of, in association tests, 168
premonition(s), 17; in semi-somnambulistic states, 25; of somnambulistic attacks, 20
preoccupation, before and after somnambulistic attacks, 47
Prevorst: *Blätter aus, see* Kerner *s.v.;* Prophetess of, see Clairvoyante of Prevorst
Preyer, William T., 49*n*
pricks: on anaesthetic hand, 57, 80, 91; insensibility to, 138; reaction to, 139, 175
Prince, Morton, 63
prison complexes, 130
prisoners: characteristic states of, 148*ff;* Ganser complex, 187; case of hysterical stupor, 137–56; hysterical psychoses, 160
prison psychosis, 156; characteristic syndrome, 151
prophecies, 17
prophets, 16
Proust, Achille Adrien, 10
pseudologia phantastica, 68, 203
psyche, abnormal affective states of, 189

psychic: complexes, disaggregation of, 53; excitation, 71*ff;* functions, automatization of, 91; processes, and hysterical attack, 77*n;* —, in misreading, 90*f;* shock, as cause of hysterical attack, 9
psychic elements: combination of, and originality, 96; conscious and unconscious, 98; disaggregation of, 67
"psychic shadow state," 46
psychogenic disturbances, dependent on external events, 184*f*
psychograph, in séances, 25*ff*
psychological possibility, 53
psychology, normal: and pathological inferiority, 4
psychopath: morally defective, 212; puberty of, 64
psychopathic illnesses, and chronic mania, 111
puberty: fantasy-making in, 70; fluctuations of character in, 44; physiological changes of character in, 64; somnambulistic symptoms in, 79; and manic mood disorder, 112, 114, 130

Q

quality of being known, 96, 98, 101*f*
questions, and senseless answers, 140*ff*
Quicherat, Jules, 60*n*

R

R., Mr., and his brother, P. R., in S. W.'s séances, 31*f*
rabbits, shooting of, in cryptomnesic image, 83, 102
Raecke, Julius, 137, 154, 172*n;* on hysterical ailments, 184*f;* on hysterical twilight state, 149; on loss of knowledge, 155; on stupor in criminals, 150

rape: attempt to simulate, 66; charge of, 165; victim's memory of attempts at, 115
reactions: meaningless, 166, 167*n;* slowness of, 165
reading, addiction to, 120
reading-tests, 90
reality, loss of, 171
Récamier, Mme., 37
red-green blindness, 197, 201
Redlich, Johann, 67*n,* 68*n*
reflexes, tests of, 6, 139, 178, 197
reincarnation, S. W.'s system of, 36*ff,* 69*f*
religious: feeling, expression of, by manic patient, 126, 129; sects, founders of, 16
remorse, as reason for simulation, 196*f,* 201
Renaudin, Louis François Émile, 63*f*
reproduction, in cryptomnesia, 103*f*
responsibility, legal, 179, 204, 213; in case of epileptic stupor, 182; juridical conception of irresponsibility, 216; limited by hysteria, 217; and moral defect, 209*ff;* and pathological self-deception, 211*ff*
rest cure, 14
restlessness, 111, 112, 116, 121*f;* inner, 133, 177, 200
retention, reduced, 197
retina, light sensations of, 59*f*
revelation, Nietzsche on, 82*n,* 105
Reynolds, Mary (Weir Mitchell's case), 61f, 79, 150*n*
Ribot, Théodule Armand, 63&*n,* 64*n*
Richarz, Franz, 180*n,* 183*f*
Richer, Paul, 9, 63
Richet, Charles, 47*f,* 87
Rieger, Conrad, 63
right and wrong, recognition of: and legal responsibility, 216
rigidity: of face, 175, 179, 192; of posture, 138, 175
Riklin, Franz, investigations with Jung, 168*ff*
role, submersion in, 66, 69, 162

romances, S. W.'s, 36*f,* 38*f,* 69
roof-climbing, 68*n*
Rüdin, Ernst, 130*n,* 151*n,* 182

S

Sabina S. (Fürstner's case), 186*f*
saint(s): hallucinations of, 67; simulation of, 186
St. Pirminsberg Mental Hospital (St. Gallen), 125, 126, 127
sanguine temperament, 109; and moral insanity, 132
saviours, 16
scarlet fever, 112
Schnitzler, Arthur, 106
Schopenhauer, Arthur, on genius, 100; "operari sequitur esse," 133
Schroeder van der Kolk, J. L. C., 62, 79, 150
Schüle, Heinrich, 58, 110, 132*n*
Schürmayer, I. H., 173*n*
science, mystic, *see* mystic science
séances, S. W.'s, 25–30; personalities in, 30–36
second sight, 17
Seeress of Prevorst, The (Kerner), *see* Clairvoyante of Prevorst
Selbruck, Anton, 66
self-: confidence, exaggerated, 110, 111, 118, 126; control, lack of, in hysteria, 99*f;* —, in malingering, 161; criticism, lack of, 99*f,* 131; deception, 210*ff;* esteem, exaggerated, 124*ff,* 130; glorification, of manic patient, 126; magnetization, 27; torture, 186
senile dementia, 90
sense(s): and cryptomnesic image, 86; functions, paralysis of, 11; hallucinations of the, 8*f;* hyperaesthetic unconscious activity of, 87; impression, strength of, and attention, 45; retention of, in hysterical lethargy, 71
senseless answers, *see* answers

sense organs: all involved in hallucinations, 22f; partial paralysis of,
65
sensibility: disturbances of, 150; and
genius, 99; and interpretation of
intended tremors, 87; tests of,
144; unconscious, of hysterical patient, 80f
sexual: excesses, 113, 213ff; symbols,
in dreams, 99
sexuality, 137f
shamming, energy required for, 163
shock neuroses, and violent affect,
164
Siefert, Ernst, 109, 111
Siemens, Fritz, 184
silence, and auditory hallucinations,
58
simulation: and auto-hypnosis, 203;
concept of, 186; confession of,
164, 196, 201f; conscious, 202; diagnosis of doubtful case, 160ff;
difficulty of diagnosis, 185, 188;
doubtful cases of, 163f; earlier
writers on, 185; effect on mental
state, 180f; excellence of, 179,
202; half-conscious, 189ff; hysterical symptoms and, 163; mistaken
diagnosis of, 186f; passage from
conscious to subconscious, 173;
passage into insanity, 202f; patient's explanation of, 176f, 196f,
201f; physical examination, 175;
unmasking of, 185f
skeletons, hallucinations of, 6f, 13
sleep: disturbed, 8, 129f; ecstatic,
71; onset of, and hallucinations,
58f; partial, and suggestibility,
13f; prodromal stage, 150; visions
at onset of, 22
sleeping state: following double
hypnosis, 154; S. W.'s, 70f
sleepwalking, see somnambulism
Smith, Hélène (Flournoy's case),
57f, 60f, 68, 79, 84; automatic
speech, 73n; Hindu cycle, 68n;
and Leopold, 73n, 74n, 86; Mar-

tian language, 85; systematic anaesthesia, 65; visions, 60
social: behaviour, in manic mood
disorder, 115ff; inadequacy, 131
solitary confinement, 127; behaviour
in, 174, 191; in darkness, 164; effect of, 150f; hallucinations in,
192
somnambulism: attacks, see somnambulistic attacks; case of Miss
S. W., 17–18; classification of, 5;
course of, 78f; development of
impressions into hallucinations,
13; and the development of new
ideas, 86n; dissociation of personality, 67; with hallucinations, 16;
hypnotic, 70f; —, response to suggestions in, 144; hysterical, following hypnosis, 147; semi-somnambulism, 24f, 33, 47ff, 64;
spontaneous, 5ff, 62f, 79, 150;
states, see somnambulistic states;
visual images objectified as hallucinations in, 57
somnambulistic attacks: course of,
19f; minor automatisms in, 21f;
nature of, 70–77
somnambulistic states: induced, 71;
second state, 61f; —, and change
of character, 61–70; —, predominance of, 79; —, with and without amnesic split, 63f
somnambulists: cryptomnesic reproduction of object, 84; intuitive
knowledge of, 86; suggestibility
of, 87
song, and feeling-toned train of
thought, 97
sparks, vision of, 58
spasms, tonic and clonic, of muscles,
186
speech: area, effect of partial hypnosis of, 52; automatic, 72f, 75;
centres, focal lesion of, 106; impulses, overflow into motor area,
51f; muscles, movements of, in
somnambulism, 73; pressure of,
128 (see also talkativeness); un-

intelligible, in somnambulistic state, 26

Spinoza, Baruch, hypnopompic vision of, 59n

spirits: appearance of, 72f; black, 34; conviction of presence of, 58; language of, 33f; S. W. and, 20ff, 27f, 33

spiritual power, and hallucinations, 61

split off: from primary unconscious personality, 72f; of subconscious personality, 56f

star-dwellers, 34f

stage fright, 164

Steffens, Paul, on hysteria and epilepsy, 4

"Stege," see "Treppe"

stimuli: cutaneous, perception of, in anaesthetic regions, 13; transmutations of, 13f

stimulus words, in association test, 221

Stockhausen, Reiner, a case of simulated insanity, 160, 183ff, 185ff; Richarz on, 180n

strangeness, feeling of, 58; and cryptomnesic image, 82

Stromboli, Mt., 82f

student, seeing apparitions and light, 60

stupidity: emotional, 185, 187; shammed, 172

stupor: catatonia-like, 182; epileptic, 182; epileptoid, 16; hysterical, characteristics of, 148ff; —, in a prisoner in detention, 137–56; somnambulistic, 65

subconscious: and auto-suggestion, 163; construction of hallucinations, 13; individualization of, 53f; suggestibility of, 54; see also unconscious

suggestibility: and the creation of an automatism, 162; in hysterical stupor, 141; influence of darkness on, 56; of somnambulists, 87; in states of partial sleep, 13f; and

unconscious orientation, 152

suggestion: and analgesia, 139; and automatic writing, 54f; dependent on psychological possibility, 53; effect of, in semi-somnambulism, 36; in hypnosis, 76; motor phenomena induced by, 48f; posthypnotic, 145, 147f; and thought-transference, 54; use of, in hypnotic somnambulism, 144; verbal, and partial hypnosis, 49; whispered, 51n, 70f; see also auto-suggestion; counter-suggestion

suicide: attempted, 15, 174, 191, 199, 200f; threat of, 123, 130, 176f

sulphuric acid, self-inflicted burn with, 163

sums, simple, tests in, 144, 178, 197f

superficiality, 112, 113f, 119

S. W., Miss, case of, 17–88; character development, 47; character in waking state, 41–47; character of, and subconscious personalities, 77; "dual" personality, 24f; educational level, 18, 19, 88; family background, 17; glossolalia, 84–86; grandfather as "guide," 22, 26, 30f; identity of ego-consciousness in all states, 72; improvement in character, 79; and Jung, 21, 35, 37ff; and Jung's grandfather, 26, 56; personal and physical traits, 18; physical state in attacks, 26, 28f; reaction to disclosure of trance behaviour, 21, 28; reaction to hallucinatory phenomena, 23; sister's dream of black and white figures, 23f; somnambulistic personality, see Ivenes; somnambulistic states, 19–25; re her spirits, 23, 27; termination of the disorder, 43

Swedenborg, Emmanuel, 36, 42; visions, 60

sweets, addiction to, 120

swindler: insight of, 217; pathological, psychology of, 66; —, skill at lying, 161f; simulated stupor, 182

swindling, pathological, 173
Swiss dialect, 18, 89ff
symbolism, in dreams, 56, 99
symptomatic actions, of artist, 100
symptoms: hypomanic, 134; hysterical, *see below;* in hysterical stupor, 138f, 145ff; manic mood disorder, 122f, 134; prodromal, 12, 15, 46; psychogenic, 160; psychopathic, 119; of psychopathic inferiority, 4ff; unmasking of, in simulation, 185
symptoms, hysterical: automatic nature of, 163; genesis of, 155; presence of, 211, 212f
syncope, hypnotic, 154n
"syndromes épisodiques des dégénérés," 130
synthesis, loss of, 171

T

table, movements of: automatic, 48–61; initial, 73; unconscious control of, 49
table-turning: and semi-somnambulistic states, 25
tachypnoea, 20
talkativeness, 113, 116, 122f, 125, 128
talking, compulsive, 105
tendovaginitis, 8, 14, 16
tests, arithmetic, in case of simulated insanity, 178
theft: charge of, 124–32, 138, 148; conviction for, 182, 191; discovery of, through feeling-toned complex of ideas relating to the crime, 220f; imprisonment for, 174ff; and lying, 163; of money, delusion *re,* 138ff, 143ff, 151
Thierfelsenburg, Elisabeth von (somnambulistic personality), 30, 37
thieves, art of shamming among, 161
thinking: disturbance of, 110; intuitive, 96f; *see also* thought-process(es)
thought-process(es): feeling-toned, 203f; in somnambulism, 57f
thought-reading: experiment in table-turning, 50f, 80; experiments with numbers, 86; from intended tremors, 54
thought transference, 25
thoughts, repressed, and the creation of subconscious personalities, 77f
threshold of consciousness, *see* consciousness, threshold of
tics, hysterical, 181
Tiling, T., 132
time consciousness, 12
toleration, threshold of, and unabreacted affects, 155
tongue, slips of, 90
touch, and hallucinatory process, 13
train of thought: and attention, 69n; feeling-toned, disappearance from conscious mind, 97f
trance: in séances, 25ff; journeys, 33ff, 43; three-day, 17
traumatic neurosis, 173
tremor(s): of hands and head, 138; writing disturbed by, 140f
tremors, intended: role of, in table-turning, 49f; sensibility and interpretation of, 87; in thought-reading experiment, 50f, 54, 80; thought-transference from, 86
"Treppe"/"Stege," 18, 89ff
tubercle bacilli, fantasy of, 38
tumbler, *see* glass
tune, and feeling-toned train of thought, 97
twilight state: amnesia for, 147, 153f; automatisms in, 73; and daydreaming, 162; epileptic, 76; and feeble-mindedness, 172f; hallucinatory, 58; hysterical, 17, 148ff, 179, 202; psychic process in, 154f; psychological mechanisms of, 163f; somnambulistic, 162; visions in, 72

typhoid fever, 5, 17

U

Ulrich von Gerbenstein, *see* Gerbenstein
"unconscious," term, as used by Jung, 95*n*
unconscious: feelings and concepts in, 87; intellectual activity of, 87; psychic complexes, 98*f*; receptivity of, 86; —, in heightened unconscious phenomena, 80; *see also* subconscious
unconscious performance, heightened, 80–87
unpleasant events: amnesia for, 172; repressed from consciousness, 153, 155

V

vagrancy, case of, 11; *see also* wandering
Valours, Berthe de (somnambulistic personality), 30, 37
Van Deventer, J., on "sanguine inferiority," 110*f*
vena, word, 84
verbal correspondences, in cryptomnesic reproduction, 103*f*
vision: field of, 144; restriction of mental field of, 151
visionaries, hallucinations of, 60*f*
visions: hypnagogic, 67; in hysterical delirium, 9; memory of, 24; S. W.'s, 22*f*
visual images, objectified as hallucinations, 57
visual sphere: automatism in, 58; excitation of, 58; irruption of hypnosis into, 74*f*
voice(s): altered tone of, 20, 27; hallucinatory, 125, 127, 128, 130
Voisin, Jules, 63
volcano, 83, 101*f*

W

wakefulness, systematic partial, 10
waking state: content of subconscious personality carried into, 65; hypnotic experiments in, 51*n*; and objectivation of dreams, 68; partial, and complex hallucinations, 61; tremors of hands and arms, 49*n*; and visual images, 14
wandering(s), 120*ff*, 124*ff*, 127, 131, 173*ff*, 190*ff*
weight-reducing course, 119
Wernicke, Carl: on chronic mania, 110; on delusions of grandeur, 151; on dream-role, 162; "levelling-down of ideas," 133; on moral insanity, 133*f*
Wertheimer, Max, 219*ff*
Westphal, A., 172*n*, 185
Westphal, C., 15
Weygandt, Wilhelm, 220
whispering: of suggestions, 51*n*, 70*f*; unconscious, 73
Wilbrand, —— (Frankfurt a. M.), 186*n*
will: influenced by abnormal affects, 217; and intellect, 132
will power, and malingering, 161
wine, 115*f*
Winslow, B. F., 10*n*
wish-fulfilment, 99; hallucinatory, 151; subconscious personality as, 70
witchcraft, 71
witch trials, glossolalia in, 84
Woltke, Sophie, *see* Guinon, Georges
word-association, Jung's studies in, 219
words: picture composition, Charcot's scheme for, 51*n*; meaningless, in partial hypnosis of speech area, 52; stimulus, in association tests, 167*n*, 221; substitutions, 18, 89–92; transposed in mediumistic communications, 25*f*

work-curve, 199, 200; tests of, 179ff
world forces, S. W.'s description of,
39–42
writing, disturbance of, by tremors,
140f
writing, automatic, 54f; in complete
darkness, 27f; experiment by
member of the Society for Psychical Research, 52f; and suggestibility, 13

Wundt, Wilhelm, 220

Z

Zarathustra, journey to hell of, 82f,
101ff
"Ziege"/"Geiss," 18, 89f
Zschokke, J. H. D., 86
Zündel, Friedrich, 84n
Zurich Clinic, 220

THE COLLECTED WORKS OF
C. G. JUNG

T HE PUBLICATION of the first complete edition, in English, of the works of C. G. Jung was undertaken by Routledge and Kegan Paul, Ltd., in England and by Bollingen Foundation in the United States. The American edition is number XX in Bollingen Series, which since 1967 has been published by Princeton University Press. The edition contains revised versions of works previously published, such as *Psychology of the Unconscious*, which is now entitled *Symbols of Transformation*; works originally written in English, such as *Psychology and Religion*; works not previously translated, such as *Aion*; and, in general, new translations of virtually all of Professor Jung's writings. Prior to his death, in 1961, the author supervised the textual revision, which in some cases is extensive. Sir Herbert Read (d. 1968), Dr. Michael Fordham, and Dr. Gerhard Adler (d. 1988) compose the Editorial Committee; the translator is R. F. C. Hull (except for Volume 2) and William McGuire is executive editor.

The price of the volumes varies according to size; they are sold separately, and may also be obtained on standing order. Several of the volumes are extensively illustrated. Each volume contains an index and, in most cases, a bibliography; the final volumes contain a complete bibliography of Professor Jung's writings and a general index to the entire edition.

In the following list, dates of original publication are given in parentheses (of original composition, in brackets). Multiple dates indicate revisions.

*1. PSYCHIATRIC STUDIES

On the Psychology and Pathology of So-Called Occult Phenomena
(1902)

On Hysterical Misreading (1904)

Cryptomnesia (1905)

On Manic Mood Disorder (1903)

A Case of Hysterical Stupor in a Prisoner in Detention (1902)

On Simulated Insanity (1903)

A Medical Opinion on a Case of Simulated Insanity (1904)

A Third and Final Opinion on Two Contradictory Psychiatric Diagnoses (1906)

On the Psychological Diagnosis of Facts (1905)

†2. EXPERIMENTAL RESEARCHES

Translated by Leopold Stein in collaboration with Diana Riviere

STUDIES IN WORD ASSOCIATION (1904–7, 1910)

The Associations of Normal Subjects (by Jung and F. Riklin)

An Analysis of the Associations of an Epileptic

The Reaction-Time Ratio in the Association Experiment

Experimental Observations on the Faculty of Memory

Psychoanalysis and Association Experiments

The Psychological Diagnosis of Evidence

Association, Dream, and Hysterical Symptom

The Psychopathological Significance of the Association Experiment

Disturbances in Reproduction in the Association Experiment

The Association Method

The Family Constellation

PSYCHOPHYSICAL RESEARCHES (1907–8)

On the Psychophysical Relations of the Association Experiment

Psychophysical Investigations with the Galvanometer and Pneumo-
graph in Normal and Insane Individuals (by F. Peterson and
Jung)

Further Investigations on the Galvanic Phenomenon and Respiration
in Normal and Insane Individuals (by C. Ricksher and Jung)

Appendix: Statistical Details of Enlistment (1906); New Aspects of
Criminal Psychology (1908); The Psychological Methods of
Investigation Used in the Psychiatric Clinic of the University of
Zurich (1910); On the Doctrine of Complexes ([1911] 1913); On
the Psychological Diagnosis of Evidence (1937)

* Published 1957; 2nd edn., 1970.   † Published 1973.

*3. THE PSYCHOGENESIS OF MENTAL DISEASE
The Psychology of Dementia Praecox (1907)
The Content of the Psychoses (1908/1914)
On Psychological Understanding (1914)
A Criticism of Bleuler's Theory of Schizophrenic Negativism (1911)
On the Importance of the Unconscious in Psychopathology (1914)
On the Problem of Psychogenesis in Mental Disease (1919)
Mental Disease and the Psyche (1928)
On the Psychogenesis of Schizophrenia (1939)
Recent Thoughts on Schizophrenia (1957)
Schizophrenia (1958)

†4. FREUD AND PSYCHOANALYSIS
Freud's Theory of Hysteria: A Reply to Aschaffenburg (1906)
The Freudian Theory of Hysteria (1908)
The Analysis of Dreams (1909)
A Contribution to the Psychology of Rumour (1910–11)
On the Significance of Number Dreams (1910–11)
Morton Prince, "The Mechanism and Interpretation of Dreams": A
    Critical Review (1911)
On the Criticism of Psychoanalysis (1910)
Concerning Psychoanalysis (1912)
The Theory of Psychoanalysis (1913)
General Aspects of Psychoanalysis (1913)
Psychoanalysis and Neurosis (1916)
Some Crucial Points in Psychoanalysis: A Correspondence between
    Dr. Jung and Dr. Loÿ (1914)
Prefaces to "Collected Papers on Analytical Psychology" (1916, 1917)
The Significance of the Father in the Destiny of the Individual
    (1909/1949)
Introduction to Kranefeldt's "Secret Ways of the Mind" (1930)
Freud and Jung: Contrasts (1929)

‡5. SYMBOLS OF TRANSFORMATION (1911–12/1952)
    PART I
Introduction
Two Kinds of Thinking
The Miller Fantasies: Anamnesis
The Hymn of Creation
The Song of the Moth   (continued)

* Published 1960.   † Published 1961.
‡ Published 1956; 2nd edn., 1967. (65 plates, 43 text figures.)

5. *(continued)*
    PART II
    Introduction
    The Concept of Libido
    The Transformation of Libido
    The Origin of the Hero
    Symbols of the Mother and of Rebirth
    The Battle for Deliverance from the Mother
    The Dual Mother
    The Sacrifice
    Epilogue
    Appendix: The Miller Fantasies

*6. PSYCHOLOGICAL TYPES (1921)
    Introduction
    The Problem of Types in the History of Classical and Medieval
        Thought
    Schiller's Ideas on the Type Problem
    The Apollinian and the Dionysian
    The Type Problem in Human Character
    The Type Problem in Poetry
    The Type Problem in Psychopathology
    The Type Problem in Aesthetics
    The Type Problem in Modern Philosophy
    The Type Problem in Biography
    General Description of the Types
    Definitions
    Epilogue
    Four Papers on Psychological Typology (1913, 1925, 1931, 1936)

†7. TWO ESSAYS ON ANALYTICAL PSYCHOLOGY
    On the Psychology of the Unconscious (1917/1926/1943)
    The Relations between the Ego and the Unconscious (1928)
    Appendix: New Paths in Psychology (1912); The Structure of the
        Unconscious (1916) (new versions, with variants, 1966)

‡8. THE STRUCTURE AND DYNAMICS OF THE PSYCHE
    On Psychic Energy (1928)
    The Transcendent Function ([1916]/1957)
    A Review of the Complex Theory (1934)
    The Significance of Constitution and Heredity in Psychology (1929)

* Published 1971.   † Published 1953; 2nd edn., 1966.
‡ Published 1960; 2nd edn., 1969.

Psychological Factors Determining Human Behavior (1937)
Instinct and the Unconscious (1919)
The Structure of the Psyche (1927/1931)
On the Nature of the Psyche (1947/1954)
General Aspects of Dream Psychology (1916/1948)
On the Nature of Dreams (1945/1948)
The Psychological Foundations of Belief in Spirits (1920/1948)
Spirit and Life (1926)
Basic Postulates of Analytical Psychology (1931)
Analytical Psychology and *Weltanschauung* (1928/1931)
The Real and the Surreal (1933)
The Stages of Life (1930–1931)
The Soul and Death (1934)
Synchronicity: An Acausal Connecting Principle (1952)
Appendix: On Synchronicity (1951)

*9. PART I. THE ARCHETYPES AND THE
COLLECTIVE UNCONSCIOUS
Archetypes of the Collective Unconscious (1934/1954)
The Concept of the Collective Unconscious (1936)
Concerning the Archetypes, with Special Reference to the Anima
    Concept (1936/1954)
Psychological Aspects of the Mother Archetype (1938/1954)
Concerning Rebirth (1940/1950)
The Psychology of the Child Archetype (1940)
The Psychological Aspects of the Kore (1941)
The Phenomenology of the Spirit in Fairytales (1945/1948)
On the Psychology of the Trickster-Figure (1954)
Conscious, Unconscious, and Individuation (1939)
A Study in the Process of Individuation (1934/1950)
Concerning Mandala Symbolism (1950)
Appendix: Mandalas (1955)

*9. PART II. AION (1951)
    RESEARCHES INTO THE PHENOMENOLOGY OF THE SELF
The Ego
The Shadow
The Syzygy: Anima and Animus
The Self
Christ, a Symbol of the Self
The Sign of the Fishes   (continued)

* Published 1959; 2nd edn., 1968. (Part I: 79 plates, with 29 in colour.)

9. *(continued)*
The Prophecies of Nostradamus
The Historical Significance of the Fish
The Ambivalence of the Fish Symbol
The Fish in Alchemy
The Alchemical Interpretation of the Fish
Background to the Psychology of Christian Alchemical Symbolism
Gnostic Symbols of the Self
The Structure and Dynamics of the Self
Conclusion

*10. CIVILIZATION IN TRANSITION
The Role of the Unconscious (1918)
Mind and Earth (1927/1931)
Archaic Man (1931)
The Spiritual Problem of Modern Man (1928/1931)
The Love Problem of a Student (1928)
Woman in Europe (1927)
The Meaning of Psychology for Modern Man (1933/1934)
The State of Psychotherapy Today (1934)
Preface and Epilogue to "Essays on Contemporary Events" (1946)
Wotan (1936)
After the Catastrophe (1945)
The Fight with the Shadow (1946)
The Undiscovered Self (Present and Future) (1957)
Flying Saucers: A Modern Myth (1958)
A Psychological View of Conscience (1958)
Good and Evil in Analytical Psychology (1959)
Introduction to Wolff's "Studies in Jungian Psychology" (1959)
The Swiss Line in the European Spectrum (1928)
Reviews of Keyserling's "America Set Free" (1930) and "La Révolution Mondiale" (1934)
The Complications of American Psychology (1930)
The Dreamlike World of India (1939)
What India Can Teach Us (1939)
Appendix: Documents (1933–1938)

†11. PSYCHOLOGY AND RELIGION: WEST AND EAST
WESTERN RELIGION
Psychology and Religion (The Terry Lectures) (1938/1940)

* Published 1964; 2nd edn., 1970. (8 plates.)
† Published 1958; 2nd edn., 1969.

A Psychological Approach to the Dogma of the Trinity (1942/1948)
Transformation Symbolism in the Mass (1942/1954)
Forewords to White's "God and the Unconscious" and Werblowsky's "Lucifer and Prometheus" (1952)
Brother Klaus (1933)
Psychotherapists or the Clergy (1932)
Psychoanalysis and the Cure of Souls (1928)
Answer to Job (1952)

EASTERN RELIGION

Psychological Commentaries on "The Tibetan Book of the Great Liberation" (1939/1954) and "The Tibetan Book of the Dead" (1935/1953)
Yoga and the West (1936)
Foreword to Suzuki's "Introductio to Zen Buddhism" (1939)
The Psychology of Eastern Meditation (1943)
The Holy Men of India: Introduction to Zimmer's "Der Weg zum Selbst" (1944)
Foreword to the "I Ching" (1950)

*12. PSYCHOLOGY AND ALCHEMY (1944)
Prefatory note to the English Edition ([1951?] added 1967)
Introduction to the Religious and Psychological Problems of Alchemy
Individual Dream Symbolism in Relation to Alchemy (1936)
Religious Ideas in Alchemy (1937)
Epilogue

†13. ALCHEMICAL STUDIES
Commentary on "The Secret of the Golden Flower" (1929)
The Visions of Zosimos (1938/1954)
Paracelsus as a Spiritual Phenomenon (1942)
The Spirit Mercurius (1943/1948)
The Philosophical Tree (1945/1954)

‡14. MYSTERIUM CONIUNCTIONIS (1955-56)
AN INQUIRY INTO THE SEPARATION AND
SYNTHESIS OF PSYCHIC OPPOSITES IN ALCHEMY
The Components of the Coniunctio
The Paradoxa
The Personification of the Opposites
Rex and Regina   (continued)

* Published 1953; 2nd edn., completely revised, 1968. (270 illustrations.)
† Published 1968. (50 plates, 4 text figures.)
‡ Published 1963; 2nd edn., 1970. (10 plates.)

14. *(continued)*
Adam and Eve
The Conjunction

*15. THE SPIRIT IN MAN, ART, AND LITERATURE
Paracelsus (1929)
Paracelsus the Physician (1941)
Sigmund Freud in His Historical Setting (1932)
In Memory of Sigmund Freud (1939)
Richard Wilhelm: In Memoriam (1930)
On the Relation of Analytical Psychology to Poetry (1922)
Psychology and Literature (1930/1950)
"Ulysses": A Monologue (1932)
Picasso (1932)

†16. THE PRACTICE OF PSYCHOTHERAPY
GENERAL PROBLEMS OF PSYCHOTHERAPY
Principles of Practical Psychotherapy (1935)
What Is Psychotherapy? (1935)
Some Aspects of Modern Psychotherapy (1930)
The Aims of Psychotherapy (1931)
Problems of Modern Psychotherapy (1929)
Psychotherapy and a Philosophy of Life (1943)
Medicine and Psychotherapy (1945)
Psychotherapy Today (1945)
Fundamental Questions of Psychotherapy (1951)
SPECIFIC PROBLEMS OF PSYCHOTHERAPY
The Therapeutic Value of Abreaction (1921/1928)
The Practical Use of Dream-Analysis (1934)
The Psychology of the Transference (1946)
Appendix: The Realities of Practical Psychotherapy ([1937] added, 1966)

‡17. THE DEVELOPMENT OF PERSONALITY
Psychic Conflicts in a Child (1910/1946)
Introduction to Wickes's "Analyses der Kinderseele" (1927/1931)
Child Development and Education (1928)
Analytical Psychology and Education: Three Lectures (1926/1946)
The Gifted Child (1943)
The Significance of the Unconscious in Individual Education (1928)

* Published 1966.
† Published 1954; 2nd edn., revised and augmented, 1966. (13 illustrations.)
‡ Published 1954.

The Development of Personality (1934)
Marriage as a Psychological Relationship (1925)

*18. THE SYMBOLIC LIFE
Miscellaneous writings

†19. COMPLETE BIBLIOGRAPHY OF C. G. JUNG'S WRITINGS

‡20. GENERAL INDEX TO THE COLLECTED WORKS

§ THE ZOFINGIA LECTURES
Supplementary Volume A to The Collected Works Edited by William
McGuire, translated by Jan van Heurck, introduction by Marie-Louise
von Franz

Related publications:
C. G. JUNG: LETTERS
Selected and edited by Gerhard Adler, in collaboration with Aniela Jaffé.
Translations from the German by R. F. C. Hull.
   VOL. 1: 1906-1950
   VOL. 2: 1951-1961

C. G. JUNG SPEAKING: Interviews and Encounters
Edited by William McGuire and R. F. C. Hull

C. G. JUNG: Word and Image
Edited by Aniela Jaffé

THE ESSENTIAL JUNG
Selected and introduced by Anthony Storr

Notes of C. G. Jung's Seminars:

‖ DREAM ANALYSIS (1928-1930)
   Edited by William McGuire

NIETZSCHE'S *ZARATHUSTRA* (1934-1939)
   Edited by James L. Jarrett (2 vols.)

**ANALYTICAL PSYCHOLOGY (1925)
   Edited by William McGuire

CHILDREN'S DREAMS (1936-1941)
   Edited by Lorenz Jung

* Published 1954.	‖ Published 1984.
† Published 1976.	# Published 1988.
‡ Published 1979.	**Published 1989.
§ Published 1983.	

Printed in the USA
CPSIA information can be obtained
at www.ICGtesting.com
JSHW022222030724
65843JS00001B/2

9 780691 259321